1974

1974

Football in the Seventies

Marvin Close

pitch

First published by Pitch Publishing, 2025
1

Pitch Publishing
9 Donnington Park,
85 Birdham Road,
Chichester, West Sussex,
PO20 7AJ

www.pitchpublishing.co.uk
info@pitchpublishing.co.uk

A CIP catalogue record is available for this book from the British Library.

ISBN 978 1 83680 139 9

Typesetting and origination by Pitch Publishing

MIX
Paper | Supporting responsible forestry
FSC® C010615

Printed and bound on FSC® certified paper in line with our continuing commitment to ethical business practices, sustainability and the environment.

Printed and bound in India by Thomson Press

Contents

Introduction

THE 1960s had been a decade of plenty for British football. Sir Alf's England lifted the World Cup and then made the semi-finals of the Euros; Celtic and Manchester United both won the European Cup, while Tottenham Hotspur, West Ham United and Manchester City all lifted the European Cup Winners' Cup. Just for good measure, Leeds United, Arsenal and Newcastle United triumphed in UEFA's Inter-Cities Fairs Cup. Denis Law, Bobby Charlton and George Best were all named European footballers of the year. Attendances were booming and record transfer fees broken year-on-year. Thanks to the abolition of the maximum wage, the top players were now earning top money and the grey, grim austerity of the 1950s was but a memory. The Beatles reigned supreme, Britain was suddenly the cultural epicentre of the world and the economy was booming. But what goes up must come down and as the 60s morphed into the 70s, that happy bubble had begun to burst.

Though this book will explore themes, events and personalities that lit up the football world throughout the 1970s, we'll be taking a particularly deep dive into 1974 – the year that Sir Alf was sacked, legendary managers Bill Shankly and Bill Nicholson called it a day and Brian Clough lasted all of 44 days at Leeds. It was the year that the softly spoken Bob Paisley very reluctantly took up the reins at Liverpool and then became the most successful manager in the history of English football. After a long-drawn-out series of rows and recriminations, George Best finally walked out of Old Trafford for ever. 1974 tragically saw the first murder inside a football ground and a hooliganism problem that was fast spinning out of control. Sunday football was introduced and England suddenly found themselves in the footballing wilderness. Amateur football was completely reorganised and the women's game began to make significant strides forward. Up and down the Football League, attendances were dropping, grounds crumbling and money was in short supply both on and off the pitch. In essence, 1974 contained pretty much everything that would have a deep and lasting impact upon the game for the remainder of the decade. This is football in the 70s.

1

Life in 1974

'This is a new year. A new beginning.
And things will change'

Taylor Swift

IN JANUARY 1974, and almost as a hangover from the festive season, Slade were still number one in the charts with 'Merry Xmas Everybody', the chorus of which joyfully proclaimed, 'So here it is, merry Christmas, everybody's having fun.' Only they weren't. Britons welcomed in 1974 amid a depressing basket of national problems – strikes, fuel shortages, power cuts, a state of emergency in Northern Ireland, IRA bombings on the mainland and the damaging effects of an oil crisis in the Middle East. To make matters worse, Britain's economy under Conservative prime minister Edward Heath was going down the toilet. In January, the nation alarmingly entered its first official post-war recession; a lot of people were seriously skint and prices were rising. The liberal, freewheeling Swinging Sixties were now but a memory and the population was struggling to make sense of a new, at times unnervingly fast-changing world. People were trying to get used to everything from the rising crime and unemployment rates and the blight of football hooliganism, to the new decimal currency, the introduction of post codes and bar codes, new telephone area codes – and increasing political instability.

In the early 1970s, most of the country's electricity was produced by coal-burning power stations, and when Britain's miners went on a lengthy national pay strike, Heath's Conservative government were forced to bring in sweeping energy-saving measures. On New Year's Day, the PM introduced a strict three-day working week. Apart from essential services like hospitals and schools, businesses, offices and factories were forced to limit their electricity usage to three consecutive days, heat premises to a maximum of 17°C, and then either close for the rest of the week or work by torch and candlelight. For a while, it was a novelty, but soon it became a complete pain in the arse. As coal reserves dwindled, Britons had to live with regular power cuts too, and in the cold, dank, dark winter weather, shivered beneath overcoats, duvets, blankets and thick woolly football scarves.

To further conserve energy, TV companies were ordered to close down at 10.30pm every day and football clubs were banned from playing floodlit midweek matches. A 50mph speed limit was imposed on all roads and motorways and the cost of petrol rose to 50p a gallon, up 20 per cent from the year before. The strain on the country was huge, the economy collapsing. Convinced that most of the electorate backed his attempts to end the miners' strike, Heath decided to go to the country and called a February general election; he had misjudged. Rather than increase his government's narrow majority, the result was a hung parliament: Harold Wilson's Labour Party gained 301 seats to the Tories' 297. Desperate to hang on to government, Heath tried to come to an agreement with the Liberals and Ulster Unionists, but failed; Wilson returned to power and formed a minority administration.

On 7 March Wilson put an end to the three-day working week and then agreed to a 35 per cent wage rise with the National Union of Miners. In modern terms, this may seem a huge jump in pay, but in truth, miners had not had a raise for a decade and many lived on subsistence wages. Just to underline what a hard and dangerous job being a miner was, four days after the strike ended ten colliers died in a methane gas explosion at Golborne Colliery near Wigan. In October, Labour would call for the year's second general election and secured a clear majority. A victory for Harold Wilson but the truth was, he had inherited a deeply poisoned chalice. Britain was in a right old mess.

Not surprisingly the tough time that the country was experiencing led many to take solace in the comfort of both nostalgia and comedy. Television's big hit of the year was the Edwardian-set drama *Upstairs, Downstairs*, the best-selling book was *The Country Diary of an Edwardian Lady*, and the pop music charts were awash with early 1960s US high-school doo-wop pastiches from the likes of Showaddywaddy, Mud and the Rubettes. The Swedish pop juggernauts that were ABBA announced themselves to the world by winning the Eurovision Song Contest with three and a bit minutes of musical comfort food, 'Waterloo'. Ear-worm novelty records proliferated with everything from Ray Stevens capitalising on the mid-70s craze for running naked through public spaces, 'The Streak' ; Sylvia's celebration of the increasingly popular Spanish package holiday, 'Y Viva Espana'; to the Wombles' celebration of, well, wombling.

From the jazz age of the 1920s and early 1930s to the dance halls of the Second World War, history shows us that in times of economic problems and strife, music that people could dance to and forget their troubles was generally at its most popular. So it was perhaps no surprise that amid the grim grey realities of 1974 Great Britain, a thrilling new dance sound would get young Brits on to their feet. The year saw the beginning of the disco explosion, with Barry White, Gloria Gaynor, the Hues Corporation and Disco Tex and His Sex-O-Lettes all charting for the first time. Clubs up and down the country went disco and a joyful, exciting new movement was born. But this all came from the USA – what was new and innovative in British music? Well, not a lot.

Now minus his Spiders From Mars, the chameleon-like David Bowie showed new chops with his album *Diamond Dogs*. A dystopian 'concept' album inspired by Orwell's *1984* and the work of American writer William Burroughs, it contained an absolute banger in 'Rebel Rebel' and was one of the best British albums of the year. Bad Company recorded their self-titled debut album in just two weeks, and powered along by the astonishing blues-rock singing of former Free vocalist Paul Rodgers, its urgency and energy propelled it towards the top of the album charts in both Britain and the USA.

Elsewhere, Genesis continued their descent into overblown, over-theatrical prog rock with their own concept album, *The Lamb Lies Down On Broadway*. And keeping them company in a year of mediocre rock music album releases were dozens of plodding, noodling British prog rock bands. Financially much further down the musical food chain, dozens of new bands went back to grass roots to form the pub rock scene. The true precursor to British punk music, it was largely concentrated in the small clubs and pubs of London and in 1974, became the petri dish for several future influential performers. Anti-glam and unflashy, pub rock was back-to-basics r'n'b, sometimes with country rock influences, and played on tiny stages in venues like the now legendary Hope and Anchor pub and the Greyhound club. In 1974, bands like Bees Make Honey, Ducks Deluxe, Ace and the Count Bishops played their socks off live night after night for very little money. Major record labels came sniffing around throughout the year, but virtually all of them concluded that pub rock had little mass-market appeal and passed on the opportunity. Snubbed by the majors and desperate to put out product, the bands signed for small independent labels like Stiff and Chiswick and the pub rock scene staggered on into 1975. But some of those bands contained singers, songwriters and performers who would soon become huge. The 101ers singer and guitarist Joe Strummer formed the Clash; Kilburn and the High Roads polio-stricken, art college teacher frontman Ian Dury would become leader of Ian Dury and the Blockheads; while Flip City's shy young bespectacled Scouse guitarist Declan MacManus morphed into the self-assured swagger of Elvis Costello. Two bands who were initially turned down by the major labels, Dr Feelgood and Eddie and the Hot Rods, went on to become chart regulars.

On the comedy front, 1974 saw the launch of a raft of classic comedy series like *Fawlty Towers*, *Porridge*, *Rising Damp* and *It Ain't Half Hot Mum*. Elsewhere in television the year saw some interesting firsts. BBC2 aired a series of single new dramas in the series *Second City Firsts*, one of which, 'Girl', featured British TV's first lesbian kiss. The BBC also debuted Britain's first fly-on-the-wall documentary series, unassumingly named *The Family*, which followed the warts-and-all daily life of the Wilkins household. It fast became the country's most controversial and talked-about television show. If it had been made today, it would have been named *The Family – Shit Happens*. Nine members of the extended Wilkins family, a dog and a dozen budgies lived cheek-by-jowl over three floors of tiny rooms above a greengrocer's shop in Reading, Berkshire. Mum Margaret worked downstairs as a shop assistant in the greengrocer's, dad Terry was a bus driver and as well as sharing their flat with grown-up children

Marion and Gary, chippy teenage daughter Heather and daydreaming ten-year-old son Christopher, the overcrowded living space was also home to Gary's wife Karen and their baby Scott, plus Marion's fiancé Tom.

Producer Paul Watson said he 'wanted to make a series about the kind of people who never got on to television'. In the end, he and the watching audience got rather more than they had bargained for. Beneath a fug of cigarette smoke – apart from baby Scott, the dog and the budgies, everyone smoked – a riveted nation watched as this 'ordinary' working-class family fought life's problems and one another. At the core of everything, matriarch Margaret battled daily to support and do the best for her kids, their partners and new grandson Scott but it was not an easy fight.

Money and the lack of it was always an issue and Margaret was desperate for Gary and Karen and Marion and Tom to stand on their own two feet, leave the flat and get their own places. Gary, Karen and their baby were on the council housing list and also keen to get their own space; Marion and Tom were a different kettle of fish. Marion worked as a hairdresser and though responsible and much like her mum, Tom knew when he was on to a good thing. He worked occasionally in furniture removals but enjoyed most of the day in the pub. Throughout the 12-episode series he was constantly pressured by Marion and her mum about committing, showing more responsibility and setting a date for their wedding. Fifteen-year-old Heather was becoming a handful. A constant problem at school, she was desperate to leave, get a job and start earning her own money. Ten-year-old son Christopher would become the subject of a revelation that genuinely shocked the watching audience – Margaret admitted to him that Terry wasn't his father but the product of a shocking affair. So far, so soap opera.

Working for 18 hours a day over a three-month period, the film crew were given a front door key to enter the flat any time they liked. As soon as it hit the screen, *The Family* divided the nation. The production team drew praise for portraying real life as lived by millions; others were offended by the bad language and swearing, which was rare on TV in 1974; many had a queasy feeling that this was nothing but an attempt to exploit ordinary people to create TV poverty porn. Predictably, opportunist politicians, moralistic campaigners and certain areas of the press jumped on the bandwagon. Clean-up TV campaigner Mary Whitehouse was characteristically appalled that the family's unmarried daughter was openly living and sleeping with her unmarried boyfriend and called for the series to be banned lest this family be seen as 'a model to imitate'.

Local Reading MP Dr Gerry Vaughan pompously declared, 'It's upset a lot of people. I've had a lot of letters from people who said it gave the town of Reading a bad name – and it's a boring programme.' And that's where he was so wrong. It was utterly absorbing and groundbreaking. Despite all their problems and perfectly normal human weaknesses and foibles, the Wilkins family showed themselves to be resilient and supportive, battling against all the odds to do their best with the poor hand of cards they'd been dealt. If you want to know what ordinary lived life was like for many people in the 70s this extraordinary TV series gets you as near to the truth as you'll find. Fortunately, every single episode from the series is still up there on YouTube. Give it a watch – you won't be disappointed.

Like families all across the country, one major problem the Wilkins family were trying to cope with was the rise in prices. The Middle East oil crisis and Britain's crashing economy sent the cost of basic essentials soaring. A year before, a gallon of petrol had cost 39p; by 1974 this had risen to 50p. In 1973, a dozen eggs cost 32p; a year later, this had risen to 45p. A large loaf of bread in 73 would put you back 11 and a half pence; a year later, 14 and a half pence. A pint of beer in 1974? Just 18 and a half pence; a year on, 22 and a half pence. All the basic food staples continued to soar in price throughout 1974 and simply putting food on the table had become a struggle. A full-time male manual worker aged 18 and over earned an average of £48.50 a week; tellingly, and it says much about the time, a full-time female manual worker earned just £27 a week, often for doing exactly the same job as their male colleagues. It was an unprecedented post-war cost-of-living crisis; does any of this sound familiar?

The dark horrors of terrorism had well and truly arrived on the British mainland. In 1973, the Provisional IRA had extended its bombing campaign to military and important infrastructure targets inside Britain, to put further pressure on the government to pull out of Northern Ireland. Throughout 1974, the reign of terror grew ever more lethal as they also began to concentrate on civilian targets, particularly in Birmingham and the West Midlands. But why was Britain's second city, with a population of over one million which in 1974 had a largely Catholic Irish community of nearly 100,000, targeted so often? Numerous theories exist; combine them together and we start to approach what may have been the reasons. Birmingham had long been a hugely important transport hub, containing major road, rail and aeroplane routes, able to take people in and out of the city at speed to other parts of the country and abroad. London, as it still remains, is England's best-policed and defended city, so Birmingham was always a softer, albeit an important and strategic, target. And certain well-established hardcore Irish Catholic families in the city offered safe houses and support to Provisional IRA players on the mainland.

Coming into November 1974, there had been 32 separate bomb attacks in the area, hitting factories, department stores, shops and offices. The IRA welcomed the West Midlands into the new year by blowing up part of Birmingham Shopping Centre. In April, a bomb wrecked the foyer of central Birmingham's impressive Rotunda building; 25 minutes later, a second blast destroyed a railway signal box in Navigation Street, knocking out local train services. On 14 July a series of bombs caused £500,000 of damage at the Rotunda (again), a factory in nearby Smethwick, a timber yard in Birmingham's Curzon Street and in an underground passageway in Watson Road, Nechells. Later the same month, five Birmingham cinemas were targeted with incendiary bombs and in October, a bomb placed under a car belonging to sports minister Denis Howell MP exploded outside his Moseley home. After over a year of trouble, the local *Daily Post* newspaper had dubbed the city 'Frontline Birmingham', but worse, much worse was to come.

After waiting in the shadows for nearly a year's worth of injuries and non-fatal wounds around Brum, the Grim Reaper strode out full and centre. In early November, Provisional IRA member James McDade was ordered to blow up a major telephone exchange in nearby Coventry. Attempting to plant the bomb, it blew up in his face, killing him instantly. But the Reaper was just getting started. On 21 November, terrorists planted time bombs at two pubs in Birmingham city centre, the Mulberry Bush and the Tavern on the Town. At the time, it was official IRA protocol to give a 30-minute advance warning of any attacks on civilian targets but on this particular night, all went badly wrong.

Well before the days of mobile phones, the operative detailed with making the warning call wasted many vital minutes desperately trying to find an unvandalised phone box. Eventually he managed to ring the *Birmingham Post* and the *Birmingham Evening Mail*, giving the IRA codeword that authenticated any warning calls. But tragically, either in panic or confusion, the caller failed to name the two city centre pubs in which the bombs had been placed. The *Post* reported that the only information the warning gave was 'there is a bomb planted at the Rotunda and a bomb planted in New Street'. Police, military and emergency services frantically raced to the city centre, but at 8.17pm, just six minutes after the first phone call had been received, the first bomb ripped apart the Mulberry Bush. The blast blew a gaping hole in the concrete floor, which caused the roof to collapse on top of dozens of customers, trapping them beneath concrete blocks and steel girders. Others were horrifically burnt in the resulting inferno and some were impaled on broken furniture. One paramedic urgently called to the scene described what he saw as 'like a slaughterhouse'.

A few minutes later, and just a few hundred yards away, the second bomb exploded in the Tavern in the Town. It had been placed in a bag at the bottom of a staircase – the only exit out of the basement pub, trapping everyone inside, underground. The blast was so powerful that several victims were blown through a brick wall, their remains shredded between the flying rubble and the thick underground cables which supplied that part of the city with electricity. On finally gaining entrance into the underground bloodbath, emergency service workers were emotionally devastated by what they found. Trapped inside the basement bar, not one single person escaped major injury – or death. Ambulances queued three abreast the entire length of New Street, constantly ferrying the worst-injured to four different local hospitals. Dozens of taxis were commandeered to take those with minor injuries to less over-run and pressured A&Es around the West Midlands. Most of the dead were aged between 17 and 30. One of the victims, 18-year-old Maxine Hambleton, had only entered the basement bar to quickly hand out tickets for her upcoming housewarming party and had been in the pub for just a few seconds before the bomb went off under her face on the stairs.

The two blasts killed 19 on the night – two would later die from their wounds. Some 184 were injured, many of them critically, losing limbs and suffering life-changing burns. The impact on Birmingham's large Irish community was immediate. Airport employees refused to work on planes travelling to and from Irish airports. Homes, shops, businesses and community centres across the city were attacked and some firebombed. People with Irish accents were regularly attacked in pubs, clubs and in the street. Alarmed at the fallout the bombings had caused, the IRA's Army Council placed the city 'strictly off limits' to its active service units and the bombings ceased for the foreseeable future.

The Troubles had impacted upon football too. In 1972, the Provisional IRA sent death threats to the SFA and individual Scottish players ahead of their British Home Championship match at Windsor Park in Belfast. Feeling they couldn't guarantee the safety of any of the British teams, the Northern Ireland football authorities suspended all home games until further notice. The game against Scotland was rescheduled and played at Hampden Park in Glasgow, where the security and safety of players and fans could be better assured. In the 1972/73 British Home Championship, Northern Ireland's 'home' games were played at Everton's Goodison Park. But the amount of security required put off the Everton board from ever staging them again. So in 1974, Northern Ireland's only scheduled 'home' British Home Championship match was once again played at Hampden Park. But no matter what the problems over the Irish Sea, English football had a lot of problems of its own and the Grim Reaper would appear again – this time, inside a football ground.

2

Hooliganism

'My best moment? I have a lot of good moments but the one I prefer is when I kicked the hooligan'

Eric Cantona

SATURDAY, 24 August 1974. Blackpool.

It was a hot day in Britain's favourite seaside resort in more ways than one. The shimmering heat in the air was melting ice-creams and burning sweaty faces. The heat on the ground had led the Lancashire Constabulary to flood Blackpool with riot police. It was Bolton Wakes Week. In the heavily industrial north-west, towns and cities each nominated a 'wakes week' during which time local mills, factories and mines were closed down for essential maintenance and workers enjoyed a week's holiday. Blackpool was packed with thousands of holidaymakers from the Bolton area. The Greater Manchester town is only 39 miles away from Blackpool by road or an hour on the train and for Bolton Wanderers fans, playing Stanley Matthews' old club on his old home ground had long been a keenly awaited local derby. Many who weren't already in the town on holiday had travelled from Bolton the day before to enjoy a night out in the fleshpots of Blackpool and some scrapping with local fans. The pubs and clubs in and around the promenade became a battle zone, with gangs of opposing fans chasing one another, throwing bottles, getting into skirmishes and punch-ups. Some Bolton fans packed into hotel and B&B rooms for the night, two and three to a single bed; many slept on the beach. They woke up the next morning, hungover and bleary-eyed, wolfed down fry-ups and started the belligerence all over again.

As match time approached, the streets around Bloomfield Road were full of broken glass, damaged cars and cracked heads. Long before the days of segregated stands or even match stewards, opposing fans were allowed to stream into the ground together and take up whatever places they fancied around the terraces. A large contingent of Bolton hooligans made a beeline for what was traditionally the home crowd end, the Spion Kop, and even before the game began, bottles, bricks and threats were being thrown across the terraces between the two sets of fans. Blackpool had narrowly missed out on promotion to the top flight the season before and had started the 1974/75 campaign with a 2-1 opening-day defeat away at Norwich and a midweek 0-0 bore draw against Leyton Orient at Bloomfield Road. Bolton had played just the once, beating Portsmouth 3-0 at Burnden Park on the opening day of the season the weekend before. Writing in the matchday programme, Tangerines manager Harry Potts described Bolton as 'our friendly foe'. A hardcore of hooligan fans on either side begged to differ. The Kop soon became the stadium's hotspot for fights and scuffles. As half-time approached, Blackpool fan Kevin Olsson and some of his mates left the terraces to buy food and drink at the Kop end tea bar. As they waited in a lengthy queue, a fight broke out between rival fans and in the melee, someone stabbed the 17-year-old local in the torso and he collapsed on to the concrete.

The wound was so deep that rather than call for an ambulance, police officers carefully scooped Olsson up from the ground and immediately drove him to the local hospital in a squad car, blue lights flashing. Medics worked on the young man from the moment he arrived at the hospital but his heart had already stopped.

The immediate reaction from the local *West Lancashire Evening Gazette* was impassioned, 'So it's happened … Britain's first soccer fan death. It is sickening that it should have happened at Blackpool. But it is equally sickening to realise that it didn't take a genius to predict its inevitability. Now the authorities will rumble into action. They will gather, shake their heads, make their pronouncements. Too late. Too bloody late.' Sports minister Denis Howell duly rumbled into action, travelled to Blackpool to visit the murder scene and vowed to consider introducing identity cards for football fans. It never happened. Shocked rigid by the tragedy, Blackpool FC did take action. They introduced segregated areas to Bloomfield Road to keep opposing fans apart, and also fenced them in. Many other clubs soon followed suit because the problem was now getting totally out of hand.

On the very afternoon of Kevin Olsson's death, a policeman was kept in hospital overnight after being pushed to the ground and repeatedly kicked in the stomach and head, after trying to separate Portsmouth and Nottingham Forest fans at Fratton Park. Thirty-eight people were removed from the ground during the game. At Tannadice Park, Dundee United and Celtic fans clashed before, during and after their match and scores were arrested. At Elland Road, there were ten arrests when hooligans from Leeds United clashed with Birmingham City's hardcore. The following Monday evening, all hell broke loose in Bristol at what would prove to be one of the decade's worst soccer riots. Local rivals

Cardiff City had travelled to Bristol City's Ashton Gate for a League Cup tie and during the match Bristol fans began to chant 'Aberfan' at the Welsh supporters. The small South Wales mining village of Aberfan was the location of a catastrophic tragedy that occurred eight years earlier, when a huge colliery spoil tip collapsed and buried the local primary school, killing 116 children and 28 adults. The despicably sick chant was designed to provoke, and it had the desired effect. After the match, which Bristol City won to further inflame the angry Cardiff fans, violent skirmishes broke out outside the ground. As police struggled to control the trouble, large groups of fans from both sides broke away and either jumped on to buses and trains at Ashton Gate or ran off towards Temple Meads railway station, continuing to fight, smash up cars and shops and generally cause absolute bloody mayhem. Well over 100 fans were arrested, 57 of them under the age of 17. Two days later, a special court handed out prison sentences, youth detention orders and heavy fines to the worst offenders.

Increasingly violent hooligan culture was becoming endemic in and around football clubs the length and breadth of the nation. Earlier in the year, the FA Cup quarter-final between Newcastle and Nottingham Forest at St James' Park was halted halfway through the second half when hundreds of fans stormed the pitch and caused mayhem. A minute earlier, Newcastle centre-back Pat Howard had been sent off for arguing with the referee after Forest's George Lyall had slotted away a penalty to put the Second Division side 3-1 up.

A section of hooligan fans began to chant, 'We're going on the pitch, we're going on the pitch,' in a clear attempt to get the match abandoned. Forest player David Serella was viciously attacked by two Newcastle fans and only saved from further violence when the referee David Smith and one of the linesmen rushed in to protect him. The two 'fans' were both found guilty of actual bodily harm at Newcastle Magistrates' Court, where Serella described the attack: 'I saw these two chaps climb over a wall and run straight at me. One of them took a flying drop kick at my chest and as I stumbled back the other one punched at me. I covered my head in my hands and I was kicked again.'

The *Newcastle Journal* talked to a home fan immediately after the match and he told them, 'It was really frightening. There had been running battles in the Gallowgate End from the start of the match, but after Forest scored their third goal the Leazes End went mad … suddenly a group of them started to surge forward. I was standing near the front of the Leazes End and I was knocked off my feet by young lads rushing past. Luckily I was in front of all the metal barriers, but people behind me were trapped against them and a number of children fainted. I saw one policeman do a diving tackle to stop a skinhead. And I saw an older man fighting three policemen at once as they tried to lead him away.'

Worried for the players' safety, David Smith led both sides off the pitch. As they ran towards the dressing rooms, several Forest players were hit by missiles thrown from the crowd. Police were forced to use dogs to clear hundreds of rioting fans from the pitch and after order was restored ten minutes later, referee Smith brought the players back out to complete the match. But the Forest players were shell-shocked – their Northern Ireland international Martin O'Neill told the press that he was genuinely scared. In the next 23 minutes, Newcastle scored three, the winner coming from skipper Bobby Moncur. Newcastle were into the semi-finals of the FA Cup. A comment piece in the *Newcastle Journal* by local journalist Ken Gorman took no pleasure in the 4-3 win, 'When supporters cannot lump defeat, sport flies out of the window. And nausea takes over.'

The Nottingham Forest staff were sick to their stomachs, too. Manager Allan Brown told a press conference, 'We were 3-1 up, playing our best football of the game, and looked like scoring more. The fans came on to stop play and that was the finish of any concentrated football. Our players just couldn't get into the game … what worries me is that fans from all over the country, having seen the effect mass invasion can have, may believe it is worth their while to invade pitches if their team is losing.'

The Forest board sent a written protest to the FA, arguing that the eventual result was not only unjust but unless Newcastle were disqualified from the cup, thugs would hold future games to ransom. The FA compromise was unprecedented – the result was declared null and void and they ordered the tie to be replayed on a neutral ground, Everton's Goodison Park. The replay was a nervy affair and even after extra time, it remained 0-0. A few days later, the two teams returned to Liverpool for the replay of the replay and a single Malcolm Macdonald goal sent Newcastle through to the last four.

Nottingham Forest's warning to the FA soon became reality. On 27 April, Manchester United played local rivals Manchester City in a match they had to win to avoid relegation to the Second Division for the first time in over 30 years. With minutes to go, former United legend Denis Law put City 1-0 up and hundreds of Red Devils fans invaded their own pitch to get the game abandoned. Fires were started in the stands and the City players were punched and kicked as they raced off to the relative safety of the dressing rooms. Even an appeal by Sir Matt Busby over the PA failed to stop the rioting and fearing for the players' wellbeing, referee David Smith abandoned the match. Yes, the same David Smith. What a spring he was having.

The People's well-respected football journalist Mike Langley had had enough, and in his weekly column the day after, he gave his verdict on the riot, 'Ten feet of unclimbable mesh, topped off by strands of First World War barbed wire. That's the hooligan-proof barrier that Manchester United must be ordered to erect around their pitch next season. No other sentence by the FA Disciplinary Commission can deal adequately with supporters who have spread terror through the First Division. Stabbings, riots, stonings, assault by spit, now arson and pitch invasions. And that's just this season. Yet the Stretford End, that nest of thugs, have flourished unchecked for years. United's board keep deploring their behaviour, but do nothing. Closing Old Trafford for a few games or even a few months, would only toy with the violence. Thousands of United's supporters are proven animals. So I say, "CAGE THEM!"'

The punishment meted out to Manchester United by the FA was little more than a gentle slap on the wrist. The Old Trafford club agreed to erect two 7ft 6in-high fences behind each goal and that was, well, about it. Like Langley in *The People,* the *Sports Argus* was appalled by the soft line the footballing authorities continued to take. A hard-hitting editorial piece suggested, 'Manchester United must be laughing their heads off. The decision of the FA Disciplinary Committee to excuse them further punishments … is a travesty of justice. No fines, no ground closure, no anything. No wonder the Manchester United directors must be rubbing their hands with glee, even though this was the first Football League match to be abandoned through crowd invasions as long as I can remember. Some clubs could do more on their own initiative to prevent it. At present they seem only too happy to accept the money hooligans pay at the gate.'

If we're being generous, perhaps at the root of the problem was that the footballing authorities and football clubs had been blindsided by events and were utterly confused. There had certainly been fighting and feuding at and around matches for decades, but never on this kind of scale. The major problem was that throughout the 1973/74 season, groups of hooligan fans had started to become ever more organised. Local kingpins with a love for power and criminality and members of the far right began to see disillusioned, mainly white working-class young men, as perfect recruits to their violent cause.

One response from the authorities was to increase the amount of 'football special trains' that ran to and from towns and cities around the nation mainly on Saturday matchdays but sometimes for midweek games too. The general public were sick to death of being threatened and terrorised by violent football thugs on normal service trains, so the decision had been made by the government, the FA and British Rail to lay on a regular network of football specials to isolate them from regular travellers. They were far from 'special'. These were trains solely intended for football fans, regularly patrolled by onboard police, ready to be received by well-armed and well-protected on-platform officers at their destination. But despite their presence, many hooligans limbered up for the fights in the towns and cities ahead by smashing up the carriages and laying into waiting opposition fans and police at stations also full of innocent train-goers.

To protect their rolling stock, which were invariably the oldest and most knackered, British Rail increasingly stripped out the football special carriages, so by 1974, many contained nothing more than bare wooden seats, no tables and a minimum of potentially trashable features or decoration. They just took the seats out of the carriages and locked the travellers up from outside for the duration of the trip. Fans had to sit on the floor, and with no toilets they had no choice but to pee in the corners. The smell of urine was just part of a heady olfactory cocktail that stank out every football special train. Although alcohol was supposedly banned, hundreds of fans smuggled booze on to the trains and soon the stink of stale ale, sweat and the male cologne de jour, Brut 33 – a cheap and cloying after shave sold in plastic bottles – began to bring nose-twitching side notes to the strong core odour of wee. The Pink News website most accurately described them as 'horse boxes for hooligans' and the very deliberate lack of comfort spurred bored football travellers on to greater damage, smashing doors and windows and sometimes fighting among themselves. For police planners, the football specials were a boon. Potential troublemaking fans were kept corralled in one place, largely away from the general public, and therefore easier to control and police.

To keep aggro to a minimum, many football specials ended their journeys not at major railway stations, but at halts and smaller stop-offs nearer to the grounds. Specials carrying opposition fans to Newcastle United's St James' Park would regularly disembark at the nearby Manors station; for Sunderland games, they'd be dropped at Seaburn station, a 20-minute walk away from the old Roker Park. In London, away fans going to Tottenham games would end up at the nearby Northumberland Park; special trains en route to Tranmere Rovers would finally halt at Rock Ferry station; New Cree, for Grimsby Town matches. Football trains visiting Sheffield Wednesday would disembark at the small nearby Wadsley Bridge station, which only ever opened on Owls matchdays. Though the specials were desperately short on comfort, the fans loved them. They were a fair bit cheaper than regular train services and allowed supporters to travel together in 'armies', meaning strength – and safety – in numbers. Not to say that travelling together with hundreds and thousands of your own fans was remotely safe.

Opposition football gangs would know exactly when the specials were due into their towns and cities and laid in wait on overhead bridges and adjacent roads, primed to attack the trains; ditto for their journeys back home. Weapons of choice were bricks, bottles, lumps of metal and stone, but more creative hooligans fashioned missiles from golf balls with nails banged into them and rocks wrapped in razor wire. Onboard police warned travelling fans to pull down their blinds when approaching or leaving their destinations, to protect them from shattered glass, as specials increasingly came under potentially lethal attack. To 'defend' themselves, football special fans invented the 'bulb shower'. Pulling in towards 'enemy' railway stations, supporters unscrewed the dozens of bulbs on the trains and then flung them at rival fans from the doors and windows. During the winter months, many fans would return home in total darkness thanks to the lack of lightbulbs, and freezing cold, as wind, rain and sometimes snow whipped in through the glass-less windows that opposition fans had smashed earlier in the day. But by and large, the football trains helped minimise the amount of time that unruly fans were in un-policed contact with the innocent general public and trouble was more efficiently contained.

Emboldened by the relative success of the football specials, the authorities then came up with a truly left-field idea – the disco train. A joint venture created by the FA, Football League clubs and British Rail, the 'League Liner' was potentially an act of genius. The 12-carriage train tried a totally new tack – give the fans so much to occupy them that trouble would be the last thing on their minds. The new venture featured state-of-the-art sound systems, DJs and flashing lights in the disco carriage, plus a chill-out carriage with a large colour TV screen that played match highlights and celebrity interviews. For those who wanted a quieter life, there was a gaming and board game carriage, and if travellers weren't keen on the disco scene, they could listen to light and classical music on headphones. FA chief Alan Hardaker enthusiastically gave his wholehearted backing to the project in a 1973 British Rail press release, 'The added touch of luxury provided by the League Liner will encourage supporters to bring wives and families – and girlfriends.'

The idea was that different clubs would take it in turns to hire the League Liner for their own fans for longer match trips, and it was no surprise that the inaugural journey took place from Burnley down to their First Division game at Queens Park Rangers in London. The Clarets' forward-thinking commercial manager Jack Butterfield had been a vocal part of the FA/Football League/British Rail special committee that was set up to make the project happen. Keen to be seen as pioneers on the side of good, Butterfield immediately signed Burnley up as the guinea pigs, telling the fans that, 'We hope that wives and girlfriends … will take the chance for this cheap excursion to London.' And indeed they did and as the authorities hoped, it had a civilising effect upon the travelling male Burnley fans, dancing themselves dizzy and distracting their partners from potentially smashing up the train. The debut trip was universally acknowledged as a success and more soon followed.

Crystal Palace then chartered the disco train to take their fans up north to Middlesbrough and again there was no trouble. In 1974, Middlesbrough booked the train for their visit over into Lancashire for their match against Preston, and even minnows Hartlepool booked out the special to take them down to South Wales to play Swansea. As a novelty, it proved to be fleetingly popular; but it wasn't cheap. Nearly three times the price of a basic football special train, the League Liner soon began to wane in popularity, and increasingly, the service ran half-full and less. British

Rail and the clubs that booked the train began to lose money on the venture and football fans increasingly lost interest. In 1976, the wonderfully unique League Liner disco train was decommissioned.

At many railway stations, police would arrive in force, often with officers on horseback, to 'kettle' visiting fans and march them to the ground. Some forces erected temporary 'holding areas' made from wire and riot fencing inside the stations, containing fans until the police were organised and ready to walk them to the ground. By 1974, the more determined supporters were second-guessing police strategy, arranging diversions and staging fights to distract their welcoming committees at the stations, and escaping off in smaller packs into the town and city centres to cause un-policed mayhem. It became a weekly cat-and-mouse battle – and Manchester United had many thousands of mice.

Back in the Second Division for the first time in decades, United's Red Army gleefully set themselves a new challenge for the 1974/75 season – to cause as much headline-grabbing chaos as they could in towns and cities they hadn't visited for years. Early in the campaign, hardcore hooligan United fans created mayhem in Cardiff city centre, overturning cars, smashing windows and setting light to market stalls and wastepaper bins. Once inside Cardiff's Ninian Park ground a hail of missiles, bricks and coins flew through the air between the now-segregated home and away sections. Even before the match began, injured fans were being carried out on stretchers and nine people were arrested outside the ground for fighting. At least 15 ringleaders from both home and away sections were dragged out of the ground; Manchester United fans tried to storm the newly erected safety fences, but were driven back by police.

On Saturday, 14 September, 5,000 United fans flooded south for the game against West Bromwich Albion. Trouble flared before they even reached the West Midlands with British Transport Police reporting serious damage to two football trains. Twenty-five United fans were arrested, as hundreds of Red Army members charged through Birmingham Shopping Centre, wrecking stores and ransacking shops. The Manchester United players had become so disturbed by the violence that they organised a public meeting inside Old Trafford with young fans to help combat hooliganism. Scottish international star Willie Morgan told the forum, 'We the players are sick to death of listening to the complaints about a small section of our so-called supporters. We do not need these villains. They should go somewhere else. This club's good name should not be jeopardised.'

Though it was laudable that the United players got involved and spoke out, Morgan had one thing badly wrong – the Red Army hooligans were by no means just 'a small section'. They had now become legion and travelled threateningly in their thousands. Henceforward, whenever and wherever they turned up, the locals were prepared. Pubs and bars were closed on matchdays and shops boarded up; streets and town centres deserted – except for the local hooligans, keen to 'defend' their home turf against the invaders. In the 70s, hooligan crews were springing up everywhere, some already earning fearsome reputations for violence – Leeds United's Service Crew, Birmingham City's early Zulu Warriors and West Ham's infamous Inter City Firm. They had become increasingly well-marshalled with their own leaders and lieutenants, several of whom were ex-military who understood the tactics of battle and ambush. Some of the leaders were older men with long strings of criminal convictions for violence and assault, who revelled in the power of leading their own little armies, demanding blind obedience from the young foot soldiers. The gangs were almost exclusively white and many had allegiances to far-right organisations like the deeply racist National Front. Though black players were still in a tiny minority in the Football League of the 70s, players like West Ham's Clyde Best, Ade Coker and Clive Charles, Bradford City's Joe Cooke and Cec Podd and the young Viv Anderson at Nottingham Forest were viciously abused by rival fans week in, week out.

As trouble increased, attendances began to fall throughout the Football League. Loyal and law-abiding fans had had enough and as TV and radio coverage of matches increased, many supporters, particularly those who took their kids, were happier to sit in the safety of their own homes rather than risk the increasingly dangerous terraces. In 1971/72, the average First Division attendance was 31,313. By the 1973/74 season this had dropped ten per cent to 28,296. In the Second Division, the 1971/72 average turnout was 14,652 – by 1973/74 this had fallen to 13,693. The Third Division, from 8,510 to 6,198 – a drop of a quarter. In the Fourth Division, 4,961 to an average of 3,927.

Throughout 1974, the so-called 'English Disease' was spreading rapidly. Tottenham Hotspur travelled to the Netherlands to play the second leg of their UEFA Cup Final against Feyenoord in front of a 67,000 crowd in Rotterdam. After drawing 2-2 in the White Hart Lane home leg, Spurs had an uphill struggle and finally went down 2-0 to a strong Feyenoord team. The players displayed an admirable dignity in defeat – a section of their fans did not. According to the *Daily Telegraph*, 'The occasion was made deplorable by the hooligan element of their supporters … they ignored public address appeals by Spurs chairman Sidney Wale and manager Bill Nicholson, who called them a disgrace to Britain.' The *Daily Mail* described a day-long orgy of violence, 'After spending the day rampaging through the streets of Rotterdam, Spurs fans ran amok on the terraces behind the Feyenoord goal when the Dutch team went into a 1-0 lead just before half-time. In one of the worst displays of hooliganism by British fans at a European soccer contest, seats were ripped from their mountings and sent spinning into crowds of Dutch supporters below. A full-scale battle raged as the fans from north London waded wildly into astonished Dutchmen with uprooted flagpoles and flying bottles.'

Baton-wielding riot police waded into the trouble and finally managed to break up the violence, but not before the terraces became littered with the fallen. About 130 people were taken to hospital, including five Dutch policemen, one of whom suffered brain damage; a fan with a perforated eyeball; and supporters suffering from serious head wounds and numerous broken arms and legs.

A Dutch Red Cross spokesman commented, 'They were like animals, these drunken English kids. We've never seen anything like this before and we never want to see it again.' A policeman who took part in the baton charges against the Spurs fans was incredulous at the state of the rioters, 'Half of them were so drunk we could have killed them and they wouldn't even have felt it.'

Thanks to the thugs' actions, Tottenham Hotspur became the first British club to be banned from Europe. Fast-forward to August 1974 and Manchester United crossed the North Sea to play a so-called pre-season friendly against A.S.V. Oostende. A gang of Red Army fans caused utter havoc in the quiet Belgian seaside resort, smashing windows, wrecking parked cars and fighting in the seafront's bars and restaurants.

As the 1970s progressed things would only get worse. The following year, the mighty Leeds United were banned from Europe after their fans rioted in Paris following their defeat to Bayern Munich in the 1975 European Cup Final. Two years later, almost inevitably, Manchester United were also banned from Europe, after a large gang of their so-called fans caused mayhem before, during and after their European Cup Winners' Cup game with Saint-Étienne, also in Paris.

3

The Managers

'Infamy! Infamy! They've all got it in for me!'
Kenneth Williams in the film *Carry On Cleo*

IT WAS a grey and rainy spring day when England's World Cup-winning manager Alf Ramsey received a phone call requesting he attend a meeting with his chairman Sir Andrew Stephen at the FA's Lancaster Gate headquarters on Friday, 19 April 1974. Ramsey asked for the date of the meeting to be postponed as it was an official day off for him and he'd arranged to have a set of inoculations for England's upcoming friendly tour of eastern Europe. The phone rang a second time and Ramsey was asked to attend the FA a day later on the Saturday. He was somewhat bemused; this was a non-work day for the FA offices and he asked what the meeting was about. Ramsey was told that it was to discuss 'operational matters', and with the British Home Championship around the corner plus the summer tour, he assumed it would be to discuss team selection, general housekeeping and travel arrangements.

It had not been an easy nine months for Ramsey. Back in October 1973 England were infamously dumped out of the World Cup in the qualifying stages after failing to overcome Poland in their two group match-ups. After losing 1-0 in a violent and bad-tempered game in Chorzów, England needed to beat the Poles at Wembley to top the group. The defeat in Poland was regarded by most football pundits as a freak result and no one was expecting anything other than an England win. After his stuttering performance in Chorzów when his over-worked defence had bailed him out numerous times, 25-year-old ŁKS Łódź goalie Jan Tomaszewski was regarded as a particularly weak link. Summarising for ITV before the game, Brian Clough famously dubbed him 'a circus clown in gloves'. It started disastrously for the stopper. With just two minutes on the clock, a Tomaszewski mistake led to his wrist being broken. As he later told the BBC, 'I was feeling the pressure and did not notice that Allan Clarke was standing two metres away from me when I rolled the ball out. I dived at his feet to make a save but he kicked me instead of the ball and I broke five tiny bones in my left wrist, like glass. They were frozen during the game and the adrenaline meant I did not feel the pain.'

Tomaszewski carried on and, for the next 88 minutes and despite the injury, he played the game of his life. He saved with hands, arms, legs and even his backside, no matter what England threw at him. Just after half-time, Norman Hunter turned out to be the clown. Picking up the ball near the halfway line, the Leeds defender, who'd been chosen ahead of Bobby Moore, got his feet in a tangle, allowing Robert Gadocha to surge forward and pick out team-mate Jan Domarski, who slid the ball under Peter Shilton. Horror of horrors: England were 1-0 down. Eight minutes later they were thrown a lifeline after Martin Peters theatrically took a dive inside Poland's penalty box – Allan Clarke put away the penalty to level.

But as England flooded forward to find the winner, the broken-wristed Tomaszewski's heroics hit new heights. At the end of 90 minutes, it remained 1-1. England were out of the World Cup. The game stats told the story of an utterly one-sided affair: England managed 36 shots to Poland's two; they forced 26 corners, hit the woodwork twice, and had four shots cleared off the line. But this was an England that struggled to score goals.

Failing to qualify hit Sir Alf hard. He'd considered quitting and constantly received offers from some of the country's top clubs. But the patriotic Ramsey decided to soldier on, convinced he had the talent, and the plan, to turn England's fortunes back around. His players still backed him and there had been no public suggestion from the FA that they wished him to leave. Since the Poland game, he'd been in charge for two friendlies against Portugal and Italy and was putting plans in place to rebuild his England side. What Ramsey didn't know was that behind the scenes, his biggest enemy at the FA, vice-chairman Professor Sir Harold Thompson, had long been plotting his downfall. An Oxford Blue in football and then a chemistry don who taught a young Margaret Thatcher, Thompson was an establishment character with an extremely high opinion of himself and his status in life.

He regarded the Dagenham-born working-class Sir Alf as his inferior in every way and despite him winning the World Cup for England, Thompson imperiously and unfailingly addressed him to his face as 'Ramsey'. When Alf was granted a knighthood in 1967, coming before his own award, the status-obsessed Thompson was enraged. In 1972, England went on a friendly tour of Europe. One morning, Ramsey and his players came down to breakfast in their hotel to find the dining room thick with pungent cigar smoke. Some of the players told their manager they couldn't eat in such an unpleasant and fuggish atmosphere and Ramsey agreed. He approached the cigar smoker, a certain Harold Thompson, politely asked him to put out his stogie and calmly explained why. Thompson stubbed out his cigar with an angry flourish and fixed Sir Alf with a look of sheer contempt. 'Ramsey' had shown him an utter lack of respect and deference – and he would not forget.

In a game against Germany, the England party needed to get a professional translator on board. A fluent German speaker, Thompson volunteered himself, but Ramsey was having none of it. Thompson was told a translator had already been appointed – they hadn't – but the truth was that Ramsey, famously protective of his players and regarding the FA vice-chair as a thoroughly negative influence on team morale, didn't want Thompson anywhere near his squad. Once again, the man who was used to getting his own way had been slighted. Thompson's dislike and disdain for Ramsey was turning to hatred. He would continue to privately but not very quietly build the case against Ramsey. Constantly in the ears of other senior FA officials, he continued to run down the manager's reputation at the Lancaster Gate HQ. Before the World Cup qualifying matches against Poland and Wales, Ramsey unwittingly gave him further ammunition. Rightly, he told the ever-parsimonious FA that he wasn't prepared to continue on his salary of £6,100 – topped up to £7,200 with a cost-of-living bonus – and wanted a significant raise to reflect the importance and prestige of being national team manager.

To put this into context, many Third and Fourth Division managers at the time were earning higher salaries and the average top-flight club boss earned three times Ramsey's wage. The Greek FA had unofficially approached Ramsey about becoming their national team manager on a salary of £30,000 a year. His customary annual increase was a measly £100 a year. Ramsey's much publicised £6,000 bonus for winning the World Cup was structured in such a way that he ended up being hammered for maximum tax. Around the same time, managers who won the First Division title were being paid up to £20,000 in bonuses. Thompson told fellow FA officials that Ramsey should be grateful he had been given the honour of being appointed England manager and was greedy. The FA told Ramsey that his salary would be discussed, as per usual, in a year's time and nothing was done. But after England failed to qualify for the 1974 World Cup, Thompson began to spread fresh bile against Ramsey at the FA's headquarters. Unbeknown to Sir Alf, some members of the FA committee had suggested they give their World Cup-winning manager a boost after the Poland disappointment by passing an official confidence vote in him. The powerful and autocratic Thompson stymied the move. According to writer Leo McKinstry in *The Guardian*, one former FA official told him, 'Sir Harold was a bullying autocrat. He was a bastard. He treated the staff like shit.'

Alf Ramsey took the train down from his Ipswich home on Saturday, 20 April for the meeting he was expecting with FA chairman Sir Andrew Stephen. Once inside the boardroom at Lancaster Gate, he was shocked to discover the room was packed with senior FA officials, sitting in silence, many nervously shuffling sheaves of papers and avoiding eye contact. Ramsey realised there was trouble afoot. He told *The People*'s Mike Langley, 'It was the most devastating half-hour of my life. I stood in a room almost full of staring committee men. It was just like I was on trial. I thought I was going to be hanged.' Ramsey was told the decision had been made to replace him as manager after 11 years in the role and then he was offered a gin and tonic, which he refused.

Ramsey left Lancaster Gate, went to watch Crystal Palace play Hull City at Selhurst Park and then began to ring around family and close friends, to warn them the announcement would soon be made public. The FA's official statement was short and shameful, 'The FA has terminated the contract of national team manager Sir Alf Ramsey with immediate effect. His successor will be announced shortly.' Not a word of thanks or appreciation. The man who had led them to England's one and only World Cup win and then third place in the 1968 European Championship and a thrilling quarter-final finish in the Mexico World Cup of 1970 was given the barest of credit for his unprecedented achievements. Long before PR, marketing and sponsorship became key parts of a manager's job, Ramsey hated talking to the media, seeing it as wasted time that took him away from his job, and he soon became characterised in the press as cold and unapproachable. But his players loved him, as did the fans. In the days following, he received hundreds and hundreds of supportive letters from England supporters – many simply addressed to Alf Ramsey, Ipswich.

The FA approached Matt Busby to become the national team's first non-English manager, albeit as short-term caretaker, but Busby had no interest in coming out of retirement. Many English football fans clamoured for Brian Clough to become new boss, but he was disliked by the powers-that-be at the FA for his forthright plain speaking and perceived cockiness. Finally, Coventry general manager and former Arsenal and England star Joe Mercer was asked to fill in on a temporary basis for seven games, because the FA had already identified the man they wanted to take over on a permanent basis. But he still had the small matter of a league championship to win. After 13 years as Leeds United manager, Don Revie duly won the Elland Road side their third league title and in August 1974 he was appointed new permanent England manager. It must have galled Ramsey. The FA agreed a salary for Revie three times the wage they had paid their former boss. The FA patted themselves on the back for 'securing the services of the best manager in English football'.

The former England international had signed as a player for Leeds when aged 30 in 1958 and was appointed player-manager in March 1961. Revie was under no illusions. Leeds were an unfashionable, not particularly well-supported club, but he had big ambitions. Two games were key to his entire philosophy on football. In 1953, and while still a striker at Manchester City, he had watched Hungary swamp England 6-3. Though he was thrilled by the Magyars' overall tactics, as a centre-forward, Revie was particularly taken by the unexpected 'withdrawn' role taken by Hungary's classy attacker Nándor Hidegkuti. He went back to Maine Road and convinced the coaching staff that he should begin to play a similar withdrawn role in the Manchester City team. It would soon bear fruit – Revie was named Football Writers' Association Footballer of the Year for the 1954/55 season. The second game that radically changed Revie's thinking about football was Real Madrid's 7-3 thrashing of Eintracht Frankfurt in the 1960 European Cup Final – a masterclass in quick, short passing and transitional play.

But to even approach a Real Madrid style, Revie needed top, intelligent players at his disposal; those he took over at mediocre Second Division Leeds were somewhat lacking. The Whites had finished 14th at the end of the 1960/61 season and were already in severe financial straits with little money available for signings. Revie, though, convinced the board to spend money on bringing Everton's tough 30-year-old midfielder Bobby Collins to Elland Road – his plan being to build a team of young, homegrown players around the influential Scot, enforcer Billy Bremner and towering centre-half Jack Charlton. Revie's first full season as player-manager, 1961/62, was a struggle, with Leeds avoiding relegation to the Third Division thanks only to a final-day 3-0 win against Newcastle at St James' Park. Trying to integrate young players like Gary Sprake, Norman Hunter, Paul Madeley and Paul Reaney proved to be a hit-and-miss affair with his tyros struggling to find any consistency on the pitch and scoring was a problem. Leeds would only win 12 of their 42 games, thanks to a meagre return of 50 goals – well over a third of those came from Charlton with eight and midfielder Bremner scoring 12.

But with his younger players bedding in, the following season would see them finish fifth. In 1964/65, Revie's side would win the Second Division championship. But questions were already being asked about his team's dark heart. Liverpool's Bill Shankly had once memorably observed, 'You can't play your way out of Division Two – you have to claw your way out.' Revie took the advice to heart. The Football League's official journal, *League Football*, placed Leeds top of its disciplinary table for bookings and sendings off. It concluded, 'This is the dirtiest team in the country.'

Throughout the 1960s and early 1970s Revie cleverly developed or signed a host of highly creative and talented players and then integrated them into his teams. Men like Eddie Gray, Peter Lorimer and Paul Madeley were the envy of the top flight. But to protect and support his flair players, Revie also put together a system of enforcers – tough, often cynical players like Bremner, Charlton, Norman 'Bites Yer Legs' Hunter, Johnny Giles and the ever-combustible Bobby Collins. Under Revie's astute leadership, Leeds enjoyed over a decade of unparalleled success, winning the league title twice, two UEFA Cups, the FA Cup, the League Cup, the Charity Shield and the Second Division. In addition they were First Division runners-up five times and Cup Winners' Cup finalists.

But Revie had always been a divisive figure. His players would run through walls for him while Leeds fans believed they had the best manager in the land. They saw him as a tactical visionary and supreme man-motivator. Elsewhere, it was a different story. Detractors viewed his management style as negative and overly pragmatic and the take-no-prisoners Elland Road team viewed as overly cynical. From his earliest days as manager corruption rumours swirled around him. Fellow boss Bob Stokoe once claimed that during his struggling Second Division years, Revie offered him a bribe if he made sure his Bury side 'went easy' on Revie's relegation-threatened team. After refusing, Stokoe was aghast to hear Revie ask if it would be OK to approach some of his players instead. *Daily Mirror* journalist Richard Stott compiled a dossier detailing other instances where Revie had attempted to fix matches and handed it to the FA. It was buried.

Dubbed 'Don Readies', Revie was always looking to top up his wages. After one England match, he demanded £200 for an exclusive post-game press interview with striker Malcolm Macdonald. Allegedly, Macdonald never saw a penny of the payment. Dour and moody, his siege mentality attitude to football and life in general made him few friends outside of Elland Road. Brian Clough was always the fan favourite and popular choice as new England manager, closely followed by the talented and likeable Bobby Robson.

Revie's record leading England was barely bang average. He failed to get them to the 1976 European Championship in Yugoslavia, and of his 29 matches in charge, his team won 14, drew eight and lost seven. To put this into further perspective, ten of his 14 wins were against international lightweights – two each against Cyprus, Finland, Northern Ireland and Wales, plus a victory apiece over Luxembourg and Switzerland. Revie's success at Leeds was based upon the loyalty and support he gave to his regular players, the culture he built at Elland Road, and in turn, his team gave him unqualified respect. Though tactically astute, Revie was now asked to pick players from lots of different clubs and find a balance and mix at top international level. Just as he had done with his Leeds teams, he would provide his England players with huge, detailed dossiers on their opponents which bored the backsides off his selections. Flair players like Tony Currie, Stan Bowles and Alan Ball disliked his pragmatism and defensive inclinations.

Revie soon learned, as Ramsey had before him, that the hierarchy at the FA were not there to help and support the England manager, but to weigh him down with bureaucracy and red tape. What's more, they demanded deference from a proud man who was used to being top dog. His first meeting with the dangerous Sir Harold Thompson did not augur well. Thompson introduced himself by saying, 'When I get to know you better, Revie, I shall call you Don.' To which a stone-faced Revie replied, 'When I get to know you better Thompson, I shall call you Sir Harold.' Their relationship went downhill from there, with Thompson effortlessly transferring his contempt for Sir Alf on to the new man. Never exactly a Positive Pete mood-wise, Revie soon became unhappy in the England job. He hated the intense media attention, the continued demands from the press – and the constant criticism. But it was out on the pitch where things were really going wrong.

By the middle of 1977, Revie was struggling to get them to qualify for the 1978 World Cup in Argentina. England had lost in their group 2-0 to Italy in Rome and now needed to win the return fixture and score an avalanche of goals against Luxembourg to better the Italians' goal difference. But before those two final group games, England embarked on a friendly tour of South America. During the trip, Revie appeared moody, depressed and withdrawn, seemingly a man with much on his mind. After two arguably fortunate draws against Argentina and Uruguay, Revie told the FA he wanted to cut short his tour to scout some Italian players back in Europe. He was being somewhat economical with the truth. Revie flew incognito to the Middle East and secretly lined up a new job and a hugely lucrative contract as manager of the United Arab Emirates national team. It was breathtakingly underhand but there was further ignominy to follow. The FA would learn about his decision not via a resignation letter, but via the front page of the *Daily Mail* in a well-paid exclusive interview with Revie. Sir Harold Thompson was reportedly apoplectic and said in a statement, 'We are all very sad that Mr Revie should not tell his employers before informing the newspapers what he is doing … he has failed to appear at meetings with me so I don't see why I should now talk to him.' The world of football was appalled and there were dark mutterings about Revie for jumping ship halfway through a poor World Cup qualifying campaign and betraying his country. The *Daily Mirror* dubbed him a 'quitter' for bailing out when things were going against him. Revie's carefully built reputation was utterly shredded.

It didn't prove to be a great year for Britain's brightest young manager, 'Ol' Big Head' Brian Clough, either. After leading Derby County to their first league championship in 1972 and then a European Cup semi-final, Cloughie and his assistant Peter Taylor downed tools and walked out of the Baseball Ground. Players and fans alike were devastated, but it hardly came from out of the blue. A hugely prolific goalscoring forward at Middlesbrough, Clough's playing career was cruelly cut short in his 20s due to a crippling knee injury. He cut his teeth as a manager in his native north-east at Hartlepools, where his breezy attacking style of play caught the eye of Derby's long-time chairman Sam Longson and Clough was tempted to the East Midlands.

At the time, Derby were a struggling Second Division club who looked to be going nowhere; Brian Clough soon changed all of that. He taught his new squad how to adapt to his trademark quick passing, attacking style and persuaded promising young players like Roy McFarland and John O'Hare to come join his project at what was a distinctly unfashionable club. In his first season, Derby finished 18th. The following season, they were crowned Second Division champions. Three years later they were league champions for the first time and then made it as far as the European Cup semi-finals, narrowly beaten by Juventus.

Players and fans alike adored him; his chairman did not. An old-school disciplinarian, Longson was thrilled by the success Clough had brought to his club but he had grown to increasingly dislike his young manager's outspoken manner and the two constantly clashed. A particular bone of contention was Clough's burgeoning media career, which often meant he was absent from the ground. Clough would argue it was putting Derby County in the spotlight, right, left and centre, but Longson cared more about the time it took Clough away from his duties. Relations between chairman and manager became rancorous. Clough and his loyal assistant Peter Taylor handed in numerous resignation letters, but each time, other board members persuaded them to stay. Eventually the inevitable happened. Another petty fall-out between Longson and Clough, another letter – but this time the chairman told the board he'd had enough of God's Gift to Football undermining his authority and would accept their resignation. The players were so distraught that they signed a letter to Longson demanding he talk Clough and Taylor around and convince them to stay. But Longson dug his heels in and the dynamic duo left the Baseball Ground.

Weeks later, they surprised the football world by turning up as the new management team not at another top First

Division club, but struggling Third Division Brighton. Clough's first match in charge saw the Seagulls hammered 8-2 by Bristol Rovers and his new side spent the rest of his six-month tenure in a relegation-battle. Eventually, a chastened Clough avoided the ignominy of a drop into the Fourth Division, but still, Brighton could only finish 19th. It was, then, perhaps no surprise that when a top-flight club came a-calling over the summer of 1974, Clough jumped at the chance to manage in the First Division again. That club, of course, was Leeds United; more, much more of that story later in the book.

Elsewhere, two footballing legends called time on their managerial careers – and one came as a seismic shock. After adding yet another cup to the Anfield trophy room by beating Newcastle 3-0 in the 1974 FA Cup Final, a couple of weeks after receiving an OBE for his services to sport and following nearly 15 golden years in charge at Anfield, Liverpool boss Bill Shankly decided to quit. Over his years as manager, the board had also become used to the fiery socialist Scot regularly handing in his resignation over disagreements about signings, team affairs and the culture he was trying to build at the club. But this time it was for real. Shankly told his directors that after 40 years in football, he was just tired out and had had enough. It was time to be with his family. For the football-mad city of Liverpool it was a bolt from the blue and totally unexpected.

Writing in the *Liverpool Echo* on 13 July 1974, journalist Alfred Green did his best to sum up the sense of shock, 'A whole city – men, women and children – were stunned into disbelief yesterday, by the bombshell that exploded in the VIP lounge at the headquarters of Liverpool FC. Shankly retiring? Never. It was a malicious rumour started by disgruntled Evertonians. It was somebody's idea of a practical joke … an announcement broadcast over the public address system in St John's market stopped shoppers in mid-stride. "What was that?" said one woman. "If it's true my old fella will be in mourning for a week. Maybe longer." People wept in the streets and even Shankly's players and close friends refused to believe the news. Reds hardman Tommy Smith told the *Echo*, "Sorry, but I just can't believe this. Retire? The close-season's always been too long for Shanks, never mind retirement." Close friend and new England caretaker manager Joe Mercer was almost lost for words when he was told the news. "That's impossible … I can't accept that … that doesn't ring true … I hope not … I prefer not to believe it. He's done everything in the game. He's the best advert the game's ever had.'"

A small group of directors had known about Shankly's decision for a few weeks, but no official announcement was made as the board desperately tried to convince Shankly to stay. The Scot later told the *Irish Independent*, 'In fact some of the offers they have made would have tempted Paul Getty.' But their long-serving manager was adamant – his last game in charge would be the FA Cup Final. Shankly's loyal number two Bob Paisley reluctantly accepted the job and only so that none of his regular boot room compatriots would face the sack under any new potential managerial regime.

Shankly almost immediately regretted his decision and as pre-season training approached, a tragedy began to play out at Liverpool's Melwood training ground. Shanks had promised the board that he would always remain available as a sounding board for the new manager, but if his replacement didn't need him around, he would respect that and step back. As the players returned from their summer break ready to start afresh under Paisley, the first person they spotted, fully kitted out, was Shankly. Paisley's first reaction was one of relief, assuming that his much-loved boss had withdrawn his resignation and was back in charge. But no. Shankly explained that though now retired, he was happy to come down to Melwood and lead the training. Paisley was crestfallen. He never wanted the manager's job but now the very man he had shown such loyalty to over so many years had returned to – unwittingly – undermine his authority. The players were still referring to Shankly as 'boss' and as pre-season training continued, he would return day after day, unable to let go. In the end, Paisley bravely took the legend aside, the man who had turned around the club, and told him, 'Bill, you don't work here any more. This is my team here, I've got things I want to do.' One can only imagine how this hurt both men.

The Liverpool board asked Shankly not to attend Melwood and, worried about further potential tinkering within the club he'd supposedly quit, decided not to give him a place on the board. They needed to move on. Having recently seen his good friend Matt Busby given a director's role at Manchester United, Shankly was outraged. Through talent, total commitment and sheer force of will he had turned around a mediocre Second Division club and transformed them into a major force domestically and across Europe. And perhaps in the emotional heat of the situation he couldn't see how much he was damaging his loyal lieutenant's task in moving Liverpool on. Massively slighted, he began to turn up at Everton's Bellfield training ground, to unofficially help coach their youth teams. With quite some degree of bitterness he told the *Liverpool Echo*, 'I have been received more warmly by Everton than I have been by Liverpool.' Truly a sad end to Shankly's amazing Anfield reign.

A few weeks after Shankly was banned from Melwood, Spurs manager Bill Nicholson quit after 16 years in charge at the club. As Tottenham boss, his record was without compare. In 1960/61 he led his attractive attacking side to the 20th century's first league and FA Cup double, scoring 115 goals along the way. In 1963, 'Bill Nick' became the first English manager to win a European title, thrashing Atlético Madrid 5-1 in the final of the Cup Winners' Cup. Throughout the 60s, Spurs won three FA Cups in eight years and under Nicholson's guidance they claimed eight major trophies in all. The 1974/75 season started badly for Spurs and after losing 4-0 to Middlesbrough in the second round of the League Cup, Nicholson decided to call it a day. He told the press, 'The simple truth was I was burnt out, I had no more to offer.'

But behind the scenes, the truth was more complicated. Nicholson had become disillusioned with modern football. He hated the negative pragmatism that was spreading throughout the top flight; a disciplinarian short back and sides man, he despaired at players' unkempt slovenliness and their increasingly high wages, and was appalled by hooliganism and the mounting aggression around the game. And like Shankly's stellar reign at Anfield, his long, committed and hugely successful spell at White Hart Lane ended in depressing acrimony. He was convinced that the best way to take Spurs forward was to appoint senior player Danny Blanchflower as new manager. The board were furious that Nicholson had actively contacted Blanchflower to discuss his 'plan' without their knowledge and appointed Terry Neill instead.

Despite everything that Nicholson had done for Spurs, the board gave him a £10,000 pay-off, then severed all ties and refused him a testimonial. In the end, common sense would prevail. In 1976, Keith Burkinshaw was appointed new Spurs manager. A huge admirer of Nicholson, he persuaded the Tottenham board to welcome 'Bill Nick' back to the club as an adviser and scout. Always a man with a rare eye for unearthing new talent, Nicholson would not disappoint. Among the many players he recommended to Burkinshaw were Gary Mabbutt, Graham Roberts and Tony Galvin, all of whom would become legends at White Hart Lane. Fittingly, Bill Nicholson was appointed club president in 1991.

1974 proved to be a crossroads year in management and tells us a great deal about the changing face of English football. Money had become king. Rewind 15 years, and the 92 Football League clubs only had five trophies to play for – four divisional titles and the FA Cup. Now the top clubs were also fighting it out in the highly lucrative European Cup, Cup Winners' Cup and the Inter-Cities Fairs Cup and for those First Division teams that didn't make it into Europe, the newly established Texaco Cup. All Football League clubs could also now have a bash at the League Cup. With more matches came more revenue and the need to succeed became ever stronger, which placed more pressure on managers. With increased sponsorship and greater media attention, the job description of the average manager was starting to change into a more front-facing business. They were expected to give more of their time to TV and press reporters, preview and review matches, and talk about players, transfers and club matters in general.

For old-school managers like Sir Alf Ramsey and Bill Nicholson, talking at any length to the press was as pleasurable as a trip to the dentist. New kids on the block like Brian Clough, Bobby Robson and Ron Atkinson were media naturals – Clough particularly lapped up the limelight and even appeared as a regular pundit on ITV. The road that Liverpool took after Bill Shankly's resignation was to trust in continuity and the collective wisdom of their Boot Room philosophy. Bob Paisley went on to become the most successful English manager of all time, winning an astonishing four European Cups, a UEFA Cup, a European Super Cup, six First Division titles, three League Cups, five FA Charity Shields and personally, five Manager of the Year awards and two European Coach of the Year titles.

Elsewhere, it was a different story. After Don Revie's 13-year reign at Elland Road, and over-desperate to replicate his success, Leeds took a different road and burnt through six different managers over the following six seasons but won nothing. Nicholson had reigned supreme at Spurs for 15 years. Following his resignation, Tottenham got through seven managers in just 13 seasons – and won nothing. Once Clough walked out at Derby after six seasons in charge, the Rams employed five different managers over the next half a dozen years. Everywhere, the shelf life of the Football League manager was lessening by the year. According to an exhaustive statistical survey done by Sky, the average tenure in 1964 was 1,400 days. By 1974, this had dropped to 1,200; in 2017, it was just 400 days.

4

The First Division

'Every team had a hardman. We had Nobby Stiles, Chelsea had "Chopper" [Ron Harris], Arsenal had Peter Storey, Liverpool had Tommy Smith. Leeds had 11 of them'

– George Best

THE BOOKMAKERS rarely get it wrong. Before the 1973/74 season began, Bill Shankly's reigning league champions Liverpool and Don Revie's Leeds United were both variously between 4/1 and 9/2 with the major firms to win the First Division title. Both retained strong squads and made few signings during the summer. At Liverpool, Shankly had already pieced together an impressive mixture of hungry, talented youth and supremely consistent older players, in a team packed with internationals. At the back: England goalie Ray Clemence and defenders Emlyn Hughes, Tommy Smith, a young Phil Thompson and Larry Lloyd. In midfield and up front: Scotland's Peter Cormack, quicksilver dribbler and Republic of Ireland winger Steve Heighway, England's new breakout star and all-round human dynamo Kevin Keegan, and top Welsh striker John Toshack. Like all Shankly sides, the 1973/74 iteration was ever-resolute at the back, gloriously easy on the eye when in possession and an irresistible force of nature up front.

Over in Yorkshire, Don Revie had created a club culture that thrived on fierce never-say-die competition, even in training. The squad he had created was, apart from Welsh goalie Gary Sprake and the Republic of Ireland's Johnny Giles, largely a split between England stars like Norman Hunter, Terry Cooper, Paul Madeley, Allan Clarke, Paul Reaney and Mick Jones and Scottish internationals Billy Bremner, Joe Jordan, Eddie Gray, Peter Lorimer, Gordon McQueen and David Harvey. To keep them all keen, Revie would deliberately play England v Scotland five-a-side matches in training and they would kick lumps out of one another. Revie remains perhaps the most complex, complicated and almost strangest of English managers. He was, on the one hand, the most logical and rational of game organisers who inspired Pep Guardiola. Pioneering the use of intense and extensive pre-match analysis to gain an advantage for his side, opponents were forensically scouted and detailed dossiers were drawn up on each of their players. But he was also deeply superstitious. Before every Leeds home game he would ritually walk to a traffic light near to Elland Road and then walk back again. He would wear the same light blue suit, the same shirt, socks and shoes for every game. Before one match he accidentally ripped the suit trousers and his biggest concern was not his pre-match team talk but whether his strides could be mended for him to wear by kick-off time.

Leeds had ended the previous season (1972/73) third in the First Division, after their form fell away in the spring. Shame, but no matter – they had two cup finals to look forward to. Odds-on favourites to beat little-fancied Second Division Sunderland in the FA Cup Final, Revie's men dominated but lost 1-0. But never mind – now they had the small matter of a European Cup Winners' Cup Final against AC Milan to win. They didn't. Following a series of shocking and controversial decisions against them made by referee Christos Michas, Leeds once again went down 1-0. Later, Michas would be banned from football for match-fixing in several other games. Leeds had looked certainties for a rare treble and ended up with nothing, the Yorkshire nearly men.

Revie was determined that the 1973/74 season would be different. It did not start well. Even before the new campaign began his team were given an honour of a most dubious nature. The Football League slapped them with a £3,000 fine and a warning about their future conduct thanks to their record crop of red and yellow cards in 1972/73. To the footballing world in general, this only confirmed what many already believed – the Whites were the thug team, 'Dirty Leeds'. It was a tag that enraged Revie. He would often argue that every successful team throughout football's history needed its hardmen and its enforcers to protect the skill and ability of the most talented players. Leeds had the latter in abundance. Forwards Eddie Gray, Peter Lorimer, Allan Clarke and Mick Jones were all top talents and any opponent who tried to rough them up had Billy Bremner and Johnny Giles to deal with. At the back, Gary Sprake, full-backs Paul Reaney and Mick Bates, and centre-halves Norman Hunter and Gordon McQueen already knew one another's games inside out, and throughout the season they would collect 21 clean sheets.

In locally born Paul Madeley, Revie had perhaps the top flight's greatest-ever utility player. During his 536 league games for Leeds, Madeley would play in every outfield position and effortlessly slot in wherever he was asked to play. A viscerally loyal Leeds fan as well as a player, Madeley was once asked into the office for contract talks by Revie's successor Jimmy Armfield. He told Armfield, 'I'm not going anywhere. I only want to play for Leeds so draw me up a contract and I'll sign it.' Used to footballers playing hardball over pay and conditions, a bemused Armfield asked Madeley whether he wanted a two- or three-year contract. Madeley shrugged and replied, 'Whatever you think's best, boss.' It probably said a great deal too about how well Revie had treated his regular players over his decade-plus in charge and gained their trust and loyalty.

On the eve of the new 1973/74 season, Revie told his squad that his aim was for them to go the entire league campaign unbeaten – and in turn, his players had a damned good go at it. They would not taste defeat until 23 February 1974, losing 3-2 at Stoke City – and after that only three more times during what was nothing other than a Mad March. Perhaps it was no great surprise that they lost out 1-0 to fierce rivals Liverpool in a tight, evenly fought match at Anfield. But then inexplicably, they lost their next game, 4-1 at home to Burnley, and then a third on the bounce with a 3-1 reverse at West Ham. The experienced Revie soon steadied the nerves and the Leeds juggernaut hurtled on towards the finishing line, ending up champions, five points ahead of runners-up Liverpool. This was the trophy that the single-minded Revie had coveted above all else for the season. So intent was he on winning the league that he fielded weakened sides in the club's UEFA Cup matches and they went out in the third round to Vitória de Setúbal. The truth is that through the late 1960s and into the 70s, Leeds had often been runners-up in competitions because they were always there in the final stages of so many league, cup and European tournaments. One honour mattered more to Revie than any other – the First Division title. And this season, he was desperate to win his second championship.

Like many clubs who had lost a successful long-serving manager, Manchester United were finding it hard to live without Matt Busby at the helm. Since his final retirement as manager in 1971, first Frank O'Farrell and then Tommy Docherty had been charged with replacing not just Sir Matt but an ageing old guard who were now past their sell-by date. Denis Law had controversially moved across Manchester to join rivals City; Bobby Charlton had gone up the M6 as player-manager at Preston North End and took team-mate Nobby Stiles along with him as assistant coach. Influential Irish midfielder Paddy Crerand was arguably past his best. But at the core of Tommy Docherty's troubles was the continuing psychodrama that had become George Best.

The previous season Docherty had done well to save United from relegation, given that his squad were a dysfunctional mess. Club captain Charlton was in constant battles with Best. Though only five or six years older than the Northern Irishman, Charlton was quite the old-school fogey and totally disapproved of Best's nightclubbing, rock star lifestyle. He complained first of all to O'Farrell and then Docherty about the mercurial Best's ill discipline, tardy timekeeping and his frequent absences from training. During the 1972/73 season, things between the two men became so bad that they not only didn't talk but sometimes refused to pass to one another. Their feud had a poor effect on morale generally and Charlton became dour and morose around Old Trafford and the training ground.

When Charlton was granted a testimonial match, Best refused to play in the United team because he 'didn't want to be a hypocrite'. He watched the first five minutes of the game and then sloped out of the ground to a local pub. The Belfast Boy was falling out of love with football and throwing all his energies into nightlife and getting legless. When Charlton left to take over at Preston, Docherty sensed an opportunity to re-motivate Best and get him back onside again. It didn't work. Throughout the first few months of the 1973/74 season, Best trained poorly and was inconsistent on the pitch. Fined for missing training, Best's hangovers had become a serious headache for Docherty.

On New Year's Day 1974, United travelled to Queens Park Rangers, where an off-the-pace Best contributed little in a depressing 3-0 defeat. The following Wednesday, he 'went out for a drink with the lads' and failed to turn up for training on the Thursday morning. Best trained the following day and Docherty said not a word to him. But the manager had plenty to say on the Saturday prior to United's FA Cup game at Old Trafford against Third Division Plymouth Argyle. Docherty pulled Best into the referee's room a couple of hours before the match and told him he was dropped. He'd not turned up for training on Thursday morning and if he wasn't punished that made it look like Best was the boss and Docherty wasn't having that. Best was furious and told Docherty that if he wouldn't play him – against a third-tier side – he would never turn out for Manchester United again. Docherty shrugged, 'So be it.' Best left the office and wandered out on to the Old Trafford pitch and then sat down in the empty Stretford End for an hour, gazing around the stadium, trying to collect his thoughts, recalling memorable matches and the joys he'd shared with his fellow players and fans. Best took one last lingering look around the stands and then left Old Trafford for the very final time.

Along with his foe Bobby Charlton, Best was one of United's greatest-ever players. The moment he walked out of his Old Trafford home signalled the end of his stellar career. Still only 27, he should have enjoyed many more years at the top. Instead, he continued to put on weight, drink heavily, train badly and see out a sad end to his career with short spells at Fulham, in the NASL in the US, and a final tragicomic act at non-league Dunstable Town. Sadly, the rest is, as they say, history.

Despite his undoubted managerial skills, Docherty struggled to lift his United side out of the relegation places. By Christmas, the Red Devils had won just four games and Best had only managed to get on the scoresheet twice. Bizarrely, Docherty had appointed goalkeeper Alex Stepney as official penalty taker and by mid-December, he was joint top scorer with two goals. Spring brought only a slight improvement in results, but by April the club who only seven years previously had been champions of Europe were looking down the barrel at relegation for the first time since the 1930s.

Their penultimate game was against local rivals Manchester City at Old Trafford and would be a derby that went down in history as one of the most significant of all time. A fairly dull 0-0 up until the final quarter, the match came alive when arch predator and recently departed United legend Denis Law reacted quicker than anyone and audaciously back-heeled a loose ball into the back of his old club's net; 1-0 to Manchester City. United huffed and puffed to little effect and then on 88 minutes, their fans rioted in the stands and invaded the pitch, in the hope the game would be replayed. With the police unable to shift the hordes from the turf, the referee had no option but to abandon the match. The Football League acted immediately – City were awarded the result and United slapped with a heavy fine. Two days later, United travelled to Stoke needing a win and relying on teams around them at the bottom to lose. In the end, it was academic – they lost 1-0.

United ended up second-bottom on 32 points, the story of their hapless season best illustrated in their goals for column. Their woeful lack of firepower saw them score just 38 times – the second-worst total in the First Division, only one ahead of bottom-placed Southampton. Twenty defeats, 12 draws and just ten victories. United's top scorer was Sammy McIlroy with just six league goals – the worst in the club's history. The mighty had fallen.

Southampton had the reverse problem – a striker who couldn't stop scoring and team-mates who totally failed to back him up with a goal or two. Mick Channon ended the season as not only his club's top scorer by a country mile, but the First Division's leading marksman with 21 goals. Badly served by a misfiring midfield and forward partners, Channon's guile and one-on-one ability gave new meaning to the phrase one-man band – he ended the season scoring two-thirds of Southampton's goals, often through sheer force of will.

The 1973/74 season saw the launch of two new football awards, the Professional Footballers' Association's Team of the Season and the PFA Players' Player of the Year. This instantly became a big deal for players, because both awards were chosen by a vote among their peers. Not surprisingly the very first team of the season included no fewer than five Leeds United players: Johnny Giles, Norman Hunter, Allan Clarke, Billy Bremner and Paul Madeley. In any age, Madeley would have been a true phenomenon. The quietly spoken and unassuming Yorkshireman brought new meaning to the word versatility. He would win 24 caps for his country, playing in seven different positions. But it was at his club where he would prove, season in, season out, that he was the ultimate all-round player. In over 700 league and cup games, Madeley would play in all ten outfield positions and not just once or twice in some of them. His record is astonishing. At right-back, he played 76 games; at left-back, 68. Wearing number four, 25 times; at centre-half, 121. As number six, he turned out 172 times; at right wing, 15. As a number eight, he played

50 times; at centre-forward, 30 times. At number ten, 21 games; number 11, 134 matches. There were an additional 13 appearances as a playing sub. The Leeds fans dubbed Madeley 'The Eleven Pauls' and 'Mr Versatile'. Team-mate Johnny Giles called him 'seven top players in one'. Don Revie simply referred to him as 'my Rolls-Royce'. To that, you might want to add 'Mr Consistency'; hardly ever injured and invariably somewhere on the Leeds team-sheet for over a decade, Madeley would be named in the team of the season for not just the 1973/74 campaign but again in 1974/75 and 1975/76.

Six feet tall and with a rangy stride, the Leeds-born player was variously a great header of the ball, an intelligent playmaker, quick and accurate with a pass and seemingly always aware of where the players were around him. He was also a cool head and calming influence among some of the more explosive and temperamental players at Leeds. In his over 700 league and cup games for the club, Madeley was only booked twice. In the new age of Total Football, Paul Madeley was the Total Footballer. His fellow PFA Team of the Season member and Leeds team-mate Billy Bremner was the Total Don Revie player. The tough, diminutive, red-haired Scot epitomised his manager's Jekyll and Hyde style: a ball-carrying box-to-box midfielder who scored goals aplenty and passed long and short with sublime precision, and often tackled, fouled and obstructed like a thug.

The team of the season's goalie was Tottenham's Northern Ireland international Pat Jennings: quite simply, one of the greatest goalkeepers of all-time. The stats are extraordinary. Jennings played over 1,000 top-class games for Watford, Spurs and then finally north London rivals Arsenal and 119 matches for Northern Ireland; the last cap gained against Brazil in 1980 was, at the time, a world record for international appearances. Jennings had everything a goalkeeper needed. First of all, there were the legendary Big Pat hands. Writing for the Gunners Town website's 'Highbury Heroes' series, David Thomas recalled, 'Pat had hands like shovels. I remember once there was a life-size photo of one of Big Pat's hands in a magazine and when I placed my own hand over it, my hand looked tiny, like a small child's in comparison. Many a time Pat's big frame would stretch acrobatically in the air and a massive paw would tip a shot over the bar or round a post that had looked like a certain goal.'

Not many keepers could catch a football one-handed, but Jennings could. He also possessed a booming long kick that once made him one of the few goalkeepers ever to score a goal in English football. Playing for Spurs in the 1967 FA Charity Shield against Manchester United, Jennings took the ball in his hands and fired it upfield; it bounced once before flying over Alex Stepney and into the back of the United net. Allied to his power, Jennings was a genius at anticipation, constantly cutting down attackers' angles with his excellent positional sense. It was rare that the Northern Irishman needed to do anything spectacular because he always seemed to be in the right place at the right time.

As well as Madeley and Hunter, the PFA's Team of the Season placed two highly talented young Derby County players in front of Jennings. There have been many great double acts in English football, Johnny Giles and Billy Bremner among them. But in the early to late 70s, there was no better a pairing than Roy McFarland and Colin Todd. Brought together by those two great jigsaw builders Brian Clough and Peter Taylor, they dovetailed deliciously well together as centre-backs. Scouser McFarland was playing for lower league Tranmere Rovers when he first came on to 'Ol'

Big Head's' radar. A Liverpool fan, McFarland knew he was also being checked up on regularly at Prenton Park by Bill Shankly and his scouts and he was desperate to get a deal at Anfield. But one fateful day in 1967 and out of the blue, the Clough–Taylor hit squad arrived at McFarland's Merseyside front door asking, nay demanding, that he sign for Derby. Taken aback, McFarland told the determined duo he needed time to think and weigh up his options. Clough and Taylor refused to leave his house until he agreed a transfer to the Baseball Ground in Derby. Clough outlined his ambitious plans for the Rams and told McFarland in no uncertain terms that if he signed for the club, he'd be in an England shirt within 18 months. Like many players before and after, McFarland caved in to the irresistible force that was Clough and Taylor.

Initially, the young McFarland would partner the powerfully inspirational and gifted Dave Mackay, who took the new tyro under his wing and schooled him in the Derby ways. But Clough knew the old warhorse was coming towards the end of his career and already had a good idea of who he wanted to replace him. In the mid-1960s, Cloughie had been the youth team coach at Sunderland and one of the young players under his tutelage was a certain Colin Todd. He wasn't tall – only 5ft 9in – and slight in build but Clough had been impressed with how he read the game, making up for a lack of size and weight with a rare gift for understanding the flow and shape of a match. Before too long, Todd had become a Sunderland regular and though only 19, Clough signed him in a record-breaking £220,000 deal. At first he switched his young new signing to right-back, still keen to get as much out of the McFarland–Mackay partnership as he could. But then it became McFarland–Todd and the remarkable double act began. McFarland had learned a bundle from Mackay and particularly how to become more aggressive, on the front foot and vociferous with his fellow defenders; he was now a commanding organiser. Clough's next job was to turn the quietly spoken and introverted Todd into his equally effective foil. The manager took part in training matches to deliberately kick and foul Todd just to get him riled up. Todd would silently pick himself up and play on, until in one session he'd had enough and gave Clough a mouthful. His manager smiled, job done. 'At last,' he told Todd, 'a human reaction.'

The PFA choice as attacking midfielder, Tony Currie, was the darling of the Bramall Lane terraces. The Sheffield United star was variously known as 'TC' or 'Top Cat' and was almost feline-like in his contrary and maverick character. Ever a player to attempt the unexpected, Currie had all the tools for the job – two-footed with a rocket shot, sublime dribbling skills and the ability to spray 50-60-yard passes around the pitch, he had now forced his way into the England team. In 1973, Currie had signed a new contract which put him on £240 a week, a small fortune at the time, and during a fairly mediocre season for the club – the Blades finished 13th – fan favourite Currie was the standout performer. Years later, supporters voted him the greatest Sheffield United player of all time, and 40 years on from retiring as a player he was still working for the club's community programme.

Up front in the PFA team was a man who had sideburns even longer and thicker than Tony Currie's demi-mutton chops, plus a self-confidence that swaggered on the edge of outrageous. 'Supermac' was a handful and a half to play against, a fearless and prolific goalscorer – and he knew it. The Newcastle fans adored Malcolm Macdonald because he was the type of player the St James' Park faithful loved more than any other – a brash, swashbuckling, larger-than-life goalscorer like the great Jackie Milburn, Hughie Gallacher,

George Robledo, Albert Stubbins and Len White. Macdonald fitted the bill perfectly. Signed from Second Division Luton Town in 1971 for a club record fee of £180,000, Macdonald had never played in the top flight before but he soon showed he was to the manor born. On his home debut at St James' Park, Supermac rifled in a hat-trick against age-old rivals Liverpool, immediately endearing himself to the Toon. The only downside? Losing two teeth in a full-blooded challenge with Liverpool goalie Ray Clemence, but that only endeared him further to the Newcastle fans. Here was a battering ram of a 21-year-old striker who was prepared to spill blood for the cause and as he was helped off for treatment, the supporters sung him off the pitch to his new anthem. Crooned to the tune of 'Jesus Christ Superstar' – 'Supermac, Superstar! How many goals have you scored so far?' His 1973/74 season had started well but in November Macdonald tore cartilage in his left knee and had to go under the knife. He returned three months later, well ahead of schedule, and promptly scored seven goals in nine games. The Londoner, born just streets away from Fulham's Craven Cottage, was utterly single-minded. Some fellow players regarded him as a greedy so and so, but Macdonald had no interest in being a team player. He was on the pitch to do one thing – score goals. And that he did in spades. Supermac played 258 times for Newcastle and scored 138 goals, more than one in every two games at the very highest level.

He was a great header of the ball and could score off either foot but what made Macdonald such an extraordinary player was his lightning pace. In 1975, he took part in the hugely popular BBC series *Superstars*, which pitted top performers from different sports against one another in a series of challenges such as steeplechase, cycling, pistol shooting and swimming. And also the 100m sprint. In one of the episodes, Macdonald surged ahead of his competitors and crossed the line metres ahead of second place. After the race finished, BBC production staff ran around in a state of disbelief and confusion, desperately trying to confirm that the timings they had were correct. It was finally confirmed that Macdonald had won the race in 10.9 seconds – an Olympic qualifying time and the second-fastest time in Europe that year. Supermac may have been big-headed, but for very good reason.

Mick Channon was named alongside Macdonald after a season of dizzying ups and downs. Now England's regular centre-forward, Channon had scored four goals in 1974's five international matches and ended the 1973/74 season as the First Division's leading goalscorer. And yet, despite his goals, he found himself relegated into the Second Division as part of a defensively frail Southampton team – hammered 7-0 by Bobby Robson's Ipswich Town; 6-2 by Derby County; and conceding four goals four times, the Saints finished a disappointing season only managing to keep 11 clean sheets in their 42 games. Arguably one of England's only world-class players in 1974, Channon now had a huge decision to make. After ten years at The Dell as a schoolboy player and then a professional, this Wiltshire country boy had deep roots in the south-west. By his own admission Channon 'loved Southampton football club like a fan' and thanks to his other great passion of horseracing, aged 26, he already had his own racing stables in Hampshire. The choice he now had was to transfer to a top First Division club worthy of his skills, that rare commodity, a goalscoring centre-forward with dazzling speed, regarded, like Macdonald, as one of the fastest players in the Football League. Or stay at his beloved Southampton, a perennially unfashionable club, who would be playing Second Division football outside of the top flight, and jeopardise his place in the England team. He chose to stay at Southampton.

Norman Hunter was not only named in the PFA Team of the Season but also honoured as the PFA Players' Player of the Year. It was wonderful redemption for the Leeds hardman. Back in 1973, it had been his poor dithering on the ball that had allowed Poland to score against England, and effectively knock them out of the World Cup. A lesser man may have allowed this costly error to hang around his neck like an albatross, but Hunter picked himself up from the depths of his disappointment and played out of his skin throughout the 1973/74 season, picking up more man of the match awards than any other Leeds player.

A la his nickname, 'Bites Yer Legs', Hunter could be hard, dirty and brutal. But he could also pick a pass, build from the back and apply his intelligent understanding of tactical shapes to constantly push Leeds forward up the pitch. Like Billy Bremner, he totally understood and bought into the DNA of Don Revie's vision – do everything you can to stop the other team from playing and expressing themselves and then impose your own power, flair and skill upon them. At the back, Hunter was sometimes far from pretty in his play; going forward, he was at times inspirational. But in many ways, the PFA award was reward for his sheer consistency. First as junior partner at the back to Big Jack, he had played in over 40 league games every season for a decade. Now that Charlton had retired and gone into management at Middlesbrough, Hunter had become senior partner and mentor to young new centre-back Gordon McQueen. Now aged 30, his wisdom and experience helped the Scot ease seamlessly into Leeds' defensive shape and in the 1973/74 season they were at the heart of a back five that only conceded 31 goals.

Despite all of the trophies Hunter won with Leeds and the 28 caps he was awarded for England, the Gateshead-born defender was particularly proud of his PFA honour. He told the *Daily Mirror*, 'I had this reputation and all that went with it ... but if all I could do was tackle and supposedly kick people, all the players would not have voted for me. So for me, personally it was the best recognition.'

Another important annual award that had been going since the early late 1940s was the Football Writers' Association's Footballer of the Year prize. Past winners included Sir Stanley Matthews, Billy Wright, Tom Finney, Bobby Moore and Bobby Charlton. There was a great deal of kudos involved in being selected for the award, by dedicated sports journalists who watched the games week in, week out, and in terms of personal achievements, it was a prize highly coveted by the Football League's top players. In 1973/74 it would be another reward for sheer consistency and would go to one of English football's most underrated post-war players. Similar to Norman Hunter, Liverpool midfielder Ian Callaghan had spent over ten seasons as a first-team regular, after making his debut for the Anfield side during the 1959/60 season as a lightning-fast and skilful right-winger. It was a position he made his own until the 1970/71 season, when a serious knee injury put him out of the game for nearly six months. After rehab and a return to training, Callaghan and Bill Shankly soon realised that the injury had robbed the winger of one of his greatest strengths: sheer pace. Callaghan confided in family and friends that he was worried this would take him out of the first-team picture at Anfield, but his shrewd boss had other ideas.

Shankly moved Callaghan into midfield, where his loss of pace wasn't as crucial. But it was a position where he knew that the former winger's vision, adaptability and passing skill would soon shine. Once again, Shankly got it right and Callaghan became the engine that now drove Liverpool's midfield. Never flash or arrogant, the unassuming Callaghan, at the age of 32, won a prestigious award that was a fitting tribute to his sheer versatility and loyalty to Liverpool. A model professional, he would play on for the Reds until the 1977/78 season, appearing 857 times.

5

The Second Division

'O Brother Where Art Thou?

– The Coen Brothers

JACK AND Bobby Charlton both became top-class footballers around the same time; they played in the same England team together, and were side by side when the red shirts won the World Cup. Now they were to go into management together and both at Second Division clubs who had seen better days. The season before, Bobby's new club Preston had narrowly escaped relegation. This was the club of Tom Finney, twice league champions, winners of two FA Cups and for decades, perennially up among the best in the top flight.

Now their hope was that arguably England's greatest-ever footballer could weave some magic as a manager at Deepdale and get North End back into the big time. Jack's new challenge was at Middlesbrough, who had finished fourth the season before. But it had been a desperately mediocre division; Boro were 12 points shy of the promotion places and yet only 14 above the relegation spots. Wor Jackie knew there was still a lot of work to do, in turning a talented but inconsistent young squad into promotion contenders. Bobby took one look at his misfiring team during the

1973/74 close-season and immediately made numerous dips into the transfer market. The eyes of the footballing world were now on the Charlton brothers, eager to see how the two World Cup winners would now fare as managers. Their respective seasons could not have panned out more differently.

On the face of it, Middlesbrough were taking a huge risk. Although Jack had already turned down a handful of work offers at other clubs both home and abroad, he had no management experience and little to no intention of studying for any coaching badges. He was brash, loud and very much still 'one of the lads'. But he came to Ayresome Park with a secret weapon – he had spent nearly 20 years watching, listening and learning at the feet of Don Revie. He also came with a strong desire to be back in his native north-east. By his own admission, he was a man who 'didn't like change' and had no desire to live and work in the south or the Midlands.

Jack arrived with a plan that shocked the Middlesbrough board, who were more than happy to open the chequebook. He told them they already had the players to take them up and, echoing Revie's inspired signing of Bobby Collins a decade before, he only needed to sign one player who would organise and pull strings – and the wily former centre-half knew he could get the man he wanted on a free transfer. The player was 29-year-old Bobby Murdoch, the Celtic player who Charlton identified as being one of the game's greatest on-field organisers. A player who could be Big Jack's major-general on the pitch and marshal the largely callow young squad of footballers the manager had inherited. The board were taken aback – their current squad seemed bang average. And they again made clear to Charlton that money was available to sign players. But Charlton was adamant – bring in Murdoch and the plan will succeed.

Like his mentor Revie, Charlton had done exhaustive research on the players at Middlesbrough and, as a highly experienced ex-player, identified why the club had not been getting the best out of them. Firstly, they were not fit enough, so Sergeant Major Charlton suggested a gruelling regime that heavily featured lengthy doses of hill climbing, army assault courses and lung-busting six-mile runs against the clock. He told them that tactically, his approach would be simple – build a strong defence and play on the break. To achieve that, he astutely pointed out that certain members of the team weren't being played in their potentially most effective positions. To wit, he wanted speedy midfielder Willie Maddren to play as a highly mobile centre-half and forward Alan Foggon to drop deeper back to play as a false nine to attack second phase balls. Maddren would end the season as Boro's player of the year, while Foggon scored 20 goals in his changed position. Murdoch would remain his one and only signing. As Revie had done before him, Charlton told the directors he would make sure his players felt appreciated, looked after and supported to the hilt. As Charlton left the boardroom, the directors looked askance at one another – they had just been given a lesson in shrewd, well-calculated football management by a tyro and quietly placed the chequebook back in the drawer.

Soon after being appointed, Charlton invited the players and staff to a meal at a country club owned by the Middlesbrough chairman. Defender Stuart Boam later recalled the event in the *Northern Echo*, 'He went round every player and discussed how good he thought they were and what abilities he thought they had … he left me to last and when he finally gave me his description of my capabilities, it wasn't very good. He had come in as player-manager so I thought it would be the end for me. But the very day after giving me a good slagging, he made me captain.'

This would be typical Jack. Like the Don Revie he had learned so much from, he knew when to hit you with a stick or smilingly hand you a carrot. In 20-year-old Scottish midfielder Graeme Souness, the new manager quickly identified a player of immense potential – but one who needed a rocket up the arse. As Souness told Sky TV in later years, 'He sorted me out as a young man, when I was maybe too full of myself. He basically said there are two doors for you. One might lead to a bit of success. The other, you'll drift out of the game and achieve nothing. You look back and there's people you meet, and if I hadn't at that time, things could have gone pear-shaped for me. If I hadn't met Jack, I might not have gone on to achieve what I did.' As Charlton would soon prove, his man-management skills created results.

Within days of Jack's arrival in the close-season, the Middlesbrough players felt like they were in the presence of greatness. As Boam remembered, 'None of us were famous players but he instilled in us a confidence in our abilities, certainly me and my defensive understanding with Willie Maddren … he was blunt, honest and open. He told you what he felt and he was always that same person. That's why we respected him so much.'

Something else that Charlton had picked up from Revie was the importance of team bonding and togetherness. Boam told the *Northern Echo*, 'What I did really like about him was that he spent a lot of time on team spirit. The team did everything together, not just training. It must have worked as well, because the ex-players all stay in touch.' Off the pitch, Charlton felt that the club had become complacent and took their fan base for granted. In true man-of-the-people style, the new boss took it upon himself to try and re-connect Middlesbrough FC to its local communities and each week he would spend two or three evenings on top of his manager's job, going out into different areas to give talks, present prizes and show his face to the people who helped pay his wages. Talking to the BBC in a 1974 documentary, *Jack Charlton – The Boss*, he explained his approach: 'I might be in Stockton or Acklam. I might finish off at Redcar or over as far as Richmond. I try and do all of the areas and fly the flag. I find this is the best way of getting around to everybody, whether it be at pigeon clubs, Rotary lunches, bankers' dinners and working men's clubs.' Just for the record, Charlton showed more than his face during that production. In one scene, and much to the hilarity of his players, the boss streaked naked through the Middlesbrough dressing room.

Charlton's first game in charge saw his new team take the long journey south to Fratton Park, Portsmouth, where a Foggon goal won it 1-0. The Middlesbrough faithful turned up to their first home match of the season against Fulham with high expectations, but the Londoners burst the north-east Charlton bubble, winning 2-0. The disappointed fans need not have worried, because Middlesbrough then went on a 24-match unbeaten run that started to put them out of sight of the chasing pack by the turn of the year. Amazingly, they would secure the Second Division title with eight games to go, and Jack became the only Second Division boss ever to win English football's Manager of the Year award. Of all England's World Cup-winning team, Jack Charlton would become the only ex-player to become a managerial success. And that young Scottish midfielder Souness? He ended 1973/74 by scoring a hat-trick in Middlesbrough's 8-0 mauling of Sheffield Wednesday in their final match.

Sir Alf Ramsey would enthuse about Bobby Moore's tactical understanding of the game and why that would make him a great manager. Ditto, his great favourite Bobby Charlton. But it would be the ever-underrated 'loping giraffe' who would better them all. When Bobby left Manchester United to become player-manager at Preston, Sir Alf said he had it within him to become one of English football's top managers – he was so wrong. Though plain-speaking and brutally honest, Jack was the better communicator. Bobby was introverted, shy and bottled up problems and concerns, finding it hard to share worries with the people around him. Still suffering the bruises from his utterly dysfunctional relationship with George Best at Manchester United, he found player-management difficult.

Unlike Jack, the younger Charlton dipped frequently into the transfer market in a bid to shore up his journeyman side. Always a naturally talented and instinctive footballer, Bobby struggled to get his ideas over to his new Preston squad, who though of decent quality were not the top-flight players Bobby had spent his whole footballing life playing alongside. In Leo McKinstry's excellent book, *Jack and Bobby*, the author recounts a training incident early in Charlton's spell as Preston manager. He tried to show one of his new players what to do if one of their wingers looked 'open'. 'Just do this,' said Bobby and with his left foot, and from a standing start, launched an inch-perfect 40-yard pass to one of the wingers' feet. 'If that's not on, try the other side,' and then whacked another inch-perfect ball to the other winger with his right foot. The Preston player's jaw dropped. The book goes on to explain how frustrated Charlton constantly became when his Second Division-standard players couldn't do what he did. He would also later admit that his biggest mistake was jumping into a manager's job without first having taken his coaching badges. Though his arrival gave the players an early season 'bounce', as winter drew in their form fell away and try as he might, Charlton couldn't provide his team with answers or any sense of tactical change that might help the cause.

The fixture calendar often plays unexpected practical jokes and towards the end of the season, on 27 April 1974 Jack's triumphant Middlesbrough would visit Deepdale to play Bobby's ailing side. To stand any chance of avoiding relegation, Preston had to win and pray that other teams around them dropped points. Already champions, Middlesbrough were chasing the all-time Second Division record points total. Keen to hype up the match, the national press portrayed it as 'The Battle of the Charltons' and 'Bobby and Jackie's War'. Clearly not having read the journalistic script, the two brothers met up for a convivial lunch before the game and wished one another well. It would prove to be a one-sided affair.

Preston were outrun and outmuscled by a rampant Boro, who were 3-0 up within the first 26 minutes. Mike Elwiss hauled the home side back into the game before half-time with a brace, but a fourth goal from the visitors early in the second half effectively ended the game as a contest and it finished 4-2. As the *Lancashire Post* ruefully pointed out, 'The damage had been done long before this match, Preston winning only one of their last 13 games. In fact they scored in just seven of their last 19 games from January to the end of the season.' Preston were relegated and Middlesbrough ended the season with a total of 65 points – in the days of two points for a win, the highest recorded in the Second Division. Bobby and Jack shook hands, but few words were exchanged. There didn't need to be. Jack jubilantly saluted the thousands of away fans who'd travelled over the Pennines, then he hugged his players, while Bobby looked momentarily lost, unsure what to do next. This was all new – he'd never been relegated in his entire footballing career and it hurt like hell. Particularly as the final blow had been delivered by his record-breaking big brother.

Jack and Bobby had long endured an oft typical on-off brother relationship. For years, Bobby had always been mum Cissie's favourite and Jack's bluff personality often rubbed the more introverted Bobby up the wrong way. Allied to that, the pair's wives were reportedly rarely happy in one another's company. Bobby had been an international regular since the age of 20, while Jack didn't win his first cap until the relatively advanced age of 29. It was classic sibling rivalry and the two continued to joust throughout their lives. But the 1973/74 season put the tin lid on what had been an increasingly new phase in their relationship. For so many years, Jack had perennially played second fiddle to the supremely talented Bobby, who was feted around the world. But as players, the tables had started to turn during the late 60s and early 70s. After winning the European Cup in 1968, Bobby's beloved Manchester United were losing their way and he would not win another trophy with them.

In comparison, Jack was the rock of a Leeds United team that during the same period, won the First Division twice, the FA Cup, the League Cup, the Inter-Cities Fairs Cup and got to the final of the Cup Winners' Cup and the semi-finals of the European Cup. And now, as they both took their first steps into management, Jack had already proved himself to be top dog. The following season his Middlesbrough side would challenge for the top-flight title for much of the campaign, finally finishing fifth. Jack, of course, would go on to become the Republic of Ireland's most successful manager. Bobby would stay at Preston in the Third Division for another largely unsuccessful season, resign over rows with the board, and never manage a football club again. But despite their constant battles and fall-outs, they were family and always stuck up for one another, no matter what. In 2008, Bobby was given the BBC Sports Personality of the Year Lifetime Achievement Award and the man who would hand him his honour? Jack Charlton. In a moving speech, he concluded, 'He's the greatest footballer in the world – and he's my brother.'

Promoted alongside Middlesbrough, two clubs who were a testament to hard work and endeavour. Like Big Jack's side, neither runners-up Luton Town nor third-placed Carlisle United had an abundance of star names but two well-settled squads of time-served pros. From early in the season it seemed clear that seven clubs would be positioned in the slipstream behind Boro, fighting it out for second and third place, as this would be the very first season when three clubs would get promoted and three come down from the First Division. Rather like today's Championship, the Second Division of 1974 was full of yo-yo clubs with recent experience of playing in the top flight and among the chasing pack were Blackpool, Sunderland, West Bromwich Albion and Nottingham Forest. What made Luton and Carlisle so different was that they had both spent the past decade patiently clawing their way up on low budgets from the Fourth Division into the second tier. Luton had last played in the First Division 14 years previously – Carlisle had never been there during their entire history. It would be a battle royal. Along with a much-improved Orient, the seven clubs all put little runs together and constantly changed places behind Boro and the final table told its own story – Luton in runners-up spot on 50 points, 15 behind Middlesbrough, with Carlisle on 49.

Carlisle's achievement led former manager Bill Shankly to somewhat loyally and hyperbolically dub their promotion 'the greatest feat in the history of the game'. The season previous, their journeymen squad of players had only escaped relegation to the Third Division by a single point. At the start of 1973/74 it looked for sure that Carlisle would struggle again, with manager Alan Ashman's men winning just two out of their first eight matches. Carlisle is only a city by virtue of it having a cathedral – in 1974, the population was under 70,000 and in truth, the Cumbrian capital was a bit of a backwater. The Football League's most northerly club, less than 50 miles from the Scottish border, Carlisle found it difficult to attract players so far off the beaten track. But himself a former Carlisle player, Ashman knew exactly what the challenge was, and to compensate for a lack of top performers he tried to create a settled side with a strong team spirit and identity.

After the first eight games, the small squad dug deep and lost just one out of their next ten. Soon, they got into the habit of winning and though their home attendances were the lowest in the division, their small but loyal fan base was having a ball. For the rest of the season, their results mirrored the personality of their squad; no flash long unbeaten runs or big wins. Steady Eddies who dug out little trills and thrills, a win here, a draw there. But as the season drew towards its end and Carlisle still found themselves within touching distance of the three promotion places, Ashman told his players that now was the time to dream the impossible dream – let's go for it, lads. Four wins out of their last five matches would see them over the line.

Ashman's team had some useful performers, but central to their success was one of modern Britain's greatest all-round sportsmen. Quiet and unassuming, midfielder Chris Balderstone had been signed from his hometown club Huddersfield Town for a bargain £7,000 in 1967. Carlisle were well aware that Balderstone lacked pace and wasn't particularly great in the tackle. They signed him because of his impressive and accurate passing range and his ability to be a great on-the-pitch organiser. And very soon, the Carlisle fans adored him for his calm, understated style;

an asset that Balderstone brought to his other summertime day job. As the football seasons finished, the Yorkshireman would swap shin guards for batting pads and regularly turn out for Leicestershire as an opening and middle-order batsman with considerable success. He played his first full county season for Leicestershire in 1973, smashing 1,222 runs at an average of 42; over the next 12 seasons he would score over 1,000 runs ten times and play two Test matches for England. Balderstone would continue to play for Leicestershire into his mid-40s and then become a county and international cricket umpire.

After leaving Carlisle to play for Doncaster Rovers in 1975, he famously became the only British sportsman to play in a professional cricket match and a football game on the same day. On 15 September 1975, the hugely committed Balderstone scored 51 not out against Derbyshire during the daylight hours at Chesterfield, then took a waiting taxi north to play in Doncaster's evening 1-1 draw against Brentford in the Fourth Division. Early the following morning, Balderstone was back in a taxi on a return to Chesterfield for the last day of Leicestershire's final game of the season. It was no ordinary match; if Leicestershire won they would lift the County Championship title. On a difficult, skiddy pitch Balderstone added a further 65 runs to end his innings on 116. Leicestershire now had three hours and 20 minutes to bowl Derbyshire out. Yet again, cometh the hour, cometh the man. Balderstone stepped up, this time with ball in hand, and his tight spin bowling took out three Derbyshire batsmen for just 28 runs. Leicestershire bowled out Derbyshire for 140 and thanks to their talisman they lifted the County Championship trophy for the first time in their history. In modern times, few sportsmen or women have been as successful in two separate professional sports as Chris Balderstone.

Down at the bottom, Preston were joined in the relegation places by Crystal Palace and Swindon Town. Not good news for Wiltshire's finest, but even worse for the Selhurst Park club. Relegated from the First Division the season before, Palace immediately found the rough and tumble of the Second Division hard to cope with and had a dire start to the campaign. They would not win their first league game until 10 November, 1-0 against Bristol City; by January 1974, they had only won three. Despite a slight upturn towards the end of the season, Palace were so far behind the game they slipped further down the football pyramid into the Third Division.

The Second Division's top scorer didn't play for any of the promoted sides, but modestly mid-table Nottingham Forest and he was one of football's maverick entertainers. Duncan McKenzie had his best season yet for the Reds, scoring 21 league goals and thanks to a successful run into the FA Cup quarter-finals, 26 in all. But the Grimsby-born McKenzie was just as famous for his off-the-pitch exploits as he was on it. A schoolboy pole vaulter, he would entertain his team-mates by leaping over a chest-high hedge after training. After one session, they each bet him a fiver he couldn't jump over their coach Tommy Kavanagh's Mini out in the car park. McKenzie did it with ease and it rapidly became his party piece. Sometimes he would do it as pre-match entertainment out on the pitch, though his car jumping soon came to a stop when he transferred to Leeds. Before a testimonial match at Elland Road, the new signing instantly endeared himself to the crowd by jumping a Mini for them. New manager Jimmy Armfield strode across the pitch towards him and said, 'Well done, lad. Now never ever do that again.' The striker was the one successful Brian Clough signing who had settled in well at Leeds, and there was no way Armfield wanted him injured doing 'circus tricks'. A few weeks later, Whites hardman Norman Hunter bet McKenzie he couldn't throw a golf ball from one end of the ground to the other. Ever a man for a challenge, McKenzie actually ended up throwing the ball right out of the stadium and so a new party trick was debuted.

It was in 1974 that the Second Division pioneered a new venture for English league football – the first matches to be played on a Sunday. Thanks to the effects of the three-day week, the miners' strike and the ongoing energy crisis, electricity was being rationed and power was in short supply. From December 1973, clubs were banned from using floodlights and evening midweek matches were put on hold. Some matches went ahead with late morning and early afternoon midweek kick-offs, but attendances plummeted as a result. To solve an ever-worsening fixture pile-up, the Football League explored the idea of holding daytime matches on Sundays. The FA had already rearranged a couple of midweek cup replays for Sunday kick-offs but were soon made aware that they would be breaking the law. Under the 1780 Sunday Observance Act it was illegal to charge money for entertainment or sporting events on the Lord's Day. The FA's legal people obviously took this as a challenge and came up with an ingenious solution; to wit, none of the clubs could charge admission to their grounds but they could charge what they liked for a match programme or single-page team sheet. Ergo, supporters were allowed into the ground free, on the proviso that they had bought their unofficial 'ticket' for the game. Accordingly, for the Bolton Wanderers v Stoke City FA Cup tie, fans could buy an optional programme for 5p but had to purchase a single-page yellow team sheet for 80p.

The first Sunday FA Cup matches were played on 6 January 1974 and something quite astonishing happened – the crowds came flocking in. At Burnden Park, Bolton

Wanderers' third-round tie against Stoke City pulled an attendance of 40,000 – nearly 20,000 more than their average gate for the season. At Cambridge's Abbey Stadium the tie against Oldham saw a gate of almost 8,500, easily United's best crowd of the season. Other clubs watched the experiment with interest and were particularly taken by the huge increase in attendances and put pressure on the Football League to follow suit. Not surprisingly the Church of England opposed the idea as did the Football League's own vice-president Bob Lord, who called it 'a disgrace'. Numerous devout players, like Swindon's Jimmy Allan, refused to play on Sundays and most of the top-flight clubs were against the idea. But given the situation and fearing a fixture pile-up, the Football League ignored Lord and gave the go-ahead for a slate of Sunday matches on 20 January.

The honour of being the first club to host a Sunday Football League game fell to Millwall, who played London rivals Fulham at The Den, kicking off at 11.30am. The match ended honours even at 1-1, but history had been made. Later in the afternoon another 11 games kicked off – another two in the Second Division, three in the Third Division and six in the Fourth Division. Nine of the matches pulled their home clubs' biggest crowds of the season. Professional football was proving to be a big Sunday hit, but the new arrangement would not last. As the energy crisis abated and the longer evenings drew in, Sunday football was abandoned and would not return for another ten years.

6

The Third and Fourth Divisions

'Trying is the first step towards failure'

– Homer Simpson

WE ALL have bad days, sometimes bad weeks and months. But to endure an entire 46-match season on a permanent down? Let us travel back in time to the knackered old stands at Spotland Park, a run-down ground in the middle of a deeply run-down economically depressed old mill town in the north of Lancashire. Rochdale had actually begun the 1973/74 season with cautiously optimistic high hopes. The board had decided that the previous campaign's 13th place was simply not good enough, and during the close-season, manager Dick Conner paid with his job. In his place came Walter Joyce, who had been impressing as youth team manager up the road at Oldham Athletic, the hope being that the 36-year-old would work a few wonders with Rochdale's youngsters, of which they had plenty. Goalie Mike Poole was just 18, as were midfielders Paul Fielding and Don Tobin; forward Alan Taylor and defender Keith Hanvey were both 20; and forward Mickey Brennan was 21. Most had been thrown into the Third Division deep end the campaign before and working with his new squad in the close-season, alarm bells had already begun to clang loudly for Joyce.

His squad was a mix of callow youth, aged injury-prone old sweats and inconsistent lower-league players who could be a man of the match one week and a four out of ten for the next five. The new campaign began innocuously enough with an opening-day 1-1 draw against Brighton at Spotland followed by a 0-0 away at Walsall. Joyce had got his side better organised, but there was a worrying lack of quality out on the pitch. On 11 September, Rochdale travelled the long journey south to play Plymouth Argyle and were hammered 5-0. They would have to wait until their eighth game to register their first win, 2-1 away at Southend, but it was nothing more than a false dawn. The wheels fell off completely and from the end of September until the very last day of the season, Rochdale would win just one more league game, 3-2 at home to Shrewsbury on 12 January.

Plagued by injuries, suspensions and hopelessly out-of-form and demoralised footballers, Joyce was often forced to draft in local amateurs and emergency loans just to make up the numbers, and by the end of the season he had started 32 different players. But whoever he selected, morale remained low and losing became a wearied habit. To add insult to injury, the club became record breakers of the most depressing kind. On Tuesday, 5 February 1974, they played at home against Cambridge United and because of the energy crisis and the resultant ban on floodlighting, the match had to be played in the afternoon. Only 458 fans turned up, the lowest post-war attendance in professional English football. Those who did turn up wouldn't have much to cheer about, with Cambridge coming away 2-0 winners. As Rochdale's sorry season stuttered to a close, three more league home games at Spotland would attract less than 1,000 fans. The Cambridge game, though, had had a demoralising effect upon the club's board members, who went public to say that even as early as February, they may as well write off the team as 'relegation certainties'.

Manager Joyce, who'd been struggling to keep his players' chins up, was horrified and went straight to the *Manchester Evening News* to tell them he was 'not throwing in the towel'. Privately fuming at the board's defeatism, he put on his diplomat's face, saying he 'respectfully disagreed with his directors' and issued a rallying cry to Rochdale fans, 'We're not yet down. As long as we have any hope at all, then we'll have to keep on fighting and hoping for a change in luck.' Joyce added that he was hopeful of signing some new players soon. In came Bradford City full-back Roger Denton on loan and Chester centre-back Jim Grummett in the hope of shoring up a hapless defence; Grummett's Chester team-mate Stan Horne was signed to bring some new life to the midfield.

Denton played twice and was memorably described thus on the unofficial Rochdale AFC.com website by a fan who'd watched him play in both matches, 'The ball seemed to mysteriously take on the shape of a cube just before it reached him. At least that's the only explanation I have for the way he misplaced every ball that came his way.' The new acquisitions made little difference. Coming into a side so very low on confidence, Rochdale continued to play it safe, tried little from an attacking point of view and set out 'not to lose'. Despite Joyce's determination, his desolate board were soon proved right. A couple of weeks after the Cambridge game, Rochdale drew 0-0 away at Southport in an abysmal encounter. The *Manchester Evening News* match report was biting in its criticism, 'If both teams go down – as they should – they won't have anything to offer Division Four.'

Rochdale would be relegated by the end of March and in the days when it was two points for a win, they would finish 21 points adrift of safety on just 21 points. Their end-of-season record was won two, drawn 17, lost 27. Thirty-eight goals for, 94 against. Down with them went Southport, Shrewsbury and Cambridge. For a full, blow-by-blow account of Rochdale's campaign, seek out Mark Hodkinson's excellent *The Longest Season: A Winter with England's Worst Ever Football Team*. His brief summation of what it was like to be a Dale fan tells its own story, 'All they had was a Saturday ritual of defeat upon defeat.'

So Rochdale fans had endured a nightmare season; surely it couldn't get any worse? It did. What can be more galling for supporters than your own team having the season from hell, while your closest rivals are enjoying one of their best? Just six miles north of Spotland, Oldham Athletic were on the crest of a wave and would end the season as Third Division champions. Key to their success would be a small, broken-nosed Scotsman who would give over 20 years of his playing and management career to the Latics. Jimmy Frizzell was signed by Oldham from Greenock Morton in 1960, and initially played as a striker, ending the club's 1961/62 and 1964/65 seasons as top scorer. Because needs must in the lower divisions and with small squads, like many older, experienced players at the time, Frizzell found himself being asked to drop back over the years to become a wing-half and then finally a full-back.

Following a spell as player-coach, aged 33, Frizzell was persuaded by the board to take on mission impossible. In March 1970 he took on the job of manager with a demoralised Oldham bobbing dangerously around the Fourth Division's bottom spots. The Scotsman's task was clear – save the Latics from a drop into non-league football. Applying a new training regime and a total change in tactics, he rejuvenated his small, poorly performing squad into a hard-to-beat side. In the season's remaining 22 matches, Frizzell inspired his men to nine wins and six draws and

Oldham ended the season 11th, in mid-table respectability. The following season, the sense of togetherness he managed to create at the club saw Oldham promoted from the basement league in third place – bizarrely, it also saw them win a now largely forgotten trophy which helped build a new stand at Boundary Park.

The Ford motor company were keen to get into football sponsorship to push their brand and proposed the idea of a new tournament that promoted fair play. With big questions being asked of the Football League and the FA about increasing ill discipline on the pitch and how it was helping to stoke hooliganism on the terraces, they were more than happy to support and promote the Ford Sporting League. The rules were simple. Each of the Football League's 92 teams were marked after every game and if they scored a home goal, they won one point. If they scored an away goal, two points. But there was a fair-play snag – if a player was booked, his club lost five points. Shown a red, they lost ten points. Ford's publicity blurb at the time outlined the philosophy behind the new tournament thus, 'The harder and cleaner your team plays the more chance they stand of winning some big prizes – and we mean big prizes. The first is £50,000; the second £30,000; and each month throughout the season, there's a prize of £2,500. All the money won must be spent on benefits for the spectator. That's part of the deal. It should produce better football. And better conditions to watch it in.'

Frizzell's attacking approach and their extraordinary on-field self-discipline soon put Oldham in the box seat. They won the first monthly £2,500 award, and then the second, the third and then, well every single one until the end of the season. At the campaign's end, Oldham were the second-highest goalscorers in the entire Football League with 88. On the disciplinary front, Oldham amazingly ended the season with just four bookings and not a single sending-off. Frizzell's attractive side won the £50,000 Ford Sporting League first prize and thanks to their monthly awards, they banked £70,000. The club's board decided to spend the money on knocking down their dilapidated Broadway stand on the north side of Boundary Park and replacing it with a modern all-seater stand. Frizzell became even more of a hero with the Oldham fans.

In 1972/73 he drove the team to a fourth-placed finish in the Third Division, so near and yet so far from a further promotion into the Second Division. By this point, Frizzell had become a cult figure with the Boundary Park faithful, who had now dubbed him 'Sir Jimmy'. But the ambitious Scot, who'd now well and truly pulled Oldham out of the doldrums, was not about to rest on his laurels. Convinced he could go one better in the 1973/74 season, Frizzell persuaded his cash-strapped board to splash some money on two – albeit ageing – big-name strikers. In came 33-year-old Scot Andy Lochhead and former top-flight centre-forward Tony Hateley. Lochhead had scored heavily for Burnley, Leicester and Aston Villa; the 33-year-old Hateley had attracted £400,000 in transfer fees playing for Aston Villa, Chelsea, Liverpool, Birmingham, Coventry and Notts County and though ungainly on the deck, he was a superb header of the ball. Already six feet tall when he left primary school, he was the Derbyshire Schools high jump champion, and spent much of his later football career in the air. Coming to Oldham, he had already scored 210 goals in 429 league games.

The two signings were a massive statement of intent, but they were also a gamble because both players had the best of their careers behind them. Lochhead's game had never particularly been based on any degree of pace but he was slowing; Hateley had been suffering from a recurring knee injury. But as a former striker himself, Frizzell was convinced that their experience would serve Oldham well in the Third Division and help to inspire the rest of his squad. The gamble partially came off. Lochhead's power and strength plus his game knowledge regularly made life extremely difficult for Third Division defenders and though he hardly scored a hatful of goals for Oldham, he proved expert in his hold-up play and getting other forward players into the game. He would score ten goals in his 44 league matches that season. It was a different story for Hateley. The gamble on his recurring injuries saw him play just five games for Oldham, scoring just the one goal. At the end of the season, Hateley was quietly moved on and ended his long career at non-league Bromsgrove Rovers, Prescot Town and Barrow.

Bristol Rovers finished as runners-up in the Third Division, having led the table for most of the season. Fired by the goal power of twin strikers Bruce Bannister and Alan Warboys, known locally as 'Smash and Grab', and the meanest defence in the third tier – that season, they conceded just 33 goals in their 46 games – Rovers had topped the table since August. But then came their season run-in and the wheels fell off. The team only managed three wins out of their last ten games and their defeats crucially included a 2-1 home loss to Oldham. They finished a single point behind the Latics, but still, Rovers were promoted and back in the Second Division for the first time since 1962. Also on 61 points, and only third due to goal difference, York City had enjoyed their best season ever and were promoted into the second tier of English football for the first time in their history.

The Third Division's top scorer for 1973/74 virtually came from nowhere. In his previous three seasons with Watford, 22-year-old Billy Jennings had been a decidedly bit-part player, managing only ten league appearances. After a good close-season, manager Mike Keen decided to give Jennings a regular slot in the Hornets' first team – the young striker repaid his faith in spades. Though not tall, Jennings had developed an impressive leap and scored a lot of goals with his head – and with both feet. By the end of the 1973/74 season he had scored 26 league goals and was named Watford's player of the year. In the close-season, Portsmouth made an offer for Jennings, but Watford were keen to hang on to their new talismanic striker and turned it down. But as the 1974/75 season progressed, First Division West Ham came in with an offer that neither Jennings nor Watford could refuse – a fee of £110,000, which was twice the club's record transfer deal for money received. Fans complained bitterly; even more so when Watford fell into a long slump and ended the season relegated into the Fourth Division. Now a Hammer, Jennings would finish his season with an FA Cup winners' medal around his neck.

The season's biggest story in the Fourth Division was all about the 'Peterborough Messiah'. Noel Euchuria Cornelius Cantwell was as unusual as his name. An Ireland cricket international, captain of the Irish football team and Manchester United, Cantwell was a sporting one-off – a deep thinker, highly articulate and a pillar of integrity. After Cantwell captained Manchester United to their first trophy win, the FA Cup, since the awful Munich air disaster, no less a luminary than Matt Busby predicted that his lantern-jawed, charismatic on-the-field leader had all the attributes to become a top-class manager. Starting his management career in the top flight at newly promoted Coventry City as successor to Jimmy Hill, who'd taken the club from the Third Division into the First Division, the charming Irishman launched a pioneering youth development policy and against the odds, twice steered them to First

Division safety. In Cantwell's third season in charge, his fast-improving young squad finished in a highly creditable sixth place. His fourth season started poorly. His side just couldn't score goals and alarmingly for the Coventry board, average home attendances had dropped from 32,000 down to 22,000. They pressed the panic button and gave Cantwell the sack in a hand-delivered letter.

The Irishman was utterly crestfallen and even considered leaving the game. But an ambitious Peterborough board tempted him back into management by offering him the top job at their struggling Fourth Division club midway through the 1972/73 season, on £5,000 a year plus bonuses and a sponsored car, as well as, for the Fourth Division, a decent, competitive transfer budget. Cantwell thought long and hard before accepting the post, because Peterborough were a club under a shadow, still trying to live down a recent stain on their name. Five years previously, the London Road outfit had pleaded guilty to poor financial governance at a joint Football Association and Football League investigation into their affairs. Illegal signing-on bonuses and under-the-counter, untaxed payments to existing players led to them being demoted to the Fourth Division – at the time, mid-season, they'd been challenging for promotion into the Second Division. In truth, there was a collective sigh of relief at London Road, as the last club to be charged with similar offences, Leeds City back in 1919, had been unceremoniously booted out of the Football League altogether. Since their demotion, Peterborough had become basement league strugglers and when they approached Cantwell, the club were rock-bottom of the Fourth Division, three points adrift. His immediate remit was to save the Posh from ending up in the re-election places. By the end of the season, the new broom had pulled them up to 19th, five points clear of the bottom four.

His next job was to rebuild a squad that could challenge for promotion and during the 1973/74 close-season, Cantwell's eye for talent brought an astutely assembled new pack of cards to London Road. As a defender himself, Cantwell was acutely aware that he'd inherited a weak back four, so in came the steel of tough-tackling left-back Jeff Lee from Halifax and rugged Notts County centre-back Micky Jones. He shocked the footballing world by convincing 23-year-old playmaker and set-piece specialist Freddie Hill to drop down two divisions from Manchester City, and to protect the classy midfielder against tough Fourth Division bruisers he signed midfield enforcer and all-round workhorse Paul Walker from Wolves. From Brighton came England under-23 international Bert Murray, a clever and pacy right-sided midfielder. They would all prove to be inspired signings and by October, Cantwell's revitalised side were top of the Fourth Division and average attendances had trebled from 3,000 to just over 9,000.

Still an extremely popular character in the East Midlands, Cantwell gave a lengthy mid-season interview to the *Coventry Evening Telegraph* to describe what life was like at his new club. He was characteristically and refreshingly honest and when asked about his successful new signings Cantwell said, 'When you are in charge of a club like Coventry City, who are aiming for the top of the First Division, there are precious few players around capable of improving the side. And the few that could do it were not available. Here at Peterborough, although I do not have the amount of money I had to spend in the First Division, I have a much wider choice of players I can sign. Instead of half a dozen there are one thousand or more players around who could make us a better team so new signings become that much easier.'

Cantwell also made clear that his unexpected Coventry sacking had taught him important lessons in the realities of football management, 'In this day and age you cannot spend much time on youth schemes and building for the future. With respect, you don't live to see the day. I'm not interested any more in what happens in five years' time. I'm only concerned about what happens this season. And if I could do here what Jimmy Hill did at Coventry City – get the club into the First Division – I'd continue to follow his example. I'd then get out and leave it to somebody else to take over.'

But not all would be plain sailing for Peterborough United because three other rival sides also had the bit between their teeth – Gillingham, Colchester United and Bury. The Gills' young manager Andy Nelson also had a great playing career captaining Ipswich Town to the First and Second Division titles under Alf Ramsey and in this, his first managerial job, he was determined to play attractive attacking possession football, rare in the old lump it long Fourth Division. Colchester had a dreadful 1972/73 season, ending up 22nd, and were forced to apply for re-election. Out went old boss Dick Graham and in came a determined and ambitious new young manager in 34-year-old Jim Smith, who although having a modest playing career in the lower leagues would go on to manage at the highest level with Newcastle United, Birmingham City and Derby County. Like Cantwell at Peterborough, 'The Bald Eagle' came into the job realising that he needed to make a major overhaul. Smith would sign ten new players and bring in five on loan and by Christmas, his quickly gelling Colchester side were top of the Fourth Division. Twenty games in, they'd won 11, drawn seven and lost only twice. Smith had looked at his best strengths and decided to approach the season in a very different way to Andy Nelson at Gillingham. Ergo, his side defended deep and hit teams on the break. They would end the season with the Fourth Division's most miserly defence, conceding just 36 goals.

The Bury manager Allan Brown and his board had made a huge and controversial decision over the close-season; they would sign a 36-year-old centre-half who had hardly played football since 1964 and was one of the most disgraced footballers in the English game. He would fast become Bury's most influential and inspirational player. Peter Swan was an England regular and hotly tipped to be in Alf Ramsey's 1966 World Cup squad. But in 1964, the *Sunday People* newspaper published an exclusive that rocked the world of football. They had incontrovertible proof that Swan and his two Sheffield Wednesday team-mates Tony Kaye and David Layne had all placed illegal bets on their own team to lose against Ipswich Town back on 1 December 1962, which they did 2-0. The taped evidence was given to the newspaper by a former player, Jimmy Gauld, a known match-fixer, who was looking at a final payday of £7,000 from the *Sunday People*, knowing that he was facing a four-year jail term for fixing several other Football League games. Gauld's footballing career had ended through injury aged just 30, after breaking a leg playing for Mansfield Town, and turning in the Sheffield Wednesday trio represented his best chance of making top money before he was incarcerated.

Why three of England's top players would have agreed to a fix still seems inexplicable. They were on good wages and bonuses, at the height of their careers. And yet agree they did. In an interview with *The Times* in 2006, Swan admitted, 'We lost the game fair and square but I still don't know what I would have done if we'd been winning. It would have been easy for me to give away a penalty or even score an own goal.' Swan pleaded guilty, served four months in Lincoln prison and was banned from football for life. The disgraced ex-player hacked out a living working as a car salesman and a pub landlord.

But in 1972, the FA decided to lift the life bans on all three players and amazingly, Sheffield Wednesday re-signed Swan, the man who had brought such shame to the club. He only managed 15 starts in his first season back in professional football and refused a short-term contract to stay at Hillsborough for the beginning of the 1973/74 season. Bury immediately smelt an opportunity.

Though now well into his 30s, Swan was still a class act and a cut above in the Fourth Division. His superb on-the-field management saw Bury lose just once in their first ten games, keeping seven clean sheets. A measure of his influence on the Gigg Lane side came during a disappointing November and December when he was injured – Bury won only twice. On his return, the Shakers were steadied and went on a seven-game unbeaten run to put them right back in the promotion mix.

Throughout the season, it was nip and tuck with all four sides constantly exchanging the top spot. By April, Gillingham were in first and the championship decider would come in their final game against rivals Peterborough away at London Road. It turned out to be an absolute thriller, played in front of the Fourth Division's biggest crowd of the season, with Peterborough coming out on top 4-2 to snatch the title from the Gills. Inevitably, they would be joined in the Third Division by Colchester and Bury.

7
The Match That Never Was

EXETER'S LOCAL tourist board describe their home as 'a small city that packs a big punch'. Its rich and serried history pre-dates the arrival of the Romans in AD50 as an important trading port on Britain's south-west coast and among the city's many landmark attractions are a magnificent 1,000-year-old cathedral, Roman walls and a thrilling catacomb of underground tunnels dating back centuries. 1974 was a landmark year for Exeter as it was finally given city status, which meant that Exeter FC became Exeter City – a small professional football club that packed, well, a fairly small punch. In their entire history, Exeter have never played above the third tier of English football and their glory days have been few and far between. Like many small clubs, Exeter's financial survival had always depended upon developing young local talent and then selling them on. Right back to the 1920s, selling star young goalkeeper Dick Pym to Bolton Wanderers for £5,000 paid for the purchase of their St James Park ground. A few years later, 17-year-old Exeter lad Cliff 'Boy' Bastin was scouted by legendary Arsenal manager Herbert Chapman and bought for £2,000, which paid for Exeter's wages that season.

But by the early 1970s, young local schoolboy players were being scouted by bigger south-coast clubs like

Plymouth, Portsmouth and Brighton and snapped up before Exeter could move in on them; the cupboard of saleable young talent was bare. To make matters worse, attendances were dropping. The average gate during Exeter's 1968/69 season was 5,371; by the 1973/74 campaign this had dropped to 4,193, and in the following season it would fall to an average of just 3,265. For a club on a shoestring budget, that was a lot of fans to lose. You might think that as one of English football's most geographically remote and financially struggling small clubs, the Football League would be looking to protect and put their support behind Exeter City. Or perhaps not. Let's go on a journey back to April 1974.

The 1973/74 Fourth Division season had proved to be a long, hard struggle for manager John Newman and his players. Newman had moved to Exeter as a player in 1967 from nearby Plymouth Argyle and soon proved to be popular with his team-mates, fans and the local press. Scrupulously conscientious, he soon earned the nickname 'Honest John' and it was no surprise to anyone when the club named him new player-manager in 1969; it was a popular appointment. Thoughtful and perceptive, he set out to create a 'one for all and all for one' culture within his small squad. When he first took over, Newman would get kitted out in the dressing room alongside the rest of his players. But when he realised this was cramping their style as they didn't want to 'banter' in front of the manager, henceforward he got changed by himself in the referee's room.

A realist and a pragmatist, Newman understood that for Exeter, thriving simply meant surviving. With attendances continuing to fall and debts to pay, the cash-starved club started the campaign with a squad of just 17 and as the season progressed injuries and suspensions began to bite. The seemingly ever-resourceful Newman was forced to juggle his available players, often playing them out of position, and if it hadn't been for the goalscoring talent of striker Fred Binney, who would end the year on 25 goals and be named PFA Fourth Division Player of the Year, his Exeter side would have been far lower than the mid-table position they managed to maintain right up until April. But then disaster struck.

On 2 April 1974 Exeter were due to take a 560-mile round trip to play a midweek match against Scunthorpe United. The week before, the Grecians had lost 2-1 at home to Peterborough when fielding a team of walking wounded. Numerous players were carrying injuries, while Jimmy Giles and Keith Bowker played despite both having flu. At the final whistle, Giles collapsed on the pitch from exhaustion. The following day's sorry roll-call revealed that the flu bug raging through the club plus other injuries and suspensions meant Exeter only had eight fit players available for the Scunthorpe game, and two of those were goalkeepers. After spending the entire season desperately struggling to rotate what few players they had to field a weekly starting 11, the club now realised the jig was up. Newman explained to the local press, 'We had the club doctor in and he issued medical certificates that nine players were unfit.'

Exeter explained their plight to the Football League at length, sent them the medical certificates and asked for the game to be postponed. A few days before, Halifax Town had been given permission to call off their match at Bournemouth and they had ten fit men, so Exeter were confident the powers-that-be would accept that they were unable to fulfil the fixture. With no reserve team because of cost-cutting, they would have had to field unregistered players just to make up an 11, which would have been against Football League rules. Exeter's board reasoned that the FL couldn't force them into a position where the authority's own laws would be broken. But to the club's utter astonishment, they were told the Scunthorpe game must go ahead or they would face serious consequences; there were even dark mutterings about them being expelled from the Football League. Irrespective of the threats, Exeter chairman Gerald Vallance decided that the team should not travel. Vallance told the *Daily Mirror*, 'I was told those players were not fit and I was not prepared to risk their health by forcing them into action.' A brave and laudable decision that showed an admirable duty of care towards his tiny, over-worked squad.

But then all hell broke loose. Enraged, the Football League swung into action immediately and imposed savage punishments upon the Devon club. As well as awarding two points to Scunthorpe, they slapped Exeter with an unprecedented £5,000 fine plus £1,300 to be paid in compensation to Scunthorpe and the match officials. The Football League refused to discuss their reasoning behind such a brutal punishment, though president Len Shipman issued a terse 17-word statement, 'Exeter cannot defy the rules like this. They should have made an effort to go and play.'

At St James Park, the reaction was one of angry disbelief. The club doctor Bryan Pepper, who'd issued the medical certificates, told the *Exeter Express and Echo*, 'The league clearly thinks they are better equipped to judge the fitness of Exeter players than I am. I still can't take in the severity of the fine. It's ridiculous ... out of all proportion. I think Exeter have every right to be shocked by this savage punishment.' Club vice-chairman Walter Rice added, 'This fine is absolutely preposterous and we must fight it. A sum of £5,000 to us represents something like £150,000 to the likes of Leeds and Liverpool.' Long-suffering manager John Newman was shell-shocked by the decision and looked visibly shattered when he gave his reaction to the local press, 'It makes one feel extremely empty and sick at this time. I just sat in a daze for a while, wondering what we were going to do next.'

In an angry editorial column, the *Exeter Express and Echo* let readers know that every question they had put to the Football League about the reasons and logic behind the punishment had been met with an imperious 'no comment' and then went on to pull no punches: 'We say that the league must not be allowed to get away with this form of dictation which amounts to almost cocking a snook at the supporters who, year after year, with no glittering prize at the end, support not just Exeter City, but league football itself.'

For a lower-league club already on its uppers, the £6,000-plus hit threatened to send Exeter into bankruptcy. Their end-of-season accounts showed that Exeter were more than £10,000 in debt – over half of that incurred as a consequence of their Football League fine. Vallance immediately called an emergency meeting of his five-man board, who unanimously agreed to appeal the decision in the strongest possible terms and to consider legal action. Sympathy was immediate and widespread. A group of concerned employees at the Department of Health and Social Security wrote a letter to the Football League Management Committee registering their disgust at the action taken by the league: 'It appears that once again the football authorities have demonstrated their failure to administer justice fairly to all clubs.' Donations began to arrive at St James Park from football fans up and down the country and *The Sun* newspaper ran a campaign to help support the club.

Prominent managers and players spoke up on Exeter's behalf. Coventry City general manager – and soon to be England's caretaker boss – Joe Mercer told the press, 'Exeter not guilty. What can John Newman do when he can't raise a team? I feel sorry for John Newman but I think that common sense will prevail.' Crystal Palace manager Malcolm Allison threw his support behind the club, saying, 'I don't think that the league took into consideration the true position of Exeter City. There are one or two who have cheated previously and this is probably one of the reasons for what happened with the league position. Exeter City, however, are sincere and honest, and the league should have postponed the game.'

Exeter MP John Hannam, himself a prominent member of the all-party Committee on Sport, weighed in with an impassioned appeal to sports minister Denis Howell to 'intervene', describing the fine as 'an unbearable load for this small club to bear'. In a letter to Howell, Hannam went on to say, 'I have long believed that some local authority assistance should be given to help maintain the smaller football clubs, as they provide a community recreation for a regular attendance of 2,000 to 5,000 supporters, but are constantly running at a loss and in debt to the bank.' Hannam had astutely opened up a wider debate which many fans agreed with. Clubs like Exeter deserved help and support in keeping football alive in small towns around the nation and for the Football League to show such callous insensitivity towards one of their own member clubs seemed quite beyond the pale. Hannam's letter to Howell went on to say, 'Exeter City have appealed against this fine and I hope that, bearing in mind the support of the doctors for the abandonment of this particular fixture on health grounds, the Football League can be influenced into changing their minds.'

Scunthorpe were less than supportive of their brothers from the south-west and it disquieted a lot of lower-league fans. United manager Ron Bradley unsympathetically told the press, 'I am simply not prepared to accept Exeter's excuse. I've had to struggle against injuries myself. I was forced to use a goalkeeper as substitute in our FA Cup fourth round tie at Newcastle – and we forced a draw.' His chairman Bill

Archer was equally dismissive, 'We are very angry about the situation. Exeter have defied the league's instructions completely.' And this despite the fact that their club, who were struggling around the bottom places in the Fourth Division, had been handed two points *gratis* and totally recompensed for the loss of the fixture.

More than anything, many fans felt that Scunthorpe were not only being tone deaf to the situation but callous about perennial lower-league problems that they themselves had experienced. This particularly rankled Exeter because the unspoken agreement had always been that small clubs should stick together, because they got little support from elsewhere. At the time, there was also very much a feeling among smaller sides that there was one law for the rich and another for the poor. Critics pointed to the make-up of the Football League board at the time – president Len Shipman had been long-time chairman of top-flight Leicester City; his vice-presidents Bob Lord and Sam Bolton were both current chairs of First Division clubs, Burnley and Leeds United respectively. It was felt that these rather more entitled authority figures didn't understand the struggles for survival that lower-league clubs faced and how important they were to the identity of their local towns and communities where football was more than just a game. For years, Exeter City had rarely made a profit.

The University of Exeter holds a fascinating archive of information about the Grecians, and in it, commenting on the 1974 fine, a club document suggests, 'The league's reason for refusing City's request was their impatience with uneconomic clubs and their acceptance that some would go bankrupt.' If this is true, then the Football League were not worthy to represent the 92 league clubs.

President Len Shipman went into damage limitation mode – not particularly to protect the Football League but to excuse himself from any responsibility for the original decision. He told the press that he had been outside of London when the decision was taken and was unaware of the issue, until his return the following day. It transpired that the decision had been taken by Shipman's two vice-presidents, Lord and Bolton. Shipman promised, 'I will see Exeter are given a fair hearing. It will be dealt with at the next Management Committee on 21 April.' But before the trouble-torn club got to learn of their fate, the week went from bad to worse.

Five days later, their much-depleted squad were forced to travel north again, this time to Scunthorpe's near-neighbours, bottom side Doncaster Rovers. In a largely dull and attritional game during which Doncaster's defensive default was to clear any attacking ball high into the stands, the Grecians held on at 0-0 for 75 minutes, until disaster struck. Exeter defender Campbell Crawford was forced to handball to save a certain goal; he was shown the red card and Doncaster scored from the spot to steal the game 1-0. Valuable points for rock-bottom Rovers, and a miserable 250-mile drive back to the south-west for Exeter. Shipman's 21 April Management Committee meeting reviewed Exeter City's appeal and double-downed on their original decision. The Grecians were guilty and must pay the consequences.

As fate would have it, Exeter WOULD play Scunthorpe before the season's end. On 22 April in their third to last league game of the season, the Iron were welcomed to St James Park but not very warmly. Club and fans alike had been disappointed, if not appalled, at not only Scunthorpe's lack of support for their plight earlier in the month, but the extreme level of criticism aimed at them by the South Humberside club. Scunthorpe trotted out on to the pitch to boos from sections of the 2,226 crowd. Exeter still only had 13 available players including two goalkeepers and versatile right-back Brian Joy, who was not fully fit and had spent the entire season filling in at different positions all around the pitch for team-mates who were out injured or suspended. But whatever their troubles throughout the season, Exeter had Fred Binney; once again, he would deliver. After the home side took control of the game in the first 35 minutes, the Exeter Exocet stepped up and rifled one in, and then two minutes later, a second. Soon after half-time Binney grabbed his hat-trick and Scunthorpe were on the ropes. Bowker scored a fourth in injury time, but Exeter could have won by six or seven.

Binney ended the season as the Fourth Division's leading goalscorer – and for the second year running. Along with team-mate and defender Jimmy Giles, Binney would be named in the PFA's Fourth Division Team of the Season. If anything, Exeter's troubles had galvanised and unified their tiny squad but the events of the season meant that local hero Binney's departure had become an inevitability – to balance the books and to allow the prolific striker, now aged 28, the opportunity to further his career. Brighton stepped in with an offer of £25,000 for Binney plus two players, John Templeman and Lammie Robertson, in exchange. Exeter survived financially, but only just.

Binney continued to thrive at Brighton. After scoring 79 goals in 160 games for Exeter, his almost metronomic goal-poaching skills brought him 35 in 70 appearances at the Goldstone Ground club. After a brief foray over in the fledgling NASL in the US, where he scored nine goals in 18 matches for St Louis Stars, Binney returned to the south-west to play for Plymouth Argyle, where he delivered more than a goal every two games, 39 in 71 appearances. In the following season, and once again working with a small player base, John Newman would lead Exeter to an admirable ninth-placed finish. Without Binney, striker

Keith Bowker would step up to the plate and score 18 league goals and Newman's tactically rearranged midfield would chip in with over 30 goals between them.

It was only right that Peterborough's Noel Cantwell ended the 1973/74 season as the Fourth Division's manager of the year, but after installing such optimism and unity in his tiny squad despite the many traumas of the campaign, John Newman should have been a very close runner-up. The man was a great manager and indeed, a great manager of men. The pressure at the top is intense; at the bottom, frantic. But without money and resources, bosses like John Newman were – and still are – part manager, part magician.

8

Up for the Cups

THE FIRST trophy up for grabs in 1974 was the League Cup, which pitched Manchester City against West Midlanders Wolverhampton Wanderers. City had almost stumbled their way to Wembley, needing two replays to overcome Third Division Walsall, one to get past Third Division York and then yet another replay to overcome Coventry City. Wolves had an easy ride to the quarter-finals, overcoming Fourth Division Exeter, Third Division Halifax Town and Tranmere Rovers, and then got into their stride by beating fellow First Division sides Liverpool and Norwich.

Wolves came into the week of the final with several key players in the treatment room and manager Bill McGarry was sweating on four late fitness tests. Top scorer John Richards had been out for three weeks, struggling with a bad muscle strain in his stomach; his iron-man captain and on-field organiser Mike Bailey last played a month before and was recovering from a broken big toe; midfielder Barry Powell had a muscle strain; and regular first-choice goalkeeper Phil Parkes had a cracked bone in his ankle. Richards, Bailey and Powell would all be passed fit, but only just. Indeed, unconvinced that Richards could manage a whole game, McGarry's plan for his star striker was to play him for as long as he could manage and then be subbed.

Parkes would miss out on the final, to be replaced by his young understudy, reserve team keeper Gary Pierce, which was a big blow for McGarry. Known as 'Lofty' both for his imposing height and his booming kicks upfield, Parkes had been the manager's trusted number one for several seasons, a commanding ever-present behind the Wolves back four.

Though neither club were enjoying a particularly good season in the league – Wolves would end up 12th, Manchester City 14th – the Blues were overwhelming favourites and oozed class. Rodney Marsh, Mike Summerbee, Mike Doyle, Colin Bell and the evergreen Denis Law all had big-match temperament and the bookies strongly fancied them to prevail in a one-off 90-minute game. But for their part, Wolves too had some cool heads on board – old warhorse Derek Dougan had been round the block a good few times, captain Bailey was a rock at the back and wingers Kenny Hibbitt and Dave Wagstaffe and exciting young midfielder Alan Sunderland could be real handfuls on their day.

With ten minutes or so to go, McGarry could see that John Richards was starting to struggle badly with his stomach injury and loath though he was, he resolved to take his striker off. He told sub Barry Powell to warm up, but as he began to stretch and sprint up and down the Wembley touchline, fate took a hand. Before Powell could enter the game, Wagstaffe pulled up sharply with a thigh strain, unable to continue. Powell replaced the winger and Richards indicated to the bench that he would try to soldier on. Three minutes later, he would defy the pain and rifle home Wolves' winner. His courageous performance was more than worthy of a man of the match award, but that would go to another Wolves player – 'the replacement'. Before the game had begun, Manchester City manager Ron Saunders had told his side to give rookie goalkeeper Gary Pierce a torrid time – constantly test him, shoot from distance and muscle him hard in the penalty box. This they did but Pierce refused to be rattled, stood tall and made a string of impressive saves. Encouraged on by skipper Bailey and defenders Geoff Palmer and Derek Parkin, Pierce grew in stature and confidence as the game progressed and thanks to his heroics, it would be Wolves who won the League Cup.

Between the staging of the League Cup and the FA Cup in May, there was another trophy to be won and it was a strange beast indeed – the invitation-only Texaco Cup. Launched in 1970, it was one of the first football tournaments in the world to be sponsored and though it would only last for five years, it initially involved a selection of top-flight sides from England, Scotland, the Republic of Ireland and Northern Ireland, all of whom had failed to qualify for any of the European competitions. In 1970, the US petroleum giant Texaco had bought the Regal chain of petrol stations in Britain and Ireland, and as part of their marketing efforts they funnelled £100,000 a year into creating the Texaco Cup competition.

In essence, the idea was to establish a 'British Cup' for club sides but after just two tournaments, the Irish and Northern Irish teams were forced to pull out because of the increased shootings and bombings during the Troubles. From then onwards, it was purely an Anglo-Scottish tournament, but the fans loved it. Like the FA Cup and League Cup, the knockout competition kicked off early in the season and had a grand final at its end. In 1973/74, 16 teams took part, with the first three rounds played on a home and away basis, the highest aggregate scorers in each tie progressing to the next round.

By far and away the form side were Burnley, who won all six of their games on the way to the final, scoring an impressive 23 goals. Their opponents would be Joe Harvey's Newcastle United, who stuttered their way to the tournament decider with three wins, two draws and a defeat. On the toss of a coin, the venue for the final would be St James' Park on the evening of 24 April, where after extra time the Magpies would triumph 2-1. It was a fairly ordinary game played in front of 34,540 fans – the real and most dramatic story of the tournament had been played out in the quarter-finals over two brutal games between Newcastle and Birmingham City, the culmination of a season-long six-match vendetta.

As well as their two First Division fixtures, the two sides had also met twice in the League Cup, drawing the first encounter 1-1 in the Midlands and then Newcastle coming out on top 1-0 in the replay. The four matches – played at St Andrew's and St James' Park – had been far from saintly. As *Goal* magazine commented at the time, 'Familiarity had bred considerable contempt.' If the first League Cup encounter had been ill-tempered and tetchy, the following three matches broke out into open warfare with an ever-increasing catalogue of old scores being settled between the two sets of players. Unlike today, footballers almost had to commit GBH to be yellow-carded or sent off. There would be a dozen bookings made in this short series of festering feuds and the Birmingham and Newcastle players had grown to loathe one another. Neither club were particularly happy about being drawn against one another in the Texaco Cup and there was a general feeling that it would end in tears. The first leg was played at St Andrew's and straight away the late challenges were flying in. Just over a minute in, Newcastle's Jimmy Smith was sent off after launching a horror tackle on City's Tony Want, breaking his leg in two places.

The atmosphere at St James' Park for the return match crackled with a rancorous electricity both in the stands and on the pitch. Minutes after kick-off Birmingham's Paul

Hendrie went studs up into United's Pat Howard, sending him flying. In agony, Howard leapt up from the pitch, got Hendrie in a stranglehold and screamed into his face; both were booked. Minutes later, Hendrie made a nasty late challenge on Newcastle's Frank Clark, leaving a gaping, bleeding hole in his shin. Inexplicably, he was not sent off, but Clark had to leave the field to get patched up. Once back on the pitch, Clark, who was obviously being targeted for his perceived 'misdemeanours' in the earlier encounters, was scythed down by City's Keith Robson, who went straight into the book. Clark then got into a feisty challenge with Paul and threw him to the ground. Into the book. Then Newcastle's Irving Nattrass's season was ended thanks to a brutal late challenge from Birmingham's Kenny Burns. Again, utterly inexplicably, Burns didn't even get a booking. Over the six games, nine players on either side had been badly injured. It was more than clear to the viewing public and the press that though both teams had gone out to win, a vengeful cabal on either side also deliberately went out on to the pitch to cripple their opponents.

The top brass at the FA were horrified. Already on the back foot because of the public outrage about the spiralling increase in football hooliganism, the on-field violence during the two games was an embarrassment. Rather than deal with it head-on, in their customary style they simply tried to play it down. Secretary Ted Croker told the assembled press that he felt 'ashamed' but accused the media of exaggerating the problem. 'There was some disgraceful behaviour, but the majority behaved very well,' he added.

On Saturday, 4 May the north came to town. Two of the most passionately supported teams in the history of the domestic game, Liverpool and Newcastle, had made it to the FA Cup Final. Sadly, a minority of those fans had travelled south with other sport in mind. What followed was described by the *Daily Mirror* as 'The Battle of Wembley' but in truth, the trouble began long before fans made it to the national stadium. During the morning of the final, tens of thousands of supporters from Liverpool and Newcastle had departed dozens of football special trains and flooded the centre of London: in their midst, a hardcore of troublemakers who once again showed the ugly side of English football. Fans of both clubs went on the rampage around the West End, breaking windows, smashing up cars and brawling with one another on the roads and pavements. Knowing that 'hardcore' from the two northern clubs would be 'in town', members of hooligan firms from Chelsea, Arsenal, Spurs, Millwall and Charlton turned up for the craic and got stuck in too. Frightened tourists and shoppers ran for cover as the 'English Disease' spread its infection through the central London streets. Black Maria horses and squad cars screamed around the area, dropping off units of riot police who frantically tried to nip the mayhem in the bud. For dozens of fans, the West End was the nearest they would get to Wembley, rounded up, arrested and locked up in local police stations.

Once at the famous old ground, the remaining hooligans reconvened their violent clashes and scores of fan fights broke out around the stadium. A 16-year-old Newcastle fan, Stephen Tempest, was stabbed several times in the side and rushed to hospital with serious injuries. To add to the mayhem, mobs of ticketless young fans rushed the fences to gain entry to the ground. The *Daily Mirror* reported, 'About 200 made it – some climbing up ropes of knotted flags and scarves lowered Colditz-style by friends already inside. Ticket touts had a good day – except for those who were beaten up. One Londoner paid £130 for two £3 tickets.'

The bookies had Liverpool as odds-on favourites, but Newcastle had history on their side, winning the FA Cup six times in their 11 final appearances. Liverpool had only won it once, back in 1965. Alongside Leeds United, reigning league champions Liverpool were the cream of 1974's crop. They had Steve Heighway, long-serving Mr Consistency Ian Callaghan, burly Welsh centre-forward John Toshack and hardman Tommy Smith among their ranks. But the player Newcastle feared the most was Kevin Keegan. Powerful, direct and a great dribbler; though only 5ft 8in tall, his muscular leap made him a real handful in the air too and Newcastle manager Joe Harvey knew he was coming into the match with something to prove. The young Keegan had not long since broken into the England team and by his own admission had not played well in his only two previous international appearances at Wembley. He was determined to show his ability on the biggest stage, and Harvey drilled his players long and hard in training, working out strategies to starve him of the ball.

Newcastle ended the season in mid-table, but many north-east fans believed they had two things strongly in their favour: one, because of their endeavours in competitions elsewhere, the final would be Liverpool's 60th game of the campaign and in a one-off challenge, they could well be gassed out. And number two, Supermac.

Though Newcastle had some top players like midfielders Terry McDermott and Tommy Cassidy, nippy wingers Terry Hibbitt and Jimmy Smith, the fans' talisman was a certain Malcolm Macdonald. All sideburns and swagger, the striker was Newcastle's not very secret weapon. Quick and powerful, Macdonald was a game-changer of a player and was never shy about letting people know about his abilities. In the build-up to the final, Supermac turned into Supermouth and confidently boasted to the press about the damage he intended to do to the Liverpool defence. He reminded them that three years previously he'd scored a hat-trick against the Reds on his Newcastle debut, and thought they had too many ageing, past-it players like Smith and Callaghan. En route to Wembley, Macdonald had scored in every round of the FA Cup and predicted that he would finish the job in the final by scoring at least once, probably more.

In fairness, it wasn't just Macdonald who was indulging in pre-match mind-games. Respective managers Bill Shankly and Joe Harvey were interviewed together at a press conference. Afterwards, Shanks made sure he was within earshot of the Newcastle staff, and loudly told his Liverpool colleagues that 'poor old' Harvey looked 'a bag of nerves'. He didn't, but the wily old Shanks had long been a master of psychological warfare. In training, he constantly reminded his players about Macdonald's bragging in the press which really got their hackles up. A brilliant football man, Shankly knew that if his side managed to neutralise Macdonald's impact upon the game, they were halfway home. Alongside captain Emlyn Hughes at the back, Shanks gave a young 20-year-old Phil Thompson the job of man-marking the Newcastle centre-forward. Showing maturity well beyond his years, Tommo shackled Supermac from start to finish, and with Hughes breathing down the neck of his Newcastle strike partner John Tudor, the Magpies struggled to make any headway up front during the first half.

Liverpool looked lively but created few chances against a tough, do-or-die Newcastle back four. At the heart of their engine room were two footballers who'd played alongside one another for over a decade at St James' Park and knew one another's game inside out. Tough Scottish international centre-back Bobby Moncur had played for Newcastle since 1962 and his uncompromising play had made him a real fan favourite. Thirty-one-year-old stalwart full-back Frank Clark would play nearly 400 league games for the Magpies – and then go on to a hugely successful late-blossoming career under Cloughie at Nottingham Forest, winning a league title and two European Cups. Alongside them were Steady Eddie centre-back Pat Howard, who played nearly 200 times for Newcastle, and the talented 19-year-old left-back Alan Kennedy, who a few seasons later would sign for Liverpool for £330,000, at the time a record transfer fee for a full-back. At Anfield, he would win two European Cups and five league titles. So no slouches there.

By half-time, both sides had pretty much cancelled one another out and trotted off back down the tunnel to the Wembley dressing rooms locked in at 0-0. As Newcastle walked off, Macdonald turned to team-mate Clark and said, 'At least we can't play as bad as that in the second half.' Behind closed doors, long-serving boss Joe Harvey was re-assuring. We're containing them, we're snuffing out their best forward threats. But let's try and get cleverer, more angled balls to Malcolm and John so they can turn Hughes and Thompson. In the Liverpool dressing room, Shanks had a more insistent message – bloody speed up play, get on the front foot, press them high; and that is exactly what his players did.

The Reds came out for the second half like a runaway train. A few minutes in, defender Alec Lindsay lashed a shot over the line from close range, but the referee disallowed the goal because Keegan was offside. But no matter. Minutes later, the 'past-it' Tommy Smith roamed dangerously upfield and swung in a teasing cross that Kevin Keegan volleyed home to make it 1-0 to Liverpool. Soon after, winger Steve Heighway banged in a second and the Reds were running the show, well on top. Thompson continued to hustle Macdonald out of shooting range and keep him off his famous left foot. The measure of his success was that Supermac's first shot on goal wasn't until the 77th minute: put under pressure by Thompson, he lost his balance and screwed it well wide. With minutes to go, Smith once again became the provider, crossing for Keegan to tap in from close range to make it 3-0 Liverpool. Commentating on the final for the BBC, David Coleman was on fine form, 'Yes, Keegan's second and Newcastle were undressed. They were absolutely stripped naked.' The Reds comfortably saw out the rest of the contest and 3-0 it would remain. When captain Emlyn Hughes was interviewed after the match, he was asked what had motivated his team the most. Without pause for thought, he immediately replied, 'Malcolm Macdonald.'

One of the most enjoyable aspects of local newspaper football coverage is how gloriously biased they can be about their own much-beloved teams. The general consensus in the national press was that the first half had been fairly tedious and lacking in incident; the second half, more enjoyable once Liverpool started to speed up their movement. From that point onwards, the *Daily Mirror* declared it 'a one-sided affair'. The *Liverpool Echo* saw it somewhat differently, 'One of the finest exhibitions of football Wembley has seen in years!' You gotta love 'em.

Despite being beaten, the Magpies decided to go ahead with an already planned open-top bus ride through Newcastle to thank their loyal fans; a staggering 250,000 crowd lined the streets ten deep to welcome them home, a measure of just how passionate they were.

Though both the League Cup and FA Cup offered up decent enough Wembley finals, the real humdinger would be played three months later between First Division champions Leeds and FA Cup winners Liverpool. It would be the first FA Charity Shield match to be televised, shown all around the world, and the first time it would be played at Wembley. Even before the game began there were intriguing subplots aplenty. Recently retired Reds boss Bill Shankly was regretting his decision; he and old friend and colleague Bob Paisley had fallen out over his continued 'interference'. New manager Paisley offered the olive branch and asked Shanks to lead out what was essentially still his team, which he did.

New Leeds manager Brian Clough claimed to have asked his predecessor Don Revie to do the same, but the England boss-in-waiting refused and sat instead in the Royal Box, glowering down at Clough as he would continue to do literally and metaphorically for the next few months. Still in regular contact with his beloved Leeds players, Revie was bristling about the way Clough was treating his league championship-winning squad. Clough had enormous respect and affection for Shankly and as they stood side-by-side in the tunnel ready to lead out their players, Clough applauded the legendary Scotsman out on to the pitch every step of the way. He also asked Shanks if they could sit together on the touchline, and throughout the match they exchanged animated chat. And as it progressed, they would have much to talk about.

Though Clough had signed Nottingham Forest's top goalscorer Duncan McKenzie in the close-season, he fielded a team solely made up of Revie's men and named McKenzie on the bench. The Leeds players were not a happy camp. From the day he walked into Elland Road, Clough had pulled no punches. Determined to let everyone know he was not overawed by Revie's reputation or the stature of the club, he told his new squad he couldn't care less how many medals they'd won – for him, they could throw them all in the bin. Now he intended to turn 'Dirty Leeds' into an attractive footballing team. The players were outraged and sullen silence soon turned into open revolt against Clough. Senior squad members had already started to complain to the board about their new manager, claiming that his arrogance and misunderstanding of the club's identity would destroy what Revie had created at Elland Road. With the right set of players, Clough had proved himself to be inspirational but the very successful Leeds team was already a well-established unit of players who had loyally long fought for one another on and off the pitch. This new Clough gig required subtle and clever diplomatic skills, and at the time, he had none.

To add extra spice to the Charity Shield game, Leeds and Liverpool had been slugging it out as the two best teams in the top flight for some years and over a series of keenly fought matches, grudges had developed between players. Though both sides contained some of the best, most skilful players in the country, neither were short on bite and muscle. But this was the Charity Shield, the season's gentle curtain-raiser – surely this was a friendly match? After a season of bad headlines over hooliganism in and around grounds, in town and city centres and on the trains, the FA were desperate to show off English football's sportsmanship at its best to the rest of the world. The match would be shown live or as lengthy TV highlight packages in many foreign countries and the FA wanted it to be a showcase. It turned out to be a shitshow.

At the time the *Sunday Mirror*'s esteemed football reporter Ken Jones put it most succinctly, 'The match was punctuated by frequent examples of nastiness.' The aggro began early when Leeds forward Allan Clarke left a boot in on Phil Thompson, who ended up in a heap on the ground. A minute or two later, Tommy Smith scythed Clarke over by way of revenge and got a booking for his trouble. One player in particular was being given constant niggle. Every time the ball came near to Kevin Keegan, the Leeds defence pushed, muscled and clipped away at his heels. Phil Boersma, who'd missed out on a place in the FA

Cup Final, started instead of an injured John Toshack, and scored a typical poacher's goal to put Liverpool ahead on 18 minutes. A loose ball in the box was hammered goalwards by Keegan, where David Harvey bravely parried it out but straight into the path of Boersma, who scuffed it home. For the rest of the half, Liverpool were on top, the pace of Steve Heighway and Brian Hall constantly pushing the Leeds defence backwards.

As the second half progressed, what started as a football game fast turned into a pretty absorbing boxing match. Keegan continued to suffer constant 'treatment' from the Leeds players and it was clear that he was starting to lose his temper. As Billy Bremner tried to control a loose ball on the edge of the box, Keegan went in studs up on the Scotsman's leg, crunched into Norman Hunter and then followed the ball across to the other side of the box, where he manhandled Johnny Giles, grabbing him by the shoulders. The tough-as-teak Irishman turned and, to everyone's amazement, smacked Keegan on the jaw with a left hook. Keegan was outraged and complained bitterly to referee Bob Matthewson. Bremner raced across and tried to show Matthewson what Keegan had just done to his leg but was waved away. During the three-way exchange between the referee and the two men, Keegan later remembered that Matthewson and Giles appeared to be on very friendly terms. As they talked, Matthewson referred to Giles as 'Johnny'. When he turned to speak with the Liverpool man, he constantly called him 'Keegan'. 'Johnny' said, 'Sorry, I shouldn't have done that,' and to the shock of the 67,000 fans in the ground, the Leeds player was only shown the yellow card.

Their shock soon turned to disbelief when a few minutes later, having escaped a certain red card, Giles went recklessly into a two-footed tackle on Keegan. Once again, the Irishman escaped a sending-off. Already wound up to breaking point, Keegan exploded with anger and launched himself at Giles. He was immediately surrounded by Leeds players, who stopped him in his tracks. According to the *Liverpool Echo*, Keegan, who by this point had totally lost it, later explained, 'Four guys came running up to me when I tackled Johnny Giles and three of them were six foot three. The fourth one was Billy and he was smaller than me. So I just fucking hit him to be honest with you. I'd done a bit of boxing and it was one of my better punches.' Bremner then gave as good as he got, and the two began to trade punches.

As the players tried to pull them apart, the two men continued to struggle, their heads gone. Matthewson had no alternative but to send them both off, the first Football League players to be sent off at Wembley. The famously emotional Keegan walked furiously down the touchline, pulled off his shirt and flung it on to the pitch. Marching off a few yards behind him, Bremner had called out, apologising to Keegan, but was rebuffed. The frustrated Scot followed suit and ripped off his own shirt. Commentating on the match for the BBC's TV coverage, Barry Davies's outrage was palpable, 'This is a side of English football we do not want to see. What do the players think they're doing? To dismiss the referee's authority in such a manner cannot be good for the game. However they feel, he is the judge and the judgement must stand.'

The ten men of Leeds began to regroup and get back into the match and it became a good, flowing affair for the final half an hour. In the dying minutes, Trevor Cherry got his head on a Peter Lorimer cross to make it 1-1, which is how it ended. To decide the encounter, it went to penalties with Liverpool winning 6-5. Ironically, David Harvey, who'd had such a good game, was the Leeds man to miss his penalty, and to this day it remains a mystery why one of Leeds' other five outfield players was not nominated to take the crucial sixth spot kick. Liverpool lifted the Charity Shield but it was nothing but a pyrrhic victory for English football. The world had seen it on screen: nasty, ill-tempered and cynically over-aggressive; the fallout was seismic and showed the domestic game to be stuck down a depressing cul-de-sac.

Clough was left fuming. Ashamed of his new players' behaviour and perhaps wanting to let them know who was boss, he told the press, 'Bremner's behaviour was scandalous. He seemed intent on making Kevin Keegan's afternoon an absolute misery. He kicked him just about everywhere, until it became only a matter of time before a confrontation exploded. Keegan was a victim, not a culprit. I told Bremner afterwards he should pay compensation for the period Keegan was suspended.'

A fortnight later, Keegan and Bremner were charged by the FA with bringing the game into disrepute, fined £500 and banned for an eye-watering ten matches each. But there were no hard feelings between Keegan, Bremner or Johnny Giles. Keegan told the *Liverpool Echo* that after the sending-offs, Bremner went into the empty Liverpool dressing room to seek him out and apologise but found him sat with his dad. With tears in his eyes, Bremner told Keegan he was really sorry. Keegan's father turned angrily on the Scot and told him, 'If you don't get out of this dressing room, I'm going to hit you as well.' Keegan recalled, 'I had to say to him, "Dad, don't hit him. He's one of my best friends."'

Many years later, Keegan would appear on the Irish internet show *Off the Ball* to help celebrate the 80th birthday of the still extremely sharp and witty Johnny Giles. The 2021 show discussed the 1974 Charity Shield at length and the love and respect between the two players was obvious.

Even before they discussed the Giles 'punch' and the Keegan–Bremner fight, the legendary Irishman said, 'In my opinion Kevin Keegan transformed Liverpool. I had the utmost respect for him as did all of the Leeds players.'

Their exchanges on the show also offered an intriguing insight into how the two ex-footballers viewed the game as it was played back in 1974 in comparison to today. Keegan observed, 'If you took the rules today and applied them to the Leeds v Liverpool games in the early to mid-70s, Johnny wouldn't have been on the pitch, Billy wouldn't have been on the pitch. Norman Hunter wouldn't. I don't think Allan Clarke would. Tommy Smith would have probably got sent off in the kick-on. It was a different time, a different era … someone like Johnny tackled you or Billy or Norman, you'd just walk away like it didn't hurt and then cry after the game when you're going back in your car. And the thing was Johnny Giles was lovely off the pitch, as was Billy. Norman Hunter was charming and a wonderful player.'

Brian Clough's disastrous reign at Leeds would last for just 44 days. Shortly after his sacking, the quick-witted news team at Yorkshire TV approached 'Ol' Big Head' to discuss and debate the events that led up to his termination – with his predecessor Don Revie. Already a TV, rent-a-quote media darling, Clough said 'yes' straight away. Curiously, almost inexplicably, the truculent, media-hating Revie agreed to take part too. The blunt, at times almost monosyllabic, Yorkshireman was not a great interview at the best of times and had a decade of beefs, gripes and grievances against the football press and media generally. But he hated Clough, a fellow manager who had consistently slagged off his Leeds team for being cynical and dirty. Partly through loyalty towards his old club and to the players he loved, he was appalled at the way Clough had treated them all. Well before the days of agents and advisors who would almost definitely have urged him to pass on the gig, Revie jumped at the opportunity to defenestrate the hated Cloughie on screen – he misjudged the situation badly.

Broadcaster and future Labour MP Austin Mitchell interviewed the two managers in a 30-minute special over the debacle at Elland Road. It remains one of the most extraordinary sports interviews ever shown on British television and I would strongly urge you to seek it out on YouTube. Mitchell was a straight news reporter on YTV and had little interest in football, but he was an expert at drawing out a story and judiciously stepped back and pitched his two interviewees against one another. He made few interventions, just a few prompts and direct questions, and allowed the two managers to go head to head. The media-savvy and genially smiling Clough constantly praised Revie and his reputation, said what a great squad he'd put together, and stressed that all he wanted to do as the new manager was to make them 'more attractive'. In response, Revie came over as aggressive and angry, constantly glowering and shaking his head. Though Leeds fans particularly may disagree, as a television drama spectacle, Cloughie made Revie look like an embittered man who couldn't let go of having moved on from his old club. If he did have advisors at the time, they had sold him a pup.

Clough clearly won the TV battle, but in reality he had lost the war. He had shown himself to be totally misguided in the manner he had approached his new job at Elland Road. Though expressed in an over-condemnatory and bitter way, Revie was right that Cloughie had shown no respect to a magnificent set of players and totally misread 'the room'. It's no surprise that this tough, together squad loathed his very presence. In the end, they could take no more and told the Leeds board that Clough must go. Faced with an unprecedented and almost unanimous vote of no confidence from their playing staff, the Elland Road directors had no choice but to give 'Ol' Big Head' the sack.

Clough would learn from his mistakes. Next up for him was Nottingham Forest where he would win a league championship, two European Cups and three League Cups. Similar to his successful spell at Derby County, this was a largely unfashionable club who needed rebuilding out on the pitch – at that, Clough was an expert. To this day, it's still a total mystery why the Leeds board decided to appoint their team's perennially most vocal and savage critic as the new manager – even more astonishing that Clough jumped to accept the job.

The once-great managerial career of Don Revie would end in scandal, controversy and disgrace. For over a decade, he had proven himself to be one of modern English football's greatest managers. After leaving Leeds to manage England, his career would be dragged down and degraded by hubris and greed. But for decades to come, his loyal Leeds players and fans would not hear a word said against him.

9
Non-League Football

'Sport must be amateur or it is not sport. Sports played professionally are entertainment'

– Avery Brundage, International Olympic Committee president 1952–72

THE YEAR 1974 saw a revolution occur in English non-league football and all thanks to a single rule change. The FA knew full well that dozens of so-called amateur clubs were secretly paying their players. Sometimes this might literally have been brown envelopes under the table stuffed with cash.

Some clubs would have board members who owned local businesses, factories and mills, and 'ghost' jobs were given to players, put on the payroll as salesmen, production line operatives or shop workers. In reality, few of them would ever work more than a few days in their 'jobs', spending the working week training as full-time footballers. Unable to police the practice, the widespread existence of 'shamateurism' had vexed the FA for years and in 1974, they finally gave in to the reality of the situation and resolved to act. They decided to abolish the distinction between 'amateur' and 'professional' players, allowing non-league clubs to pay their footballers if they so wished.

The immediate ramifications of this decision were huge. Overnight, the FA Amateur Cup, the annual highlight of non-league football for 80 years, was disbanded. From 1974 onwards, the top non-league sides would compete in the FA Trophy, a still relatively new competition created five years earlier. For those clubs further down the pyramid, another new tournament, the FA Vase. The FA's rule change also meant that the Great Britain Olympic team was disbanded, though this was not a huge loss to the nation. Curiously, successive GB sides perennially underperformed. The last time the team actually qualified for the Olympics was way back in 1960 in Rome and they crashed out in the first round. The side failed to qualify for the next three Olympics. A Great Britain men's football team would not appear at the Olympics again until London 2012.

The loss of England's amateur national side was more heartbreaking. Formed in 1901 as a consequence of the FA's decision to officially make a distinction between paid and unpaid players and clubs, the amateur team set out to determinedly extol the virtues of 'Corinthian sport', fair play and gentlemanly conduct. Their early history was astonishing. Up to the outbreak of the First World War, they steamrollered the best amateur national teams in Europe, beating France 15-0, Germany 12-0 and 9-0, the Netherlands and Sweden both 12-2, Switzerland and Hungary both 7-0 and Belgium 11-2. The amateur England players made up most of the Great Britain Olympic football team and won golds in 1908 and 1912.

After the Great War, the amateur side contained so many outstanding unpaid players that some were selected to play for the full professional England team as well. In 1923, three members of the Corinthians club – Graham Doggart, Basil Patchitt and Jackie Hegan – all won full caps. Hegan would actually win four caps that year, playing in three friendlies

– twice against Belgium and once versus France – and then in that year's British Home Championship game against Northern Ireland. His four-cap full international career ended with a 100 per cent scoring record of four goals in four games. He also ended the year as England's top scorer. In 1929, Dulwich Hamlet's Edgar Kail played for England in a friendly against Spain. Bernard Joy of the Corinthians earned his only cap in 1935 against Belgium and became the last amateur to play in the senior England side.

Without a doubt, amateur football was still full of some top-flight players. In October 1925, the England amateur team played a side made up of the country's top professional players and thrashed them 6-1. But as the decades passed and more and more countries professionalised their leagues and national teams, interest in international amateur matches began to fade. The England side would soldier on playing a dozen or more games every year to increasingly smaller and smaller attendances. By 1974, the game was up.

On 5 April 1974, they played their final international, against the Auld Enemy Scotland in the last match of the annual British Amateur Championship at Coventry City's Highfield Road. It was a dull 1-1 draw, which meant that England shared the last title with Wales. A meagre crowd of 1,221 was testament to an atrophying lack of interest in international amateur football – 20 years previously, the same England v Scotland fixture saw a crowd of 27,000 rock up at Wembley. A month before the England amateurs' final match, a friendly against Malta at Reading's Elm Park was watched by only 496 fans. The message was clear and England's amateur national side sadly went out not with a bang but a very small whimper.

It would be another five years before non-league footballers got the opportunity to play for their own national side, when the FA created a new team first called the England Semi-Professional team, then England Non-League, finally settling on the rather snappier England C. The team's first gaffer was a promising young non-league manager called Howard Wilkinson, who later, of course, would manage Sheffield Wednesday and win the league title with Leeds United. From day one, it almost exclusively featured players from the very top non-league clubs but their first and biggest problem was finding other national or representative teams of an equivalent level to play against. Between 1979 and 2003, they competed in the annual Four Nations tournament alongside a Scotland side made up of players from outside the Scottish Premier League, international minnows Gibraltar, and a semi-professional Wales team. England C won the tournament seven times. Beyond those annual fixtures, they played professional under-23 teams from the likes of Italy, Belgium and Turkey and smaller nation states like Grenada and Barbados. England C still play today and their manager, former Stevenage and Barnet boss Paul Fairclough, has been in the position since 2003 as of the time of writing.

Though this was the very last time that the FA Amateur Cup would be contested, it was Isthmian League Bishop's Stortford's first final and it could not have been more timely. The Hertfordshire side were celebrating their 100th anniversary and this was their one and only shot at ever lifting the Amateur Cup. The season before, the Bishops had gone close, narrowly losing 1-0 against Slough Town in the semi-finals. In 1973/74 their route to the final had been a tough one – the first three rounds had matched them against three of the south-east's best amateur teams in Hayes, Hitchin Town and Walton & Hersham; the quarter- and semi-finals, two of the north-east's finest and most historic clubs, Blyth Spartans and Ashington. But this was a side on form, who had enjoyed a successful league season by finishing in third place, and manager Ted Hardy had put together a team that had a wealth of past Wembley experience behind them. Midfielder John Payne had played in four previous FA Amateur Cup finals for Enfield and Hendon and was twice on the winning side. Full-back Tony Gibson was a losing finalist with Enfield in 1972. Midfielder Peter Leakey had played in two losing finals for Dagenham, as had forward John Dear and defender Martin Smith. Centre-forward Tony Bass played in two finals for Hendon and Dagenham.

Their opponents on the day were fellow Isthmian League side Ilford, who were a fast-improving outfit. During their first ten 1973/74 league matches, Ilford had not managed a single win and were looking like serious relegation fodder. The board brought in John Evans as new manager, and after looking at his squad he realised he had to perform major surgery. In a total revamp, he got rid of all but three of the Ilford squad and as the new players began to gel, the team continued to climb the table, ending the season in a very creditable ninth place. Key to Ilford's success were their two amateur England internationals, Roger Day and Tony Turley. Day was generally regarded as one of amateur football's greatest midfield schemers. Hugely experienced, not only had Day won 33 England caps but he'd also played in five previous Amateur Cup finals for other clubs at Wembley. Right-winger Turley was now 28 years old and before Evans signed him he had played for a host of top amateur clubs like Enfield, Barnet and St Albans. With Day pulling the strings in midfield and Turley providing the bullets from out on the wing, both would be vital to the Ilford challenge. This would be their fifth FA Amateur Cup Final, having won it in 1929 and 1930 and lost in 1936 and 1958. Although both sides' average home gates hovered around the 2,000 mark, 34,000 fans turned up for this last showpiece occasion. Good support no doubt, but to put this in perspective, 20 years previously Pegasus had beaten Harwich 5-0 in front of a sell-out 90,000 Wembley crowd. The simple truth was that fans were losing their appetite for amateur football's biggest days out.

The final final got off to an explosive start. After 12 minutes, Stortford's John Dear ploughed through the back of Roger Day and after lengthy treatment down on the pitch, Ilford's influential playmaker was stretchered off with heavy bruising and abrasions to a battered right leg. Dear was fortunate to only receive a yellow card and without Day to organise them, Ilford were soon on the back foot. Stortford attacked relentlessly and halfway through the first half captain Dave Lawrence latched on to a teasing ball ten yards out and lashed it past the Ilford keeper. Early in the second half, Stortford's Denis Murphy doubled their lead but much against the run of play, Ilford's Peter Drabwell nodded in from close range to put his side back in the game. But it wasn't for long; winger Peter Leakey made it 3-1 to Stortford and then striker Tony Bass was upended in the Ilford area and Martin Smith made it 4-1 from the penalty spot. For the first – and last – time in their 100-year history, Bishop's Stortford lifted the FA Amateur Cup.

Parts of the match report in *The Times* read more like an obituary, 'Amateur football in England was quietly buried without ceremony at Wembley on Saturday.' In truth, much of non-league football continued to be played on a totally amateur basis, with only the bigger clubs able to pay players as either full- or part-time. And arguably, by replacing the FA Amateur Cup with two separate competitions, the FA Trophy and the FA Vase, smaller amateur clubs further down the pyramid suddenly stood a far greater chance of winning a major national cup. A look at the last dozen FA

Amateur Cup finals reveals that the finalists all came from amateur football's top leagues, the Northern, Isthmian and Athenian.

In a year of seismic changes within amateur, now non-league football, the south-east's most prestigious league, the Isthmian, also underwent a fundamental shake-up. For the first time in its 59-year history it split into two divisions, enrolling 16 new clubs to help make up its second tier. Fifteen of them migrated from a step further down the football pyramid from different divisions of the Athenian League plus little Hertford Town from the Eastern Counties League.

Free-scoring Wycombe Wanderers won Division One of the Isthmian League in 1973/74, scoring 96 goals and notching up a record 90 points, though to put that into its proper context, this would be the first season that the Isthmian applied three points for a win. This was Wycombe's fifth Isthmian League title win and the following season they would win it for a sixth time. Hendon finished second and despite the long haul of extra matches they played in to finally lift the FA Amateur Cup, Bishop's Stortford ended the season in third. Down at the bottom, the sad demise of Corinthian-Casuals continued after a nightmare season saw them relegated into the new Isthmian League Division Two, after winning just three games and drawing four. Which embarrassingly meant that the club lost a demoralising 35 games, some of them punishingly.

Further up the country, the well-established Northern League based in the footballing hotbed of the north-east was now in its 76th season. The 1973/74 campaign saw a fierce two-horse race between a pair of the region's most venerable and strongest teams, Spennymoor United and Blyth Spartans. They went through the entire season matching one another at the top point for point, both winning a truly impressive 30 games apiece, drawing four and losing four, both finishing on 64 points; Spennymoor edged it on goal difference. Some measure of their dominance comes in the simple facts that third-placed Willington ended the season a full 16 points behind the two clubs; and that between 1968 and 1979, Spennymoor and Blyth would win the Northern League title nine times between them. Rock-bottom Stanley United won just four games all season and ended on a miserable 18 points. Things would get worse during the summer: beset with financial problems, Stanley were forced to resign from the Northern League and folded.

The much newer Northern Premier League was now in its sixth season and two clubs, Boston United and Wigan Athletic, had dominated in what was a strong regional division. Covering northern England and clubs from the north Midlands and Wales, the 1973/74 season would involve six teams who would go on to reach the Football League – Morecambe, Fleetwood, Macclesfield, Barrow, Scarborough and Wigan. But top of the pile in 1974 were Boston. The Lincolnshire side had also won the title the season before, and would do so again in 1977 and 1978. 1973/74 runners-up Wigan had been Northern Premier League champions in 1971 and would win it again in 1975. The two clubs were enjoying seasons of great success – Wigan of course, would go on to enjoy many more in the Premier League and the Championship, as well as winning the FA Cup, four second-tier titles and the old Fourth Division championship.

As they had started their rise in the early 1970s, another former top-flight club had fallen into a tragic decline. Just four seasons after being kicked out of the Football League, Bradford Park Avenue were on life support and the club's shareholders were now forced to switch it off. Finishing fourth to bottom in the Northern Premier League's 1973/74 season, attendances had plummeted into the low hundreds and Park Avenue were in heavy, unsustainable debt. The board had made the heartbreaking decision to sell off their quirky, iconic Park Avenue ground to property developers and played their home games at arch-rivals Bradford City's Valley Parade. The loss of their home ripped the guts out of the club. Designed by the doyenne of British football stadium architects, Archibald Leitch, it contained a unique double-sided stand – one side looking out on to the football pitch, the other on to the next-door Park Avenue cricket ground, a venue where over the years, Yorkshire played more than 300 matches. But even this move had merely allowed the club to stagger on further into indebtedness, and after the season finished, on 3 May 1974, shareholders decided that with an overdraft of nearly £60,000 and other debts aplenty, there was no option but to wind up the club.

It was a huge loss to the city of Bradford but also to English football. In the early 20th century, Park Avenue had spent a decade in the First Division, and then before and after the Second World War, 20 years in the Second Division. Famous former players included swashbuckling England centre-forward Len Shackleton and future national team manager Ron Greenwood. In the 1960s, young local lad Kevin Hector became a goalscoring sensation at the club. At the age of 21 he became the third-youngest striker – behind Dixie Dean and Jimmy Greaves – to reach 100 league goals; in the 1965/66 season he was the Football League's top goalscorer with 44 goals. Inevitably, Hector left for Derby County and England caps, and without his goals Bradford Park Avenue fell into a total slump and had to apply for re-election four times on the trot. In 1970, the game was up and the club were booted out of the Football League. Four years later, they were out of business.

Distraught fans clubbed together to register the Bradford Park Avenue name as a company and for years, the new, reconstituted club played their football in the parks and on the recreation fields of the Bradford Amateur League Division Four.

10
Women's Football

'Whatever women do they must do twice as well as men to be thought half as good. Luckily, this is not difficult'
– Charlotte Whitton, Canadian politician and social reformer

ON 17 March 1974, the England international women's team proudly strode out at Slough Town's Wexham Park Stadium to play Wales Women. It ended 5-0 to England and to mark their fine victory, the FA gave each of the players a memento none of them would ever forget – not a plaque or a shield or even an official cap, but an egg box containing, well, six eggs. This perhaps gives you some indication of how seriously the powers-that-be took women's football. The FA didn't even have to pay for them, having just taken on the Egg Marketing Board as one of their sponsors. Some of the players even debated returning the eggs – thrown against the windows of the FA's Lancaster Gate headquarters in London – it was such an insult.

Hopes had been raised three years previously, when the FA lifted their near-50-year ban on women's teams playing on any officially recognised FA grounds, a vengeful act that had driven the women's game underground.

Women's football had become hugely popular during the First World War in armaments factories up and down the country. After men's football was stopped in 1915 and as women replaced the men in the factories, they also took their place on the football pitch. Armaments factories were dangerous places to work not just because of accidents and explosions, of which there were many, but also due to the toxic chemicals used in the manufacture of bombs, bullets and missiles. To try and make the workplace a little healthier, munitions managers urged their women workers to get out in the fresh air during their breaks to exercise and play sport. There was only one game they wanted to play and that was football.

Works teams began to challenge one another and soon, as the standard of play improved, women's matches were pulling big crowds. The Munitionettes Cup was created and charity games organised to raise money for injured soldiers. Matches began to be played at big professional grounds like Old Trafford, Ewood Park and Highbury, often in front of 20,000 and 30,000 crowds. Pre-eminent among these new teams were Dick, Kerr Ladies, a side based at a major munitions factory in Preston, Lancashire. When the First World War ended, female factory workers were shown the door and demobbed soldiers returned to their old jobs. But many women were not prepared to give up their football and new clubs were formed around the nuclei of the old factory teams and charity and exhibition matches continued.

On Boxing Day in 1920, a match took place that became a hugely significant landmark in English women's football and ultimately, for all the wrong reasons. The now hugely popular Dick, Kerr Ladies took on a well-supported and skilful St Helens Ladies team at Everton's Goodison Park and it created astonishing interest. The totally packed-out crowd numbered 53,000, with 14,000 other fans unable to gain entry, locked outside. Everton's average First Division crowd that season was 37,215 and for football's male establishment the huge popularity of the match represented the final straw. Most women had been forced to leave their wartime jobs to allow the returning men to take up their old posts. Now the sporting authorities – and the government – were intent on getting women out of football. They had condemned several women's teams from holding 'politically charged' games that were held in industrial areas in the north, Midlands and Wales to financially support striking miners. Though the truth was, many of the footballers came from communities that mine owners were trying to starve out and they were fully aware of the privations that were affecting their own families and neighbours, the women wanted to help through what they did best: play football. In a male-dominated world, a lot of men were also uncomfortable about women playing the men's game. The huge gate at Goodison Park was proof positive that the buggers were taking over. The powers-that-be decided it must be nipped in the bud.

On 5 December 1921, the FA held a meeting in London at which they not only banned women from playing on any professional grounds or pitches affiliated to the national body, they also stopped male referees from officiating the games, under threat of being expelled from men's football. In justification, the FA very selectively chose several ill-researched medical 'studies' that sought to prove, without much attention to actual facts or research, that playing football made women sterile. It was of course propaganda rubbish, but the meeting's committee minutes concluded in uncompromising terms, 'Complaints have been made as to football being played by women, the council feels impelled to express their strong opinion that the game of football is quite unsuitable for females and ought not be encouraged.'

English women's football was effectively cast out into the darkness and driven underground. Women would continue to play at local levels in parks and sometimes on 'friendly' rugby grounds, but there were no officially organised leagues or cups; no funding, no support, no nothing.

So why did the FA finally decide to lift their ban? One thing's for sure, it wasn't for altruistic reasons or because of any change in the hard-wired male chauvinism at Lancaster Gate. With women's football developing fast in Germany, and particularly in Italy, UEFA were putting increasing pressure on England's governing body to rescind their ban. Also, women footballers were making their voices increasingly heard. By the mid-to-late 1960s, and buoyed by England's World Cup win, more and more unofficial local and regional women's leagues had been set up and existing ones increased in popularity.

There was next to no funding and they still struggled to find non-FA pitches to play on, but the sport had a dedicated and enthusiastic base of both players and fans. All it needed was to get itself organised on a more national level, with or without help or sanction from the FA. Accordingly, on 1 November 1969, representatives from 44 women's clubs from England, Scotland and Wales met up at the Caxton Hall in London where the Women's Football Association was launched; six months later, seven regional leagues would affiliate to the newly born WFA.

With the ban lifted, 1971 saw the launch of the Women's FA Cup, an invitation-only tournament that sought to involve the best teams from around the regional leagues of England, Scotland and Wales. In a first for domestic women's football they even gained a sponsor in Mitre and though the deal only extended to free footballs, help with marketing plus a little cash it was a step in the right direction. The early 'superpower' was Southampton, who would win the first three WFA Cup finals against three Scottish sides, Stewart Thistle, Lee's Ladies and Westthorn United. So coming into the 1974 final, the Saints were still the unbeaten winners of the tournament.

Their opponents were a team from Cheshire called Fodens, most of whose players worked for a Sandbach bus and lorry manufacturing firm called Edward Foden and Sons. What was essentially a works team had started up in the early 1960s and as the company grew to enjoy their women's success in local friendlies they started to take it more seriously. Rare for the time, the company paid for their players' travel to away matches and gave them expenses. Fodens started to run football camps for girls and women and began to scout around the region for good young players. They soon found Pat Firth, Alison Leatherbarrow and Sylvia Gore, all of whom were or would become England internationals. Attacking midfielder Gore had already put her name into the record books of women's football. On 21 November 1972 she was in the starting line-up for England Women's first official international match, against Scotland, and scored England's first goal. Though the fixture was a landmark for English – and Scottish – women's football, the narrative surrounding the run-up to the game gives an at-times shocking insight into the battles women footballers, coaches and organisers had to fight in the early to mid-1970s. For Scotland's team secretary, and later manager, Elsie Cook, it cost her her marriage.

In a moving five-part BBC podcast series about that first England v Scotland match, *My Moment in History: Kicking Off the Women's Game*, Elsie recalled how her then-husband had told her to quit the job as secretary because 'he would not tolerate the idea that women played football'. He gave her an ultimatum, 'It's either me or the football.' Elsie chose the Scotland team and explained during the documentary,

'That was the male attitude in Scotland in those days. The women should be at the sink, they shouldn't be daring to pull on football boots ... I was a football suffragette, I had to prove that women could play football, simple.'

But to play, there was no pay, and rarely even any expenses. For that first international, teenage England player Jeannie Allott took the road less travelled and hitchhiked from Crewe to Scotland. She told the BBC, 'I always hitchhiked, whether it was for Fodens Ladies or for the England team ... there was no money, I had no choice. I couldn't afford a train ticket, but when somebody loves football as much as I do – and still do – you'll do anything.' Things for several of the Scots players were little different. A coach had been booked for players who lived further afield, to ferry them to Greenock on the west coast where the game was taking place, but it never turned up. The ever-resourceful Elsie got them a last-minute, seat-of-the-pants lift to the venue in the back of a furniture removal van. Elsie and a small team of volunteers had also spent the previous week hand-stitching Scotland badges and shirt numbers on to the team strip.

The match took place in extremely challenging conditions at Greenock's athletics ground, Ravenscraig Stadium, also home to the Greenock Juniors Football Club. Used to playing on park pitches, several players on either side had never played at a ground that had an actual stand and proper dressing rooms. Across Scotland, the weather on 21 November was atrocious and all but one professional men's match had been called off. The pitch at Ravenscraig was treacherously icy and the snow had begun to blow in squalls. But no matter; there was not one woman on either side who would countenance this historic landmark game being called off. The two sides trotted proudly out on to a treacherous frozen pitch and as the snow blew into them, a bagpipe band welcomed them with the inspiring skirls of 'Scotland the Brave'. Scotland came out hard and scored through diminutive striker Mary Carter. A few minutes later, 17-year-old winger Rose Reilly made it 2-0 Scotland, direct from a corner.

Reilly's own back story was typical of the experience several girls had at the time as footballers. As a schoolgirl, and desperate to play the game, Rose had 'changed' her name to 'Ross', cut her hair short and arrived to play in some of Glasgow's top schoolboy teams, already in her kit so she didn't have to change with the others in the dressing rooms. During one game, in which she scored eight goals, a watching Celtic scout picked 'Ross' Reilly out as the outstanding talent on the pitch and approached the team's coach about signing 'him' up on schoolboy terms at Celtic Park. The coach had to tell the scout that yes, Reilly was the team's best player by far, but 'Ross' was Rose, and already an outstanding player. Not long after the England match, and at a time when few male British footballers were playing abroad, Reilly was scouted by top French professional club Reims, where she spent sixth months before moving to Italy to play full-time football for ACF Milan. There, Reilly spent four seasons, winning two league titles, and then moving on to play professionally with ACF Napoli, ACF Firenze, Bari, Catania and Lecce. Rose Reilly twice won the Serie A Golden Boot award and eventually retired aged 40, having won eight Serie A titles, a French championship and four Italian Cups.

Towards the end of the first half at Ravenscraig Stadium, the weather was worsening but it didn't seem to cramp the style of England's Sylvia Gore, who showed her class and determination by picking up the ball just outside her own box. She ran almost the length of the pitch and somehow managed to navigate her way through the slippery, frozen, threadbare turf to expertly slide the ball past Scottish goalie Janie Houghton to make it 2-1.

England would go on to win 3-2, though it's still debatable who scored their second and third goals. The official record says that Gore got her second with the equaliser and Southampton's Pat Davies put in the winner. But many of those watching on at the match, including team-mate Sue Lopez, were convinced that Pat Davies got the final touch on both goals. As there's no existing film coverage of the two goals, we'll never know. But one thing was for sure – women's international football in England and Scotland was off and running.

At the end of the 1973/74 season, Fodens went into the WFA Mitre Challenge Cup Final completely unbeaten in their regional league and their cup games thus far. But they were under no illusions. In later years, Fodens duo Pat Firth and Alison Leatherbarrow would give absorbing interviews to *Our Game* magazine about their experiences of the final. Pat immediately put the match into perspective, 'Fodens at the time was the team to beat in the north, but Southampton was the team to beat full stop.' The Saints contained no fewer than seven current England internationals, including the highly regarded forwards Sue Lopez and Pat Richardson, both early stars of the women's game. Southampton weren't just good, they were ruthless. Once ahead in games they would continue to relentlessly apply the pressure and won a lot of their matches by wide margins.

Fodens went into the game as complete underdogs, though their journey to the final was making the press sit up and take notice. Alison Leatherbarrow earned her living working at a Woolworths store in Leigh and two evenings a week, she worked behind the bar of a local pub. One night, as she recalled, a national newspaper came a-calling, 'The *Daily Mirror* came down to the pub to do a story and I couldn't stop laughing. They wanted me to show a red card to this big six foot six bloke from the bar and I couldn't do it, I couldn't stop laughing. Every time I got mentioned in the local papers, Woolworths got a free advert.'

Even though the FA ban had been lifted, not one single professional men's football club was willing to stage women's football's most important game of the year, so it was 'hats off' to non-league Bedford Town who stepped in to host the final for the second year running, plus a third-place play-off between beaten semi-finalists Swindon Spitfires and Westthorn as a curtain-raiser for the afternoon's main event. The Fodens team had set off in a coach from Sandbach at 8am, followed by a small caravan of cars and buses containing a couple of hundred or so of their fans. In total, nearly 1,000 supporters turned up at The Eyrie to watch the two matches. Pat Firth and Alison Leatherbarrow sat in the stands before their final to watch the third-place game, which Westthorn won 5-0. Both recently capped for the first time by England and both only 18 years of age, they soon became aware of mutterings around them. Leatherbarrow remembered, 'Fans largely from down south were asking, "Who are Fodens?" And saying things like, "They don't stand a chance against Southampton."' After Westthorn, the Fodens duo trooped off down to the dressing rooms and Alison told Pat, 'What have we got to lose? And after that we had no nerves.'

Leatherbarrow played out of her skin and opened the scoring in the first half with a 20-yard screamer into the top-right corner. Southampton piled on the pressure and eventually Pat Davies got the almost inevitable equaliser midway through the second half. With five minutes to go, it looked like the tie would go to extra time, but a rare mix-up in the Southampton defence allowed Leatherbarrow to slip in and score the winner. Winger Jeannie Allott was named player of the match and Fodens were WFA Mitre

Challenge Cup winners. But it took a long time to sink in. Leatherbarrow remembered the atmosphere on the coach back to Cheshire as strangely subdued, 'Everyone was very quiet. If they were like me, the other players were thinking – did that just happen? Did we really beat Southampton? But we did.'

The international players at Southampton and Fodens would meet up again for three official England friendlies during 1974. First was the Wales eggstravaganza; the second away in Groningen against a fit, well-organised Netherlands side on 31 May. This would be much more of a true measure of how the nascent England team was progressing in terms of skill, ability and tactical knowhow, because the Dutch women had a much longer history of competitive involvement. The Netherlands played their first unofficial women's match as far back as September 1956, beating West Germany 4-2. On 17 April 1971 they played the first international women's match recognised by FIFA, against France. It was a day for them of mixed emotions – the French won 4-0. The Dutch also had long-established women's amateur leagues where standards were high in terms of coaching and training. Impressed with flying England winger Jeannie Allott, several Dutch clubs tried to tempt her across the North Sea. In 1976 she finally succumbed and signed for Zwart Wit '28 Rotterdam and worked as a shipping planner at the port authority. Allott played for several Dutch sides well into the late 1980s. At KFC '71 she spent a season playing alongside a young Sarina Wiegman – a woman who would of course have a massive future impact on English football.

On 7 November, England would play their third official international friendly of the year, against France at Wimbledon's Plough Lane. This was well before the Dons would so spectacularly make it into the Football League and at the time, Wimbledon were a modest side playing in the old Southern League. The game may have been a full international, but the never-supportive FA still wouldn't let the national team play on professional Football League grounds. But whatever, this was a hugely important game for England. Along with Denmark, France were one of the early European leaders in women's football and this was a challenging match-up. The night before the game, the Daily Express National Five-a-Side Championship took place at Wembley Arena in front of 9,000 fans. Before the official games kicked off, five of the England women's team took on a quintet of their French counterparts in a short-sided exhibition match. France won 1-0, but the more important result for English women's football was that the word was beginning to spread.

Twenty-four hours later on a freezing cold night at Plough Lane, 2,000 fans would turn out to watch the full England XI beat France 2-0 – the eighth win in England's first eight matches. It was still early days, but women's football in this country was making important progress on all fronts. Any kind of national league was years away and full-time professional football, decades. Women were still only allowed to play two 35-minute halves and everything was achieved on the most threadbare of shoestrings, with players having to buy their own kit and pay subs to travel for matches. Many, including early sponsors, still regarded the women's game as an entertaining novelty rather than a sport and most male football fans saw it as nothing more than 'a laugh'. But the women players – their coaches, managers and administrators – were deadly serious and battled against all the odds to make it the game it is today. Throughout the 70s more and more women were pulling on their football boots. By 1979, nearly 300 clubs were affiliated to the WFA, embracing over 6,000 players and 21 regional leagues.

Let's leave the last word to Jeannie Allott, who told *The Independent* in 2022, 'It's fantastic what's happening now but don't forget the girls who started it off for you. We played for England and set the ball rolling.'

11

North of the Border

'It is up to us, to everyone at Celtic Park, to build up our own legends. We don't want to live with history, to be compared with legends from the past. We must make new legends'

– Jock Stein

SQUARE-JAWED, BROAD-SHOULDERED John 'Jock' Stein started working life aged 14 as a coal miner in the Lanarkshire coalfields, an area of small working-class communities where most boys finished school and went straight underground. Life as a miner in the 1940s and 50s was a physically hard and often dangerous job and through the decades, countless disasters at Lanarkshire's collieries claimed the lives of young Scotsmen. Working as a miner taught the young Jock Stein several valuable life lessons that he would adapt expertly into his later job as first a footballer and then a manager. Life underground was all about teamwork. Make a mistake or shirk a responsibility and it could quite literally lead to injury or even death. Attention to detail was everything. Focus, focus, focus. Men had to stick together and constantly look out for one another. And to get through long, tough, muscle-burning shifts, they needed to create a community spirit and a sense of togetherness.

Above ground, Stein spent his Saturdays playing part-time football for tiny Albion Rovers for over a decade. Though a tough defender who was hard into the tackle, Stein was never flair-heavy. By his own admission he was never better than an average passer of the ball, lacked pace and full-time football seemed way beyond his capabilities; but sheer, bloody-minded tenacity got him there at the ripe old age of 28. Ambitious Southern League Llanelli Town, based in another hardcore mining area, signed Stein and 'looked after' him financially so he didn't have to go down the pit. It would end in tears for Llanelli, who overstretched themselves financially, and missing his family, Stein returned home to Glasgow, where he resigned himself to going back underground and playing part-time or amateur football again.

But fate took an unexpected hand. Celtic's reserve team coach Jimmy Gribbins had been impressed by Stein's man-management on and off the pitch and offered him an unexpected professional contract opportunity – to wit, come back to Parkhead, captain the reserves and become a mentor to Celtic's youngsters. A few months later, fate once again gave Stein's hitherto unspectacular playing career another fortunate leg-up. A serious injury crisis saw the Big Man promoted into the Celtic first team and he would become a regular for the next four seasons, ultimately becoming captain.

Again, it wasn't down to any great individual footballing skill but because of his supreme man-management talents on the pitch. He knew where his players should be and what they should be doing and let them know in no uncertain terms how they should organise themselves. Surely management beckoned: in July 1957, Stein was appointed Celtic reserve team manager and his impact was immediate. Over three years, he turned the reserves into a fast and furious, fit and fearless, supremely well-organised side. Surely this was a first-team manager in waiting? Or perhaps not.

Though a highly influential former Celtic player and now manager of the Parkhead reserves, the board had been extremely reluctant to take him on as Celtic's overall boss. With the reserves, he was a hands-on manager, who spent every day on the training pitch with his players, tutoring them in tactics and teaching them how to think about the game. Stein was a skilled communicator who talked simply and with great clarity and his work with the second string was much admired by Celtic's directors. But they were nervous about offering him the first-team job. There was no doubting his impressive nascent managerial abilities but there was one very important box Stein could not tick – he wasn't a Catholic and in deeply sectarian Glasgow that mattered.

Celtic had never appointed a Protestant as first-team boss throughout their entire history, and in March 1960, Stein was forced to move on from his beloved Parkhead in order to advance his managerial ambitions at struggling Dunfermline. When Stein took over, the Pars were mired in a Division One relegation battle with six games left to go, not only low on confidence but results – it was four months since their last league win and they'd taken some five- and six-goal batterings along the way. As a former no-nonsense defender, Stein's first job was to reorganise his back five and though they conceded two in his initial game, they scored three and got their first win since January. The fans were jubilant but it was a bittersweet victory for Jock Stein – his debut 3-2 home win was against Celtic. The irony, however, was that the former Parkhead favourite had immediately shown the Celtic board just what they were missing out on. Coming into their last five matches, Dunfermline had only kept three clean sheets all season; Stein ramped up his new defensive drills in training and not only did the Pars win their last five games, they kept another three clean sheets. Stein's impact had been instant and from being a club in meltdown, Dunfermline comfortably escaped relegation to Division Two, finishing in 13th place, seven points clear of the drop zone.

The following season, Big Jock would guide the small, unfashionable Fife-based club to their first major honour. After a 0-0 draw at Hampden Park in front of 113,000 fans, they won the Scottish Cup in a 2-0 replay against – yes, you guessed it – Celtic. In the next campaign, Stein not only led Dunfermline to a best-ever fourth-place finish in Scottish Division One but to the quarter-finals of the European Cup Winners' Cup. South of the border, Wolves and Newcastle were now sniffing around after Stein, but in the end he moved on to Edinburgh and ironically, became boss of another Scottish Catholic club, Hibernian. There, Stein continued to impress and at the end of 1964/65 Celtic finally came a-calling.

Fast-forward to the 1973/74 season and Jock Stein was enjoying his ninth year as Celtic manager having already brought them unparalleled success. During his first year in charge, the Hoops won the 1965 Scottish League Cup and in 1966 he led them to their first championship in 12 years. The following season, Celtic won an unprecedented quadruple – the First Division, Scottish Cup, Scottish League Cup and the European Cup, beating Italy's mighty Inter Milan 2-1 in Lisbon to become the first British team to win the trophy. Remarkably, his entire Lisbon Lions team were born within 30 miles of Parkhead. As fellow Scottish manager Bill Shankly memorably told Stein, 'John, you're immortal now.'

In 1969, Stein won another domestic treble, and in 1970 a league and League Cup double. Perhaps most staggeringly, between 1966 and 1974, Celtic would win nine Scottish league titles in a row. Coming into the 1973/74 season, the squad was one of his best ever. At the back, Billy McNeill and Danny McGrain were not only tough and ruthless enforcers but comfortable on the ball. Younger players coming through like Kenny Dalglish and David Hay had, despite their tender years, already made it into the Scotland national squad and up front, top scorer John 'Dixie' Deans, nicknamed after the legendary Everton and England striker Dixie Dean, continued to bang them in. Up until 22 February 1974, the Bhoys had won 16, drawn two and lost only four. Along the way, they'd hammered Partick Thistle 7-0, Falkirk and Dunfermline 6-0, and Clyde 5-0 and kept 12 clean sheets.

But the season wasn't just about Celtic. Runners-up Hibernian had run the Hoops close throughout the campaign. By 22 February, Hibs had won 13, drawn five and lost only three. Like Stein at Celtic, the Hibernian manager was nothing less than a club legend in his own right; Eddie Turnbull had been one of Hibernian's Famous Five. Throughout the late 1940s into the mid-50s, the attacking force of Lawrie Reilly, Bobby Johnstone, Gordon Smith, Willie Ormond and Turnbull himself shone like diamonds during what would be Hibernian's greatest period of success. Between 1948 and 1952, the Famous Five's goals powered the Hibees to three Scottish league titles and, in 1956, as far as the semi-finals in the inaugural European Cup. Scottish football had never seen anything like them. Playing an early proto-form of Total Football, the quintet were constantly on the front foot, switching positions and bamboozling opposition defences with their sheer unpredictability. The great Rangers centre-forward Willie Thorne was captivated by them, telling *The Scotsman*, 'They are like a swarm of wasps, the way they buzz around you, interchanging at will.' Between them, the five men scored an astonishing 695 league goals for Hibernian, one-club man Turnbull weighing in with 150 over 349 games. After serving for seven years as manager of Aberdeen, the Easter Road faithful were thrilled when Turnbull returned to the scene of his former triumphs in 1971 as their new boss.

By February 1974, Hibernian and Celtic had almost been matching one another game for game and things were exceedingly tight between them at the top of the table. On the 23rd of that month, Celtic's team coach made the hour or so trip from Glasgow to Edinburgh for a showdown at Easter Road, a match that both managers knew may well have a significant bearing on in which city the championship trophy would end up. Played in front of 48,554 fans – by far Hibernian's biggest crowd of the season – it proved to be a pulsating thriller of a game. After only 75 seconds, the ever-opportunist Dixie Deans poked in a loose ball to make it 1-0 to Celtic. Hibernian began to press high and on 23 minutes, Arthur Duncan stroked in the equaliser. From there, the match went from end to end in a thrillingly even battle between Scotland's top two. On 37 minutes Deans passed on to Kenny Dalglish, who lashed it home to regain the lead, 2-1 Celtic. The visiting Glasgow fans were loving it, and to the theme tune of television's *Rupert Bear* kids' series, they joyfully serenaded their striker, 'Kenny, Kenny Dalglish, everyone knows his name.'

On 53 minutes, Hibernian's own fan favourite Jimmy O'Rourke made it 2-2. The lifelong Hibees supporter had been at Easter Road since 1962 and became the youngest player to make his debut for the club, aged just 16 years and 85 days. Three days later, he scored against Dunfermline, also making him Hibs' youngest-ever goalscorer. For 12 seasons, O'Rourke had sweated blood for his hometown team and it was his goal that had won Hibernian their first major silverware for 20 years, when the Edinburgh green and whites had beaten Celtic to lift the Scottish League Cup in 1972. Eddie Turnbull's early to mid-1970s side was generally regarded as the best to wear the Hibs shirt since his early 1950s team and O'Rourke was not only a pivotal member of the side that became known as 'Turnbull's Tornadoes', he was much-beloved by the fans. He ran through walls for the crowd because he was one of their own. But seconds after he'd celebrated scoring the equaliser against Celtic, O'Rourke couldn't resist a glance towards the Hibernian bench that spoke of deep, mixed emotions. Sat on the touchline was new signing Joe Harper, who O'Rourke knew had arrived to potentially replace him. This despite the fact that his goal against Celtic was his 14th league strike of the season and though now 32, he was in the scoring form of his life. But boss Turnbull, who'd managed Harper at Aberdeen, believed that Hibernian stood a genuine chance of winning the title if they could just find an extra edge up front and it was time to start replacing the older Tornadoes.

At Montrose and then Aberdeen, Joe Harper had been Scotland's top goalscorer for three seasons running and then moved south to First Division Everton in 1972. With 12 goals in 43 games, Harper was hardly pulling up trees but Turnbull was certain that he could get the best out of him again if he returned to Scotland. He was named on the subs' bench for the Celtic game, giving the Hibernian fans their first look at him in the flesh and, well, there was a lot of it. Though only 5ft 6in tall, Harper had always carried extra weight but his spell away in England had added more pounds. Future Scotland manager Ally MacLeod famously described him as looking like a Toby jug but still capped him, because Harper's gift in life was that he scored goals. A player who enjoyed a drink and was never afraid to speak his mind, the striker was self-willed and obstinate – particularly in the penalty area.

Back on the turf at Easter Road, Jock Stein urged his Celtic team forward and on 62 minutes, winger Paul Wilson put them 3-2 ahead. After scoring at the very start of the game, Dixie Deans bookended a man-of-the-match performance by getting a second in the last minute to make it Hibernian 2 Celtic 4. Though an utterly thrilling game, there was disappointment for Hibs and particularly for lifelong fan Jimmy O'Rourke. Days later he was sold to St Johnstone. Thirty-year-old strike partner Alan Gordon went to Dundee. For the past few seasons, the pairing had been a match made in heaven. Playing alongside O'Rourke, Gordon had cracked in an impressive 51 goals in 84 games for Hibs and, like his striking buddy, he was shocked to be shown the door. But Turnbull had decided to rebuild. Many fans thought he'd jumped the gun.

For a while, Turnbull's hunch about the albeit overweight and not fully fit Joe Harper paid off. In the 12 league games after the Celtic defeat Harper would score ten times but during his short, season-and-a-half stay at Easter Road, he would divide the fans – and the players. Harper had turned up for his record £140,000 signing-on in front of the press, full of himself and wearing an expensive fur coat, cockily boasting about his abilities. Fans had really taken O'Rourke and Gordon to their hearts, and this brash new man was making all the wrong noises. In the dressing room, he was soon getting into disagreements with his new team-mates and generally making it clear that he liked life at Hibernian as much as the fans and players enjoyed him being there. Harper moved back to his beloved Aberdeen and continued to bang in the goals. As Turnbull's Tornadoes were broken up, Hibernian's fortunes soon began to fade.

The 1974 Scottish Cup Final at Hampden Park on 4 May matched Jock Stein's Celtic up against Jim McLean's young Dundee United, who included a 19-year-old Andy Gray up front. The bald facts were these. This was United's first Scottish Cup Final and they came into it as rank outsiders with the bookies. Their biggest hope, a sickness bug had ripped through the Celtic squad in the days leading up the final and several of their regulars trotted out on to the pitch as effectively walking wounded, still ill and looking decidedly off-colour. But on the day, the occasion was just too big for McLean's tyros, who played like rabbits in the headlights. The game was effectively over inside 25 minutes, when goals from Harry Hood and Stevie Murray put Celtic two up. With seconds to go, top scorer Dixie Deans fired in to make it three but in truth, Celtic never needed to get out of second gear. The *Glasgow Evening Times* headlined their report on the game, 'Powder-Puff United!'

Tragically, most of the action took place off the pitch. Earlier in the week, Rangers fans had rioted during a so-called friendly against Everton, so the police were out in force to counter any trouble at the cup final and sadly there would be much of it to contend with. Celtic and Dundee United hooligans fought ferocious running battles inside and outside the ground. Forty fans were carted off to local hospitals, many with head wounds caused by flying bottles, bricks and bovver boots. Some 125 thugs were arrested and over a dozen policemen injured.

It would be another black day for British football's fast-growing hooliganism problem. The *Glasgow Herald*'s verdict on the event concisely summed up the sad story of a forgettable encounter, 'This was not a great final on the field, for Celtic were drab by their own high standards and Dundee United diffident to the point of invisibility. Many of the 75,000 crowd were walking the streets of Mount Florida by the finish, bored by the play, distracted by the bottles and fists thrown on the terraces, and tired by a campaign that through summer, autumn, winter then spring, had lasted far too long.' Nonetheless, Celtic had won the Division One and Scottish Cup double. In two other competitions, the Hoops would not fare so well.

Stein was desperate to win a second European Cup, ambitious to position his team among the very best club sides in Europe. Their 1973/74 campaign had been an in-and-out affair. After thrashing Finland's TPS 9-1 on aggregate, their second-round tie against Danish amateurs Vejle presented them with an unexpectedly far tougher proposition. Before the first leg in Glasgow, the Vejle players spent the day walking around the city's shops – Celtic spent the evening on walkabout. Without inspirational captain Billy McNeill, who was injured, the Hoops turned in a shocker of a performance to draw 0-0. Seasoned sports reporter Malcolm Munro had more attack than the whole Celtic team put together when he analysed the match in the *Glasgow Evening Times*: 'Tinkers, tailors and candlemakers of Jutland, playing under the name of Vejle (pronounced Wily, and weren't they just that?), reduced Celtic to a jerry-built side. Never in a long career of covering football have I seen Celtic so ineffectual.' In the away second leg, Celtic didn't fare much better, a solitary Bobby Lennox goal finally dividing the two sides.

In the quarter-finals, Celtic once again avoided any of the European big boys, drawing Switzerland's Basel. Though a largely unfancied side and in the middle of their winter break, Basel played out of their skins in the freezing home leg and beat Celtic 3-2; it was game on for the Parkhead return tie and it would prove to be a roller coaster. After five minutes, defender George Connelly was stretchered off with an ankle fracture that would tragically cost him his place for

Scotland at the 1974 World Cup. Inside 15 minutes, Celtic's all-out attacking approach saw them two up through Kenny Dalglish and Dixie Deans, but just before half-time, Basel took advantage of two defensive lapses to make it 2-2. In the second half, Celtic attacked relentlessly and on 57 minutes Tommy Callaghan netted with a thundering volley, levelling the tie on aggregate. But try as they might, Celtic couldn't find a way through a resolute Basel defence and the match went into extra time. On 99 minutes, Harry Hood crossed, Jimmy Johnstone flicked on and Stevie Murray looped a header over the Basel goalie to make it 6-5 on aggregate and Celtic squeaked through.

In the semi-finals Celtic would face a much tougher task – La Liga champions Atlético Madrid, a footballing Jekyll and Hyde, a highly skilful team who also had a dark side. Their Argentinian coach Juan Carlos Lorenzo was a man who regularly dabbled in football's black arts and encouraged his players to seize any advantage they could on and off the pitch, by fair means or foul. They travelled to Glasgow for the first leg on 12 April not to show off their undoubted footballing skills, but with malfeasance in mind.

The fixture was a bloodbath on and off the pitch, with Atlético determined to intimidate and close down the match with the most brutal of game plans. The Celtic players were forced to endure 90 minutes of continual cynical fouls, flying elbows and scything tackles; three Atlético players were given their marching orders and seven were booked. Finishing the second half playing backs-to-the-wall, boot-it-out-of-the-ground football, the heavily depleted Madrid side ground out what they had come to Parkhead for, an away 0-0 draw. Celtic's diminutive winger Jimmy Johnstone was attacked in the tunnel coming off after the game and fights broke out among opposing players. The *Aberdeen Evening Express* simply described the encounter as 'one of the roughest and most brutal affairs ever to take place on a Scottish football field'.

The following day, manager Jock Stein talked to the press and despite a night's sleep, he was still incandescent with rage about Atlético's performance, 'The match was terrible – the worst game of football in which Celtic have ever been involved. We have played all the famous teams like AC Milan, Benfica and Real Madrid, but we have never encountered such tactics as last night. Frankly, this game was never football.' Perhaps unsurprisingly, the Spaniards saw things differently. Atlético Madrid's president Vicente Calderón had seemingly watched a different game, telling the Spanish press, 'You could not see how our team could play because of the crazy referee from Turkey. We are angry at his handling of the game.' The Spanish newspaper *Nuevo Diario* levelled serious allegations against the Scottish police and dubbed the match 'the night of a thousand blows'. The tabloid claimed that Glasgow officers charged into Atlético players, officials and Spanish reporters at the end of the match and quoted the team's masseur, Carlos Rodrigo, who said, 'They beat us without mercy in the tunnel.' He said Eusebio Bejarano was hit several times and that he limped into the dressing room with a busted lip, 'He wanted to go to the defence of [Rubén Oswaldo] Díaz and two policemen grabbed him while another two beat him without mercy and brutally.' Both club and press regarded their team as the injured party; the football authorities sided with Celtic's concerns.

Celtic immediately lodged a complaint with UEFA and the governing body were unequivocal in their view of the game. A cable was sent to Atlético Madrid which read, 'The committee warns you now that your club shall be entirely responsible for any incident whatsoever at the return match on April 24, on which may depend the future participation of your club in this competition or in future competitions of UEFA.' Atlético, and a section of the Spanish press, were appalled at what they regarded as an unjustified warning and during the intervening two weeks before the return leg, rancour began to rise. Celtic were so concerned about the bad feeling surrounding the away tie that they advised fans not to travel to Spain. Their worries were not unfounded.

According to the *Belfast Evening Telegraph*, 'The Spanish hate campaign, which forced Celtic to live under armed guard every minute of their stay in Madrid, reached a peak of ferocity when Stein sent his players out for a pre-match warm-up. The abuse from the 60,000 fans was so harsh he had to take them off after only two minutes.' Playing in such a cauldron of seething hatred, Celtic did well to shut out the baying crowd and were the better side in the first half. But come the second, Atlético showed their Jekyll side, constantly pressing Celtic back, playing fast, attractive football. Two goals in the last 15 minutes put them through to the European Cup Final. Jock Stein told the assembled press after the game, 'Atlético won, but football has lost.' When Bayern Munich beat Atlético 4-0 in the final's replay, the green and white half of Glasgow rejoiced.

Earlier in the season there was one domestic trophy that Celtic failed to win. After beating fierce Glasgow rivals Rangers 3-1 in the Scottish League Cup semi-finals, Stein's men went into the final as overwhelming favourites. Opponents Dundee were given no chance by the pre-match critics, but it would turn out to be an extraordinary day. In the grim midst of the national energy crisis, floodlighting at British football grounds had been banned, so the final's kick-off time was brought forward to 1.30pm. When the two team coaches arrived at Hampden Park midway through the morning, neither side wanted to play. Parts of the pitch were frozen and driving snow and sleet blew a gale through the stadium, but despite the clubs' pleas, referee Bobby Davidson decreed that the final must go ahead. By the time the players entered the field of play, the snow and sleet had turned to pouring rain and the frozen parts of the pitch were now slushy puddles. Despite the precarious conditions, and much slipping and sliding around, the two teams served up an entertaining first half, with Dundee edging it, four shots on goal to Celtic's one. The two sides would squelch in at half-time 0-0, drenched and plastered in mud.

Given the conditions and the earlier kick-off, it was no surprise that only 29,974 turned up to watch – the lowest-ever attendance at a Scottish League Cup Final. But in the second half, it would be the hugely outnumbered contingent of fans who'd travelled the 80 miles from Dundee who did all the celebrating. On 75 minutes, the Dens Park men won a free kick in the centre circle. Up stepped right-back Bobby Wilson, who lofted a high ball on to the edge of the Celtic box. Striker Gordon Wallace rose majestically, chested it down, took it on the spin and drilled a bullet past Ally Hunter in the Celtic goal. Marshalled superbly by inspirational captain Tommy Gemmell, who Dundee had astutely signed from Nottingham Forest in the summer, the men from the east smothered Celtic's increasingly desperate attacks and the match ended 1-0; Dundee won their first League Cup for 21 years.

Under Gemmell's leadership, it would prove to be a sterling season for the Dark Blues. The club finished fifth in the league, reached the semi-finals of the Scottish Cup and thanks to their League Cup win, they qualified for the following season's UEFA Cup. Celtic would end the season exhausted. Through the regular season, they played 63 matches and four of the squad – Danny McGrain, Jimmy Johnstone, Kenny Dalglish and David Hay – would barely have time to draw breath before travelling to Germany to play for Scotland in the 1974 World Cup.

In Division Two, three teams dominated from the first day of the season onwards. Airdrieonians had been relegated from the top flight the year before and were desperate to bounce back immediately. A club from the 35,000-population Lanarkshire town of Airdrie, their home attendances had grown, thanks to visits from big clubs like Celtic, Rangers, Hibs, Hearts, Aberdeen and the two Dundee sides. They were not keen to hang around Division Two for any longer than was necessary. Not only would Airdrieonians end the 1973/74 season as champions, they set an extraordinary record. Their home form was simply astonishing; in their 18 league games at Broomfield Park, Airdrieonians won 16, drew two and lost none. Averaging over three goals a game, they handed out an 8-0 battering to Brechin, beat St Mirren 6-1, Cowdenbeath 5-0 and Alloa 5-2, as well as scoring four on four occasions. It was, though, their defensive record that was truly unparalleled in Scottish league football. Over the entire season at their quirky home ground, which had three vastly different-shaped stands and a cricket pavilion tight up to the edge of the pitch, Airdrieonians conceded just six goals in 18 games. The driving force behind their success was talismanic skipper Derek Whiteford, a deep-lying midfielder who constantly gave added protection to his lanky and muscular back four. Whiteford had been shown the door by Hibernian aged 20 and with seemingly little interest from elsewhere, he thought his professional career was over. But in 1967, Airdrieonians stepped in and signed him up. He would be eternally grateful to the Broomfield Road outfit for resurrecting his career and over a ten-year spell at the club, would repay them in spades. Though a largely defensive midfielder, he scored 116 goals in 438 appearances for the Diamonds.

Kilmarnock were promoted as runners-up having fought Airdrieonians all the way. Their last 11 games saw them win ten and draw one. They too, had an impressive home record, winning 15, drawing two and losing just the once and scoring 96 goals. It was no surprise that ever-dependable striker Eddie Morrison scored 22 league goals – in his time at Kilmarnock Steady Eddie fired in 149 goals in 341 appearances. The astonishing Killie surprise was that his team-mate John Fleming ended the season as Scotland's top scorer with an impressive 33. This is the rare story of a footballer who managed to play out of his skin and way above his normal capabilities for just one bright, shining season in the sun. Coming into the 1973/74 season, the hitherto largely uncelebrated midfielder rocked up having scored just two goals during three previous campaigns, totally failing to pin down a regular first-team place. But once given his chance Fleming caught fire. A confidence player, he scored early in the season and never stopped. If Fleming scored once in a match, he would often score again. As well as hat-tricks against Forfar Athletic and Queen's Park, he scored twice in seven further league games.

In the following season at Killie, he scored 11 goals and just five the next. Fleming would then move on to Aberdeen, and in four seasons was on the mark just 12 times. Though they missed out on the title, Kilmarnock gained bragging rights by becoming the only Second Division side to finish the campaign unbeaten against champs Airdrieonians. In February, they drew 0-0 in a hard-fought away game at Broomfield Park, in front of Airdrieonians' biggest crowd of the season, 7,824. But before that they gave the Diamonds their biggest beating by far, overcoming the future champions 4-0 at Dens Park. Predictably, both Morrison and Fleming would be on the scoresheet.

Hamilton Academical ended the campaign as the extremely unlucky third-place promotion losers on 55 points. They'd challenged at the top all season and ended up just an agonising three points shy of Kilmarnock, eight points ahead of fourth-placed Queen of the South. In the previous ten Division Two seasons, 55 points would have got the Accies promoted nine times and crowned champions twice.

Down at the bottom, it proved to be another depressing season for Brechin. In last place for the third time in four seasons, the tiny Angus-based club won only five times in their 36 games, the same number they'd achieved the campaign before. Based in a town of only 6,000 people, Brechin perennially struggled for crowds and money. Most of their players were semi-pro, amateur or untried local youth players and even half-decent lower-level professionals continued to resist the call to Brechin's tiny Glebe Park ground.

As the lengthy season finally came to an end, Scottish club fans turned all their attention towards a rare summer of hope on the international stage. For the first time since 1958, Scotland's finest were off to compete in the World Cup finals.

12

The British Home Championship

'How many countries ARE
there in this country?'

– Ted Lasso

THE ANNUAL four-nation championship of the British Isles was now into its 90th year and by far, the oldest international football tournament in the world. But as more international competitions had been established, notably the World Cup and the European Championship, the British Home Championship had lost much of its prestige as the decades passed by. In 1974, the scourge of hooliganism, the fall in home international attendances – apart from the England v Scotland games – the Troubles in Northern Ireland and England's desire to play against 'stronger' international opposition were already beginning to threaten the future of the tournament. The far smaller nations, Wales and Northern Ireland, continued to have to cast their nets wider and deeper down in football's lower leagues to make up the numbers.

England were on a down and though Scotland had made it to the World Cup finals in Germany to be played a month later, European national sides like West Germany, Italy and Spain were now regularly outperforming the best of Britain. The Germans had won the 1972 European Championship and got to the semi-finals of the 1970 World Cup, where Italy were losing finalists. Since winning the 1964 European Championship, a resurgent Spain were on a fine run of form. From the beginning of 1970 to the end of 1974, the Spanish match record was won 14, drawn nine and lost four, including impressive victories over West Germany, Italy, Uruguay, Argentina – and Scotland. During the previous two years, England had played Italy twice and West Germany once, and lost each encounter.

Scotland came into the 1974 British Home Championship desperately hoping to generate some momentum going into the upcoming World Cup. Though they were the only team from the British Isles to qualify for the tournament in Germany, the Scots were on a bad run of form. Manager Willie Ormond had taken over from the Manchester United-bound Tommy Docherty the year before and during his 11 games in charge, Scotland had won only twice. Their major problem was lack of goals, an irony not lost on Ormond. As a player, he had been one of Hibernian's high-scoring Famous Five forward line in the 1950s. As a manager at unfashionable St Johnstone, Ormond developed a thrilling attacking style that saw them reach their first national final, the Scottish League Cup in 1969, narrowly losing 1-0 to Celtic, and the 1970/71 season saw them finish third in Division One behind Celtic and Aberdeen. His Scotland side included a slowing 34-year-old Denis Law whose international career had delivered 30 goals in 54 appearances, but he had only scored three times since 1968.

Aside from the veteran Law, the team he would choose to face Northern Ireland in their first 1974 Home Championship game had only managed to score eight international goals between them. The Irish were a cheerful bunch who enjoyed playing under their genial young 32-year-old manager Terry Neill and came into the Scotland match with a particularly strong defensive unit that featured the ever-dependable Pat Jennings and the talented Arsenal full-back pairing of Pat Rice and Sammy Nelson. In 1974, the Northern Irish had to face three away games because increasing violence and civil unrest back in Ulster had made Belfast an unsafe place for footballers to visit. Since the tragic happenings on Bloody Sunday back in 1972, bombings, burnings, murders and kidnappings had escalated across the ever-more fractious Catholic/Protestant divide. Euphemistically called 'the Troubles', the violence had made Northern Ireland a 'no-go' area for international football. The respective FAs of England, Scotland and Wales did not feel that the safety of their players and staff could be fully guaranteed in Belfast, so the Northern Ireland team became nomads. An unexpected consequence of this was that the World Cup-bound Scotland would get to play all three of their Home Championship internationals at Hampden Park.

Ireland went into the game as 7/1 underdogs. On the coach from their hotel to the ground, Neill told his players to 'go out there and enjoy yourselves' and that they did. It was a bad-tempered first ten minutes with three Northern Ireland players going into the book for some clattering tackles, but once the Irish got into their stride, they began to play cool, short passing possession football and smothered a pedestrian Scotland in midfield. Just before half-time Newcastle United's Tommy Cassidy gave them the lead and the *Glasgow Herald* was not impressed. Describing the goal, their match report observed, 'The goal proved all that was wrong with Scotland. Cassidy emerged from a sandwich between [David] Hay and [Billy] Bremner – few escape from such a vice – then sprinted 40 yards, taking a return pass and sliding the ball into the net past David Harvey's late and desperate intervention.' In the second half, Scotland continued to huff, puff and toil in vain. A measure of their lack of potency in the final third was that their first strike on goal, and it would eventually prove to be their only one, came as late as the 58th minute. The fans inside Hampden Park had hoped to see their team turn on the style as they prepared for the World Cup finals. They would return home disgruntled and confused by their side's weak capitulation. And what rankled underneath the Scottish skin was that only three of the starting 11 played their club football in Scotland – Sandy Jardine at Rangers plus David Hay and Kenny Dalglish at Celtic.

Of the English-based players, no one stood out. After a long, exhausting season with English champions Leeds, the usually talismanic Billy Bremner had looked knackered and off the pace. Denis Law proved that his best days were now behind him and delivered a lacklustre performance and on the opposite wing, the recently relegated Manchester United player Willie Morgan had a shocker. The *Glasgow Herald* concluded, 'The sad hard truth is that just four weeks before the start of the World Cup, Scotland cannot score a goal, cannot win a match and cannot inspire confidence.' Defeat was not the only blow for Ormond – regular left-back Willie Donachie was taken to hospital at half-time with an ankle injury and his leg put in plaster.

England came into the Home Championship with problems of their own. World Cup winners in 1966 and one of the best teams at Mexico 1970, their inability to qualify for Germany 1974 was nothing short of a national sporting humiliation. The badly handled sacking of Sir Alf Ramsey had sent shockwaves through the regular squad and morale was low. But for once, the FA came up with an ingenious idea. Knowing that their chosen new manager Don Revie still had to wait patiently in the wings because of further commitments to Leeds, the powers-that-be appointed the avuncular Coventry City general manager Joe Mercer as caretaker boss. The 60-year-old was already a legend in the domestic game. As a player, the Ellesmere Port-born Mercer had captained Arsenal to two league championship wins, an FA Cup and two Charity Shield successes in the late 1940s and early 1950s. Beloved by team-mates and fans alike, Mercer became the beating heart and soul of life at the old Highbury Stadium. As a manager, he had early success in his first job at Aston Villa, winning the inaugural League Cup in 1961. But it was his work at Manchester City that really put him on the managerial map. In 1966, he got City back into the top flight, winning the Second Division championship. Two years later they won the First Division title, and the FA Cup the year after. In 1970, the Blues won the European Cup Winners' Cup and the League Cup.

His appointment was hugely popular with the England players, who responded immediately to his chirpy and cheerful positivism; a total contrast to the far more distant and stand-offish style of Sir Alf.

To say that Mercer had inherited a squad that was in transition would be an understatement. For 'transition', read total churn. Not one single player remained from the England team's final starting 11 against West Germany in the Mexico World Cup less than four years earlier. After years of happy stability based around the likes of Bobby Moore, Geoff Hurst, Martin Peters, the Charlton brothers and Gordon Banks, Sir Alf had been desperately trying to rebuild and rejuvenate an ageing squad. Between England's departure in Mexico up to his sacking less than 46 months later, Ramsey would hand England debuts to 25 different players and half of those would go on to play ten games or less for the national side, seven only gaining one cap. As he continued to chop and change, England failed to get past the qualifying tournament for the 1972 European Championship and then, of course, in the following year they did not get to the 1974 World Cup finals. Ramsey's last eight games in charge brought two wins, three draws and three losses, just not good enough for an international side who still regarded themselves, delusionally or not, as one of the game's world powers. Joe Mercer came into his eight-game caretaker reign with nothing to lose. It would be Revie's job to mastermind a return to football's top table – smiley old Joe wanted to do his very best for the national team, but so disenchanted were England fans, anything was going to be a bonus.

Never one to bother much about the intricacies of on-field tactics, on the eve of England's first game, against Wales in Cardiff, Mercer would tell his new charges, 'Just go out there and play the same way you do for your clubs.' Manna from heaven for new players he picked for the match, like Queens Park Rangers' mercurial forward Stan Bowles, Leicester City's Keith Weller and Stoke defender Mike Pejic. Mercer's laid-back style took the pressure off a bruised and wounded England; it bore immediate results at Ninian Park. Crowd-pleaser Bowles had a grand old game and scored, as did Kevin Keegan, in a comfortable 2-0 win. Though the game was scrappy and far from a classic, it was a welcome winning start for Mercer. But writing in the *Sunday Mirror*, well-respected football writer Ken Jones was less than impressed, 'Scoring twice on a day when they might have taken six from a brave but uninspired Welsh side, they are still inflicted with inadequacy up front.' This was not news to Mercer, who knew the potential of the available players he had to work with. Apart from a fast-developing young Kevin Keegan, the safe hands of Peter Shilton and the sheer industry of striker Mick Channon, the larder of top-class international English players in 1974 was rather bare. Mercer's major aim was to raise morale and get some wins under the England belt. So game one, job done.

As ever, long-time Wales manager Dave Bowen had to include several Second and Third Division players in his British Home Championship squad and though he could call on top talent like Leeds' Terry Yorath and flying Burnley winger Leighton James, his side were short on quality. They made up for it with hard work and endeavour, inspired by a manager who'd already been ten years in the job. Bowen was a Welsh legend. As a player, he had captained the Red Dragons at the 1958 World Cup and won 19 caps for his country. Unusually, Bowen entered management with two jobs. As well as being appointed part-time as Wales boss in 1964, he also took the reins at Northampton Town, who he led from the Fourth Division to the top flight in just five seasons. As if the demands of those two jobs weren't enough, Bowen also regularly worked as a sports journalist and a TV pundit.

In the second round of matches, Scotland manager Willie Ormond was feeling the pressure of expectation and, desperate to get his side into winning ways before their journey to the World Cup, he decided to make three key changes for their next game against Wales. Leeds' battering ram Joe Jordan was given a start up front alongside the prolific Hearts striker Don Ford. And to create more chances, Ormond recalled Scotland's prodigal son and loveable rogue Jimmy Johnstone. Variously known as 'Jinky', 'the Wee Man' and 'the Lord of the Wings', the 5ft 4in, red-haired Johnstone was already a legend at Parkhead, the ultimate fan favourite. The late, great, award-winning sports writer Hugh McIlvanney memorably described him thus: 'It was his capacity to express effervescent, outrageous, almost surreal mischief through his play – and to make all his darting runs and surges of convoluted trickery a deadly weapon for his team – that rendered him unforgettable. That and the ability not only to thrill but, with his antics on the field, to evoke smiles and sometimes laughter.'

Off the pitch, Johnstone liked a drink, a prank and a wind-up and was outspokenly irreverent. He was no lover of authority and as far as the Scottish FA was concerned, the feeling was reciprocal. Though widely regarded by many pundits to be as good, if not better, than George Best, the Wee Man only gained a paltry 23 Scotland caps.

As well as the three changes in personnel, Ormond also made a key tactical change that did offer some hope for Scotland's World Cup journey. Instead of playing Kenny Dalglish up front, the manager asked the hugely talented young Celtic player to operate in his more familiar club role behind the attack. According to *The Observer* the change was a big success that augured well for Scotland's future, 'The Celtic player looked far happier than he has done recently and as a bonus, opened the scoring.' Scotland 1-0 after 22 minutes and just before half-time, a powerful surging run into the box saw Dalglish hauled over in the area and the ever-reliable Sandy Jardine made it 2-0 from the penalty spot; it effectively ended the match for the toiling Welsh. In the second half, it would not be fair to claim that Ormond's changes had completely rejuvenated his Scottish side, but they showed enough ability to manage Wales out of the game. Johnstone was a constant thorn in their side and the newly restored Joe Jordan and Don Ford continued to frighten the life out of a nervy Welsh defence with their sheer power and physicality. The 45,000 Hampden crowd went home cautiously optimistic about their final match in the tournament, against the Auld Enemy, and at least a little more hopeful for their World Cup prospects. And for only the second time in ten games, they had managed to score more than a single goal.

England took on Terry Neill's Northern Ireland at Wembley and the Ulstermen did what they did best – smother, spoil and then counter-attack. The first half was a dull affair and thanks to a characteristically calm, confident performance from the ever-dependable Irish defence, England created few threats up front. On 36 minutes disaster struck when England's highly influential defensive organiser Roy McFarland limped painfully off the pitch with an Achilles tendon injury that would put him out of football for the next six months. Norman Hunter replaced him, but for the next 20 minutes the English defence seemed edgy and indecisive. Ten minutes into the second period, and revelling in his new short-term role, Joe Mercer went for broke and brought on one of English football's most charismatic players for his international bow.

Leicester City striker Frank Worthington was the ultimate showman. Long-haired and moustachioed, the playboy Yorkshireman had a penchant for long fur coats, rhinestoned Elvis Presley suits and driving his showy red Ford Mustang around at high speeds. His impact on the Wembley game was immediate. Worthington's power and directness began to frighten the life out of the normally cool and collected Northern Ireland defence. Along with fellow striker Keith Weller, the debutant began to pull them out of shape and set up a string of chances. Finally the pressure paid off. In the 67th minute, Mick Channon delivered an inviting ball on to Worthington's head. The footballing *flâneur* deftly nodded it across to Weller, who headed powerfully home from the edge of the penalty box; 1-0 it was, and 1-0 it would remain.

Mercer's gamble had worked with Worthington paying back his faith in him in spades. Amazingly, the mercurial striker would only gain eight caps for England – six of them during Mercer's short reign. The manager would later say of Worthington, 'He's one of the best centre-forwards of all time.'

It could be argued that the maverick Worthington never fully realised his immense potential, but heck, he lived one hell of a life. On the pitch, Worthington would play until he was 44 years old, travelling the world and playing for 24 different professional and non-league clubs. In the USA, he signed highly lucrative deals with Philadelphia Fury and then Tampa Bay Rowdies; in South Africa, he enjoyed a season with Cape Town Spurs; he also had a successful spell with Mjällby AIF in Sweden; late in his career, he turned out for Shelbourne in the League of Ireland. In the Football League, he played for everyone from Huddersfield Town, Leicester, Birmingham City, Leeds United and Sunderland to Brighton, Tranmere, Preston and Stockport. Frank would finally end his career as player-manager at Halifax Town in 1992.

England would go into their final match against Scotland at Hampden Park with two wins, no goals conceded and only needing a draw to lift the trophy. Nomadic Northern Ireland would travel to Wrexham for their third away game of the tournament, knowing that a win would give them an outside chance of winning the championship themselves. The Welsh though were desperate not to be handed the wooden spoon and the game was a proper war of attrition full of hard work and endeavour. Wrexham's 21-year-old striker Dave Smallman scored the only goal of the match with a well-placed lob over the keeper in the 26th minute – by the second half he was lying in a hospital bed after being stretchered off injured. Smallman's goal was the first for Wales in eight matches and was enough to secure them equal bottom spot with Northern Ireland.

What was desperately disappointing for the Welsh was the poor crowd at the Racecourse Ground. The atmosphere in the stadium was flat throughout and only 9,500 paid to watch on the day. By comparison and playing in the third tier of the Football League, Wrexham's highest attendance during 1973/74 was 9,883. It's fair to say that Welsh international football was in the doldrums in 1974. Prior to their Northern Ireland victory, Wales's previous 20 games contained 13 defeats and just five wins.

And so it all came down to the final match. Scotland desperate to go into the World Cup with another win under their belts; England determined to spoil the party and get their own show firmly back on the road. The bookies were overwhelmingly predicting an England victory but Scotland had other ideas. Roared on by a raucous Hampden crowd, they flew out of the blocks, playing high and constantly pressuring a nervy English defence with pace and skill. On four minutes, Joe Jordan lashed in a powerful goal-bound strike, which Peter Shilton seemed to have got covered. But agonisingly, Mike Pejic lunged at the shot and diverted it well away from his wrong-footed keeper and into the back of the England net; 1-0 Scotland. On 30 minutes, England took on a further self-inflicted wound when an innocuous-looking cross was deflected past Shilton by a hapless David Nish. England were 2-0 down to two own goals; they were being outfought and outplayed.

Scotland now had the bit between their teeth and continued to bombard the overworked England back four. Key to their success was the Wee Man, who laid on a dribbling masterclass. Time and time again, Jimmy Johnstone demanded the ball from his team-mates and ran relentlessly at the English. Being a Celtic player, he'd always been given a hard time by the Hampden Park fans but this was different. A supremely talented Scotsman was making fools out of the Auld Enemy and even Rangers fans began to loudly chant his name. Soon the ground was a cauldron of noise and all England could do was shrink back into damage limitation mode. Scotland peppered the English goal and could and should have won by a lot more than the eventual 2-0 scoreline. When the final whistle blew, the Hampden crowd roared Johnstone's name to the rafters.

Summing up the Scotland performance, the *Glasgow Herald* observed, 'Jordan was great, Bremner immense, Lorimer brilliant. But it was perhaps Jimmy Johnstone who took greatest satisfaction from this Hampden triumph … he had his best game in a Scottish jersey.'

After the game a jubilant and defiant Johnstone told the assembled press, 'We have been regarded as second-raters by a lot of people and were written off before the game against England. Now everyone must take us seriously. We proved that we are the best side in Britain and are worthy of our place in the World Cup finals.'

Having so ruthlessly destroyed England's defence and reminded Willie Ormond of his potent box of tricks, Jimmy Johnstone was rightly handed a place in Scotland's 22-man World Cup squad. Jinky was elated but then once again blotted his copybook in a series of off-the-field shenanigans, turning Ormond against him. Despite Scotland's poor record of creating scoring chances, the manager would not play Johnstone for a single minute during the team's three group matches. Jinky would return home to Scotland frustrated and dejected; worse was to come. A year later, manager Jock Stein showed him the door at Celtic. For years, Stein had treated the diminutive Johnstone like a son but even his great patience had its limits. Sick of Johnstone's behaviour, turning up late and hungover to training and generally clowning around in the most inopportune of moments, Stein informed the Wee Man that his contract was not being renewed and he was given a free transfer. A hardcore Celtic fan before he became a player, Johnstone was devastated to be let go, aged just 31. He would have short spells at San Jose Earthquakes, Sheffield United, Dundee and League of Ireland side Shelbourne. Jinky played his last competitive game on 18 August 1979, for non-league Elgin City against Deveronvale in front of 495 fans. Now drinking perhaps far more than he should have done, Johnstone was released shortly afterwards.

For Scotland, it was now on to Germany for the World Cup. For the Home Championship, it was another season of dwindling attendances and an increasing disenchantment with the tournament as a whole. In 1984, the British Home Championship would sadly mark its centenary by disbanding for ever.

13

The 1974 World Cup

'The World Cup is on a disaster course. The players have become money-mad'
– former Brazilian manager João Saldanha

FIFA WERE understandably nervous about Germany holding the World Cup finals in 1974. Two years previously, the country had hosted the Olympic Games, which for the first week of competition had gone like a dream. Held in Munich, the event's official motto was 'Die Heiteren Spiele' – the cheerful Games – and the enthusiastic local crowds had packed out the various stadia for virtually every sport on offer, 195 events in 28 different disciplines. The world, too, watching on TV, was massively impressed by each of the spectacular and ultra-modern sporting sites, all designed by groundbreaking architect Gunter Behnisch. Everything was supremely well organised and the athletes loved the facilities at their Olympic Village. All except the Israelis.

Ever aware of the dark spectre cast over the event by the 1936 Nazi Olympics, the organising committee were eager for the world to see a democratic, open and optimistic West Germany and had deliberately planned security to be discreet and low-key. But the Israeli team felt it to be anything but sufficient, concerned that their accommodation was in a fairly isolated location in the Olympic Village and far too easily accessible. They asked the German authorities to beef up their security protection, but just before dawn on 5 September, a detachment of Palestinian Black September militants scaled a chain-link fence adjacent to the Israeli team apartments. Carrying machine guns and grenades in their duffel bags, they stormed the accommodation base. Two Israelis were killed during the attack and nine taken hostage. After hours of tense and largely unsuccessful negotiations between the hostage-takers and the German and Israeli governments, Germany's military intelligence launched a botched rescue attempt. The remaining nine Israeli hostages were all killed and all but three of the terrorists, the rest captured. It shocked the world.

After lengthy discussions between FIFA and the German government, the security measures taken for the 1974 World Cup were understandably much more high profile. Military and police helicopters patrolled the skies above the stadiums, and on the ground, heavily armed officers protected the different countries' hotels and training facilities. For the grand opening ceremony at Frankfurt's impressive new stadium, there was a crowd of 60,000 – one in 60 of them were members of the German security forces. It would be the biggest police and military presence at any stadium in the history of sport.

The two debutants at the tournament, Zaire and Haiti, were no strangers to heavy security and gun-toting uniforms. Zaire, the first side from sub-Saharan Africa ever to appear at the World Cup, lived under a deeply militarised tyrannical dictatorship. Caribbeans Haiti hailed from the most repressive country in the Western world, where their autocratic leader François 'Papa Doc' Duvalier led a vast 'voodoo army', the heavily armed and much-feared Tonton Macoute. His torture chambers were invariably full to capacity and it's estimated that 60,000 of his 'opponents' were killed during his 14-year reign. On his death in 1971, the country came under the control of his indulged obese 19-year-old son Jean-Claude 'Baby Doc' Duvalier, who continued to run 'the family business' with cruel and careless brutality.

Both Zaire and Haiti arrived at the 1974 World Cup with talented though largely untested squads and were not expected to do anything but make up the numbers. The real favourites were hosts West Germany, Johan Cruyff's Netherlands, South American giants Brazil and the ever-ruthless Italy. But before the first match had kicked off, there were rows aplenty about money, with major unrest in the Dutch and West German camps over pay and bonuses with players even threatening to go on strike. Netherlands maestro Johan Cruyff blindsided his manager Rinus Michels and the country's FA with a different commercial problem. The Dutch strip was sponsored by Adidas, but Cruyff had a very lucrative boot deal with Puma Kings and refused to wear the famous Adidas three stripes down the sleeves of his shirt. He told Michels, 'It's my head sticking out of the shirt and I have a deal with Puma.' In a face-saving compromise, Cruyff was allowed to play with just two black stripes down the arms of his jersey.

According to the *Daily Telegraph*, 'Everywhere, players seemed to have their hands out – for interviews, for having their pictures taken or for wearing a certain manufacturer's product. The Scots fell out with their football boot company and erased its symbols with black boot polish.' Much of this may appear to signal a new era of player entitlement, desperate to squeeze as much money out of the game as they could. But the truth is, FIFA and the national participating FAs made a fortune from the 1974 World Cup's worldwide broadcasting rights, actual match attendances and licensed merchandise and very much gained the lion's share of the huge profits that rolled in. Over the previous decade or so, the World Cup had become big business. But it was the players who contested the World Cup and gave us the joy, the excitement and the great sporting moments, not the well-remunerated officials and their organising bodies.

And so to the runners and riders. Forming the core of the German side were five genuinely world-class Bayern Munich players – goalie Sepp Maier, Franz Beckenbauer and Paul Breitner at the back, plus arch goal poacher Gerd Müller and the powerful Uli Hoeneß up front. As well as the advantage of being hosts, Germany were in form – their ten matches before the tournament saw them win seven, draw two and lose only once, 1-0 against Spain in Barcelona. They were also reigning European champions. Surprisingly, the Netherlands only qualified for the finals thanks to an outrageous error in their final group match against Belgium. Their fierce rivals and neighbours had finished third in Euro 72 and were a strong side. They went into the final qualifying group decider level on points with the Netherlands. Both sides had steamrollered Norway and Iceland home and away and then drew 0-0 in a bad-tempered Antwerp encounter, but the Dutch had a far superior goal difference. The Belgians knew they had to win the last match in Amsterdam to qualify; only the group winners went through.

Their approach was the antithesis of Total Football. Concerned that if they were too attack-minded then the Dutch had the capability to tear them apart, Belgium played ultra-conservatively, putting ten men behind the ball and defending deep, in the hope of catching their opponents on the break. By the 89th minute and with the game still locked at 0-0, Belgium won a free kick just inside the Dutch half. Paul Van Himst launched a Hail Mary high into the box, where keeper Piet Schrijvers misjudged the flight of the ball, flapped and missed, and Jan Verheyen was Johnny on the Spot to stroke it home into an empty net. The Dutch had been denied and Belgium thought they were through to the World Cup finals.

But then the referee Pavel Kazakov blew for offside. The Belgians went ape and angrily surrounded Kazakov, but he waved them away and the decision stood. A couple of minutes later he blew the whistle again, this time for full time, and scandalously the Belgians, who'd not conceded a single goal in the qualification group, were out. Television replays clearly showed that at the very moment Van Himst had touched the free kick no less than three Dutch defenders were unequivocally playing Verheyen onside. Belgium had been robbed, but the Dutch were through and despite the narrow squeak, they would arrive as one of the pre-tournament favourites and with a new manager. As well as the mercurial Cruyff, who the new Dutch boss Rinus Michels had just managed at Barcelona, the key players in his team – Ruud Krol, Johan Neeskens, Piet Keizer, Johnny Rep and Arie Haan – all played for Ajax, who had just won three European Cups on the trot with some irresistible attacking football.

Although Brazil came into the 1974 tournament without a recently retired Pelé, they did have the sublimely skilled Rivelino, Jairzinho, Zé Maria, César, Edu and Mirandinha. Brazil had won three out of the previous four World Cups, and at the time they were the only South American side to lift the trophy in Europe, in Sweden back in 1958. They also came with a tough, rugged new attitude. Fellow South Americans Argentina, Uruguay and Chile were all fancied, but Italy were many people's pre-tournament favourites. They came into the World Cup unbeaten in international matches since June 1972, seeing off Brazil and England, twice, along the way. The 1968 Euros champions had a good balance of youth and experience in their squad and included household names like goalie Dino Zoff, influential skipper Giacinto Facchetti, classy midfielders Sandro Mazzola and Gianni Rivera plus a young Fabio Capello.

There would of course be no England. Scotland came into the 1974 tournament as the only side to qualify from the British Isles and it was their first time at the finals since 1958. In their group, the Scots faced the mighty Brazil, a strong Yugoslavia and the relative unknowns of Zaire. But manager Willy Ormond's squad had genuine strength in depth and included highly rated international-class performers like Kenny Dalglish, David Hay and Jimmy Johnstone plus the inspirational Leeds quartet Billy Bremner, Peter Lorimer, Gordon McQueen and Joe Jordan.

Even before the group matches got under way, Scotland made a big splash at the World Cup. The grand opening ceremony's 'main event' was a cute concept that aimed to highlight the traditional music of each competing nation. Fans streamed into the ground to see 16 huge prefabricated half-football structures strategically placed around the Frankfurt pitch. Under each one, a hidden band or group of musicians, singers and dancers from every country. One by one, the panels of each half football fell away to reveal the groups of performers who played traditional music from their own nation. The first ball was opened and an inspirational Yugoslav folk music and dance ensemble, all in national dress, got proceedings off to a rousing start. The next football was opened to reveal, and to huge applause, a troupe of impassioned German musicians and dancers. And then a tango team from Brazil. Wonderful musicians and dancers from Sweden, Chile, Australia, Zaire and Bulgaria. By this point in the proceedings, the 20-man bagpipe and drum City of Glasgow Police Band had been waiting in the dark concealed beneath the outer casing of their football for

45 minutes. Before the ceremony had begun, the Scottish musicians enjoyed a great deal of German hospitality and particularly, the local lagers. With bladders now close to bursting, the pipe band had no option but to urinate long and hard on to the floor of their structure. When their turn to perform finally came around, the segments of their ball fell away and the band marched proudly out through frothy puddles of urine.

The first match in Scotland's group was between reigning world champions Brazil and Yugoslavia. It was a disappointing 0-0 draw played out on a sodden pitch – no, it wasn't due to urine – and uncharacteristically, Brazil were physical and uncompromising in the tackle. Scotland went into their opening game knowing a win against Zaire would see them top the group. Ormond and his coaching team knew little about the Africans, but memorably told the press, 'If we can't beat Zaire we may as well pack our bags and go home.' They did beat them, 2-0 with goals from Lorimer and Jordan, but it was a tough battle. Ormond's team were outplayed for long periods by a relentlessly attacking and maverick Zaire, who made world football pundits sit up and take serious notice of this 'unknown' African side.

They had arrived on the world stage with a bang, which put a smile on the face of Zaire's former army general turned ruthless dictator President Mobutu. Like many tyrants before him, Mobutu had looked to sport as a political tool to both promote his regime and massage his ego. From the late 1960s onwards, the Zaire national setup had vast resources and money pumped into it. Most of the country's best footballers played abroad around Europe but they were ordered to return home by the dictator and Zaireans knew what happened if you said 'no' to Mobutu. The project soon began to bear fruit. In 1968, Zaire won the African Cup of Nations and then for a second time, in 1974. But the cream on the cake for Mobutu was World Cup qualification where 'his boys' would show the globe how superior his Zaire team had become. He genuinely expected them to lift the Jules Rimet Trophy and showered houses, cars and jewellery upon the players by way of 'carrots'. He didn't need to tell them about the 'sticks' – they knew him of old. The squad travelled to Germany in a febrile mix of fear, stress and excitement. For a number, their real hope was to perform well enough to get offered professional contracts back in Europe and simply 'defect' and stay there.

They had certainly impressed against Scotland and next up were a confident Yugoslavia side. But during the intervening four days something went horribly wrong for the Zaire players. Senior government officials had been sent to the World Cup with a huge kitty of cash for the squad. Alongside them were an army of Mobutu lackeys and hangers-on who'd been making merry with the cash and the players soon discovered two things. One, even before the Yugoslavia game, the kitty had been totally plundered and spent. Two, it had included their wages, expenses and bonuses. The squad was left penniless. Incensed, the players rebelled and went on strike. FIFA secretly stepped in and offered the Zaire players 3,000 Deutschmarks each in cash as long as they went ahead and played the game. If Zaire's players had refused, it would have been a global humiliation that football's governing body could not possibly countenance.

Under huge pressure, Zaire's edgy, angry and worried team agreed to go ahead with the match but the whole affair had demoralised them and they'd hardly trained. After 20 minutes, they were 3-0 down to a slick Yugoslavia and looking ragged. Worse, much worse, was to come. After the third goal went in, coach Blagoje Vidinić, himself a Yugoslav, was ordered by a Zaire government official to sub the goalie Kazadi Mwamba. His replacement? Tubilandu Ndimbi, a 5ft 4in friend of the government official who was keen to see him play. A minute later, the hapless Ndimbi let in the fourth. A few minutes after that, midfielder Ndaye Mulamba was sent off. On the half-hour, Zaire were down to ten men and 4-0 behind. By half-time, that would be six. By full time it was 9-0 to Yugoslavia.

Mobutu was incandescent with rage. The result was an international humiliation for his regime and on the president's orders, senior government officials arranged a sinister secret meeting with the playing squad, behind closed doors, the press banned from attending. To the players' horror, they were told in no uncertain terms that if they lost to Brazil by four or more goals they would not be allowed to return to Zaire, and all their assets and the assets of their families confiscated. Other threats were largely unsaid, deeply implicit, but the players all knew the score. The dictator had brought chilling new meaning to the phrase 'group of death'.

Scotland's second group match, against Brazil, ended 0-0, no bad result against the reigning world champions, and for long spells the Scots had the better of an attritional, ill-tempered match. Once again, Brazil showed their ruthless side and three of their men went into the book for late tackles. One of them, Rivelino, should have been sent off for striking Scottish skipper Billy Bremner in the second half. In truth, the rugged, physical Scots gave as good as they got and put in a few tasty tackles and off-the-ball provocations themselves. It was in no way pretty to watch, but Scotland came closest to breaking the deadlock in the second half, when a towering Joe Jordan header was fumbled by the Brazilian keeper into the path of Bremner, who raked it agonisingly wide. Typically one-eyed, Willie Ormond was not impressed by Brazil and told a post-match press conference, 'We did enough to win, but the Brazilians just stopped us by fair means or foul and I feel we should have had a better deal from the referee.' Fellow Scot and Liverpool legend Bill Shankly had a different and scathingly honest view of the goalless draw, telling the press, 'Great game! You know what that was? Two Third Division teams trying to kick each other to death, that's what it was.'

Scotland's task was now clear. If they could beat Yugoslavia, they were through to the second group stage. Even a draw would have got them there, as long as Brazil didn't score three or more in their final group match against Zaire. At the time, no one had a clue what pressure the Zairean footballers would be playing under. But Scotland's challenge was clear. Before the game began, the omens were not good. As the Scotland XI lined up for the national anthems, 'God Save the Queen' began to boom out of the stadium's loudspeakers. The players exchanged bemused looks and shrugged – some began to laugh. Everyone was expecting to hear the inspirational 'Flower of Scotland'. The players remained silent, refusing to sing, but thousands of Scots fans in the stadium began to boo loudly. The Yugoslavs looked utterly confused – surely you cat-called your opponents' national anthem, not your own?

Like Brazil before them, Yugoslavia had obviously looked at tough, hard-tackling, rugged players like Bremner, Hay, Jordan and McGrain and decided to get the aggression in first. It was a dour and bruising game and remained 0-0 until the 81st minute, when Stanislav Karasi was brought on and headed Yugoslavia into the lead with his first touch. Scotland battled back like crazy and finally, with a minute to go, Jordan equalised with a downward half-volley. The Scots sent everyone up front, but to no avail. The whistle blew at

1-1 and Scots fans everywhere awaited the final encounter in the group with bated breath.

Against Brazil, Zaire showed the world an unexpected new side to their game. Secretly playing under so much threat and fear, they were throwing in potentially leg-breaking tackles against Rivelino and his men and it was a dirty, bad-tempered first half. But by the hour point, the Brazilians had managed to ride enough lunging tackles to be 2-0 up. And then they won a direct free kick dead centre just outside the Zaire box and up stepped Rivelino, at the time probably the greatest free-kick specialist in the world. Zaire formed a defensive wall, while Rivelino discussed options with his team-mates. But before the Brazilian could take the kick, defender Mwepu Ilunga broke from the wall and kicked the stationary ball far away to the other end of the pitch. It was an extraordinary act that silenced the crowd.

On air, BBC commentator John Motson did Zaire a huge disservice by describing the incident as 'a bizarre moment of African ignorance'. Nothing could have been further from the truth. This was a highly professional Zaire team, many of whom had shone in Europe's leagues and twice won the African Cup of Nations, and they knew the rules of football as well as any other side at the World Cup. Secondly, as Ilunga would later reveal to the BBC, he knew exactly what he was doing in kicking the ball away. Angry and exasperated by his president's threats and the unrelenting pressure his team-mates were being put under, Ilunga snapped emotionally and hoiked the ball as a protest, expecting to be sent off – in the end, the referee only punished him with a yellow. Brazil would win 3-0, enough to qualify them for the next stage. This would leave Scotland in an unprecedented position in World Cup history. Yugoslavia, Brazil and Scotland all ended on four points but the South Americans' 3-0 victory would edge them ahead of the Scots on a goal difference of one. With eventual winners West Germany surprisingly losing to fierce Iron Curtain rivals East Germany in the group stages, and more of that soon, Willie Ormond's men would end the tournament as the World Cup's only unbeaten team.

The Zaire squad were immediately bundled on to a plane back to Africa and though they'd prevented Brazil beating them by four or more, the players knew they would not be returning home to smiles and handshakes. When the jet touched down in Kinshasa, an empty grey army truck was sitting on the runway waiting for them. They were ushered into the back and driven straight to President Mobutu's palace, where they were subjected to a vicious hour-long rant from their dear leader. The players were 'traitors' and 'subversives' who had 'shamed the nation'. Mobutu issued many threats, most of which he carried out. All funding to the national squad was cancelled and the international team was disbanded. Every single player was banned from playing football again and to ensure that none of them tried to play abroad, their photos and personal details were prominently displayed at every port, airport and border crossing in Zaire. Some of the squad became homeless, most were denied any kind of future employment and lived on in poverty. Ilunga became a taxi driver using the Volkswagen given to him by Mobutu before the World Cup, the final irony.

In Group One, pre-tournament favourites West Germany had already beaten Chile and Australia to qualify for the second stage – their third group game would be against East Germany. This would be the first – and last – time that the two nations would meet on the football pitch, and to say that the match was politically charged would be an understatement. This was east versus west, capitalism versus communism, and both were desperate to prevail.

Against all the odds, East Germany would win through a single Jürgen Sparwasser goal and there was jubilation behind the Iron Curtain. The West German side stayed up all night drinking away their sorrows, but the following day manager Helmut Schön, himself an East German, and captain Franz Beckenbauer began to rethink and realign their tactics. Though West Germany had beaten Chile and Australia, they were lacklustre in both games and the embarrassing defeat to East Germany was the final straw. It had not been a happy camp. There were constant fall-outs over bonus money and Schön's tactical approach, rows between player cliques and about match selections. But the loss against their 'enemy' seemed to focus minds and unite the fractious squad.

East Germany's famous victory would see them top the group but ironically, this did them no favours. As it panned out, this placed them in a tough second stage group against big hitters Brazil, Argentina and Johan Cruyff's Dutch. As group runners-up, hosts West Germany joined, on paper, a much easier second phase group containing Poland, Sweden and Yugoslavia. The format of the tournament did not have quarter- or semi-finals; the winners of both groups would contest the World Cup Final.

Thus far, the Netherlands had been by far the most thrilling team at the World Cup. A side that boasted truly world-class performers like Cruyff, Neeskens, Rep and Rensenbrink, the Dutch played a fast and fluid brand of Total Football that bamboozled all who were put before them. Constantly exchanging positions to outmanoeuvre opponents, their highly adaptable and intelligent players created acres of space for one another. In the first group stage they had cruised through unbeaten, defeating a strong Uruguay side 2-0; ending up 0-0 in a bore draw against an obdurate and ultra-defensive Sweden; and then hammering

Bulgaria 4-1 in a glory of a game. The Netherlands were getting well into their stride. Dutch players were long-haired, hip and liberal, effortlessly moving within the zeitgeist of the time and worshipped like rock stars, particularly at home.

They would storm the second group stage with a 4-0 thrashing of Argentina, a 2-0 win over a deeply negative East Germany followed by a joyous 2-0 victory over an equally negative Brazil, the beauty of their Mexico approach now lost to a depressing, rough-house cynicism. Brazil would end the tournament after failing to score in four of their seven appearances and to compound their disappointing campaign, Luís Perreira was shown a red card in the defeat to the Netherlands after he brutally hacked down Johan Neeskens. The Dutch were in the World Cup Final, the toast of the footballing world.

In their second-round group, West Germany were starting to get into their stride. Goals from Paul Breitner and, inevitably, Gerd Müller, saw off Yugoslavia 2-0, then Germany were up against the hard-to-beat, rugged Sweden side. Though down 1-0 at half-time, the Germans overran the Scandinavians in the second half and cruised home 4-2 winners.

Surprise package Poland had also won their first two games, which meant that the last second-round match against Germany would provide the other finalist. Unlike the brilliant bright sunshine of Mexico 1970, the 1974 World Cup was blighted by torrential rain and many games were played in tricky conditions. The West Germany v Poland decider in Frankfurt would prove to be the worst. Hours before kick-off, the gunmetal grey skies over the Waldstadion turned black and a Wagner-esque *Sturm und Drang* dropped a deluge of rain on to the pitch. The kick-off time was put back, while the local fire service were drafted in to help an army of volunteers drain the

Don Revie and his Leeds United league champions.

The weird and wonderful Soccer Liner disco train.

Franz Beckenbauer proudly lifts the World Cup for West Germany.

Jack Charlton makes himself useful at Middlesbrough.

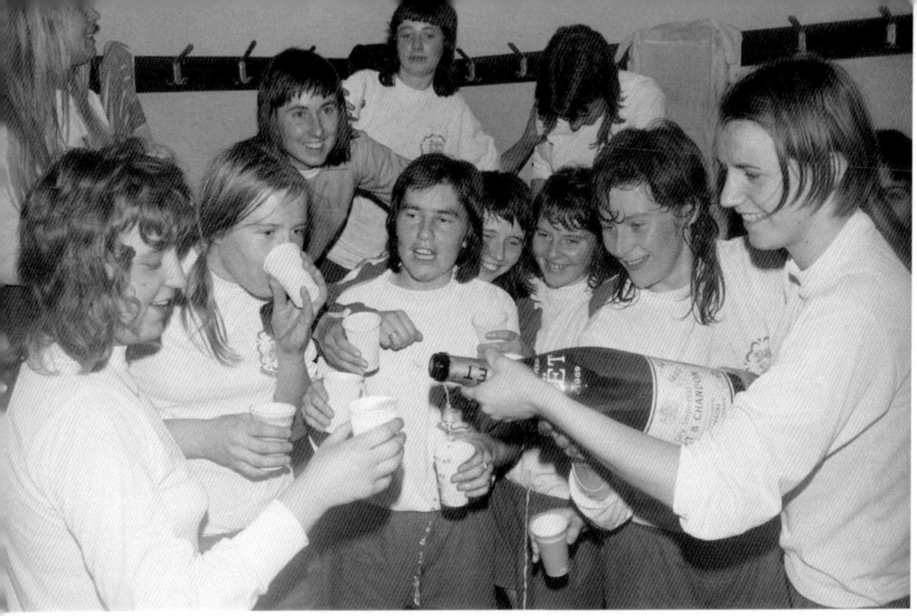

The newly created England women's football team celebrate a win.

Ref Reg Matthewson shows red cards to the brawling Billy Bremner and Kevin Keegan.

A football hooligan feels the long armlock of the law.

Legends shake on it – Cloughie and Shanks at Wembley for the Charity Shield.

Footballer of the Year Norman Hunter bossing it for Leeds.

The great Jock Stein stands guard over Celtic Park.

Johan Cruyff turns it on against Argentina at the World Cup.

Liverpool show off the UEFA Cup and the league championship trophy at the start of the 1973/74 season.

waterlogged surface and eventually the decision was taken to go ahead with the game. But it was still a quagmire and what might have been a classic encounter between two of the tournament's best sides turned into a bit of a farce. With puddles all over the pitch, passes were constantly caught up in the mud and water and the game became a lottery. With minutes to go, that supreme poacher Müller once again popped up in the box and scored the winner. It would be hosts West Germany versus the extravagantly talented Dutch in the final.

On the eve of the match, the Poles completed a highly impressive campaign by beating Brazil 1-0 for third place. Speedy winger Grzegorz Lato bagged the winner and ended the tournament as top scorer with seven goals. The highly unfancied team, who'd shocked the world of football by knocking England out in the qualifying group stages, had grown stronger and more confident as they'd gone along. Jan 'The Clown' Tomaszewski had an impressive World Cup and won a well-deserved third-place medal for his endeavours.

The German newspapers were disgruntled by the rave reviews the Dutch were garnering from the world's press while their own team was, they felt, being underestimated and before the final, they went on the attack. Scurrilous stories, but possibly true, appeared in German tabloids claiming that the Dutch had celebrated their famous victory over Brazil by drunkenly partying late into the night with local prostitutes. They characterised Cruyff's men as arrogant, disrespectful and hedonistic, their own men as serious, well-disciplined sportsmen. The Dutch couldn't give a stuff – they were enjoying their World Cup. There was, too, a distinct historical undercurrent to the Netherlands' footballing mission. They were desperate to play a German side in the final because only 30 years before, the Nazis had conquered and enslaved their country, committing many atrocities along the way. This would be the first time that the Netherlands played Germany in a major tournament final.

The Dutch went into the decider supremely confident that their skill and swagger would be too much for the pragmatic Germans. It would turn out to be Total Football versus total discipline. Cruyff and his colleagues flew out of the blocks and in the first minute, the Barcelona superstar waltzed through the German defence, was legged over in the box and won a penalty. Germany hadn't even touched the ball. Neeskens stepped up to hammer home and in the process score the first penalty in a World Cup Final. It was 1-0 to the Netherlands and for the next 20 minutes they toyed and played with the Germans, mocking their opponents, goading them to come forward and then constantly changing and exchanging positions to close down space. Dutch forward Johnny Rep would say after the game, 'We wanted to make fun of the Germans … but we forgot to score the second goal.'

One Dutch player began to be starved of the ball. Defender Berti Vogts, nicknamed *Der Terrier*, was handed the task of man-marking Johan Cruyff out of the game. The tactic was no surprise to manager Rinus Michels' men, as they knew Germany often employed Vogts to cancel out the opposition's best attacking player, but they were supremely confident that Cruyff was too abundantly talented to be chained by the workmanlike German defender. Thus far, the man who had invented the sublime, wrong-footing 'Cruyff turn' had been the standout player of the tournament. It was testament to how well Vogts played on the day that Cruyff was so subdued. The defender stuck to him like a limpet, effectively starving the Dutchman of service, and gradually West Germany were getting back into the game. In the 25th minute Bernd Hölzenbein was fouled in the Dutch area and the Germans were awarded a penalty of their own. Paul Breitner stepped up and stroked it in to make it 1-1. Game on.

After 43 minutes, striker Gerd Müller showed why he was one of the best goal predators in the world when he latched on to a ball inside the box and, showing exquisite touch and balance, he swivelled and lashed it into the net. This would be his 68th goal for West Germany and his 14th in World Cup tournaments. Vogts' key performance and the generally shrewd pragmatism of the German side saw them go in at half-time 2-1 to the good. The Netherlands would not be denied and during the second half launched attack after attack on the German goal, but keeper Sepp Maier responded by playing probably his best 45 minutes in an international shirt. It would remain 2-1 Germany and total discipline won out over Total Football. Franz Beckenbauer lifted West Germany's second World Cup and the dreamers of the Netherlands woke up with a bump.

The 'bad losers' of the tournament were Brazil. The head of their FA, João Havelange, offered up a bizarre and damaging conspiracy theory – to wit, the 1966 and 1974 World Cups had been deliberately rigged to prevent Brazil from winning. He told the Brazilian newspaper *Folha de São Paulo*, 'In the three matches that the Brazilian national team played in 1966, of the three referees and six linesmen, seven were British and two were German. Brazil went out, Pelé "exited" through injury [following some rough defensive play] and England and Germany entered into the final, just as the Englishman Sir Stanley Rous, who was the president of FIFA at the time, had wanted. In Germany in 1974, the same thing happened. During the Brazil–Holland game, the referee was German, we lost 2-0 and Germany won the title. We were the best team in the world and had the same team that had won the World Cup in 1962 in

Chile and 1970 in Mexico, but it was planned for the home countries to win.'

Just a little fact-checking – Brazil's 22-man squad in Germany contained only eight players from their Mexico selection and just one, Pelé, from the win in Chile.

14

The Summer of 74

'Saturday comes again, welcome or not, it comes again like it always does, welcome or not, wanted or not, another judgment day – the chance to be saved, the chance to be damned'

– Brian Clough

AS THE whistle blew at The Valley on the windy evening of Friday, 3 May, Charlton Athletic had signed off on another fairly ordinary season with a 2-0 win over Aldershot. Relegated into the Third Division two seasons previously – and for the first time since 1934 – they were now enduring the sharp end of a decade in decline. In the 1940s and 1950s, the big old south London ground rocked to the din and noise created by regular 40,000-plus crowds. Finishing 14th in the 1973/74 third tier, their average gates had plummeted to 5,600. For that last match of the campaign against Aldershot, only 3,245 bothered to turn up. The club's coffers were near empty and, desperate to earn some much-needed ready cash and get The Valley rocking again, the board decided to enrol the help of Messrs Townshend, Daltrey, Entwistle and Moon.

Two weeks later, the ground would reopen during the close-season to host a 12-hour one-day rock festival headlined by the Who, supported by ex-Velvet Undergrounder Lou Reed, Steve Marriott's Humble Pie, the newly formed Bad Company, Geordie chart favourites Lindisfarne, American rock band Montrose and former Stone the Crows singer Maggie Bell – the 'Scottish Janis Joplin'. It was not the first rock gig in English football stadium history. During the early summer of 1971, cash-strapped Hartlepool had pioneered the idea to help keep themselves afloat over the off-season months by putting on a stadium gig for minor Scottish prog-rockers Beggars Opera. Great idea, but they didn't think big enough. The show was by all accounts a great gig, but Beggars Opera had no hits and nothing much more than a cult following, and though an interesting novelty for the good folks of the north-east, it didn't pull a significant crowd.

A couple of months later, equally cash-strapped Hereford United dreamed a little bigger and hosted a full show on their Edgar Street ground headlined by local boys Mott the Hoople, supported by ace guitarist Albert Lee's band Heads, Hands and Feet, plus folky duo the Amazing Blondell. Mott the Hoople had just become a major chart act, scoring hits with 'All the Young Dudes', 'All the Way from Memphis' and 'Honaloochie Boogie', and though a fair crowd turned up, the sheer logistics of putting on the show, allied to the modest profits made, didn't see Hereford repeat the venture any time soon. Charlton, however, and the promoters who worked with them, had done their homework and believed the only way to make a stadium gig work financially was to think big. And in 1974 there were few bigger bands in the world than the Who.

In addition, the artistes on the rest of the bill were virtually potential venue-fillers in their own right. The one-day festival was a resounding success on all fronts. Over 50,000 music fans packed into The Valley to watch the supporting cast play storming sets. Then on came the Who with the madcap Keith Moon debuting his new outrageously large drum kit, which featured three sets of tom-toms (11 in all), extra cymbals and two bass drums. This would be the biggest crowd the band had played in front of since the legendary Woodstock Festival five years before and in front of a well-oiled and at times overly rowdy crowd, delivered a scorching set.

Pete Townshend's verdict on the day – and night – was ambivalent. He told *Melody Maker*, 'Charlton was very disappointing, because when we went out the first thing I felt in the air was violence … the only way I could get it together was by shutting out the audience and working with the group.'

But despite the guitarist's misgivings, the Who returned to The Valley two summers later to headline another major show. At this, they would set a new record for becoming the loudest band of all time, hitting 126 decibels. By comparison, the average clap of thunder overhead hits the ground at around 120 decibels. The sonic racket didn't go down well with local residents, but it did earn both Charlton Athletic and the Who a place in the *Guinness Book of Records*.

The sound of music for England's national team had been in a particularly mournful and minor low key since the sacking of Alf Ramsey. Having missed out on Germany 1974, England found themselves in the rare position of warm-up act and bit-part players for three World Cup-bound eastern European sides. In June, England flew out to play friendlies in East Germany, Bulgaria and Yugoslavia but new caretaker manager Joe Mercer was determined to change the mood music surrounding the players into a far more positive major key. On his first meeting with the squad, he told more jokes in an hour than the serious-minded and introverted Ramsey had managed during a decade at the helm. After jokingly telling his new players he was clearly insane to be there, because 'I never wanted the bloody job', Mercer assured his men he wanted them to express themselves and play their natural game. The cheery and avuncular old pro implored the squad to trust in their talent and flair and added, 'Let's all at least bloody smile, eh lads?'

After years of dealing with the taciturn and uncommunicative Ramsey, the media revelled in Mercer's open and witty banter and within days of his appointment as caretaker boss, the popular press had dubbed him 'Uncle Joe'. Those in the know realised that Mercer was a man who knew struggle, having bravely clawed his way back from serious mental health problems to now stand where he stood. As a left-half with Arsenal, he'd captained the Gunners to two league titles and an FA Cup win, gaining five England caps along the way. Starting off in management, he'd suffered two relegations from the top flight with his first two clubs, Sheffield United and Aston Villa, but at the latter he then bounced back with a refreshing new philosophy that combined the development of youth with a forward-looking attacking style. The talented young side he built at Villa Park became known as 'Mercer's Minors' and they rewarded his faith in them by first winning the Second Division championship and then the 1961 League Cup.

But the long hours and stressful total commitment that he put into the job soon began to take a toll on his mental health. After suffering a debilitating nervous breakdown in 1964, Mercer was forced to leave football for over a year to get himself back on to any kind of even keel. It was a struggle, but with help and support, he returned to the game rejuvenated and Second Division Manchester City took him on as their new manager in 1965. Older and wiser from his illness, Mercer realised he needed to appoint a number two who could take pressure and stress off him; his first appointment was inspirational. Visionary young coach Malcolm Allison was impressing as manager at Plymouth Argyle and Mercer knew him from coaching courses at the FA's Lilleshall base. Together, the two men brought a new golden age to the long-underperforming and underachieving sleeping Manchester giants. First they won the Second Division to get the Blues back into the top flight, following relegation three seasons earlier. The pair assembled a stellar squad of talented young players like Mike Summerbee, Colin Bell and Francis Lee and on they went to win the First Division title, the FA Cup, the European Cup Winners' Cup and the League Cup.

When Mercer took the call from the FA, he was working as general manager at Coventry City with Gordon Milne as first-team boss. Milne was thought by many to be a serious contender for the full-time England job, but it was Mercer who was put in temporary charge. Mercer immediately drafted two great entertainers into his squad: the mercurial Frank Worthington, and the king of the dribble, Stan Bowles. For Mercer's first match in charge against East Germany, he picked eight players with seven caps or less and they attacked with a freshness rarely seen from England in recent years. Coming into the second half, they'd already hit the woodwork four times but it would be East Germany who scored first on 66 minutes through centre-forward Joachim Streich. A minute later, Mick Channon smashed in the equaliser direct from a free kick and the game ended in a lucky draw for an outplayed East Germany. After the match, Mercer quipped, 'We hit the woodwork more times than a team of lumberjacks.'

Next up, England flew to Sofia to take on Bulgaria, an obdurate and well-organised side who they carved apart. The biggest surprise on the night was that they only triumphed by a single goal, inevitably scored by Mercer's flair pick, Frank Worthington. In the 44th minute, Kevin Keegan flicked a carefully placed Ray Clemence goal kick into the path of the Leicester forward, who rifled it past the memorably named Bulgarian goalie Rumyancho Goranov Radev. Up front, the pace, decision-making and mobility of Worthington, Keegan and Channon scared the life out of the home defence, but somehow the score remained 1-0 England, and Bulgaria were given the tough workout they needed to prepare them for the World Cup. England's third tour match against Yugoslavia started badly, with Keegan being falsely arrested for affray at Belgrade airport and then treated to a beating by overzealous local police; more about that later.

The match itself was an end-to-end thriller, Mercer's 'new' England keen to get on the front foot and press high. In the sixth minute, Yugoslav goalie Enver Maric fumbled a fierce Trevor Brooking shot and arch predator Channon scrambled home from close in. The Yugoslavs equalised on 23 minutes through Ilija Petković, and shortly after half-time Branko Oblak put them 2-1 up. But England continued to swarm forward and on 75 minutes, Keegan equalised with a deft header as the match ended honours even. Less than a week later, all three eastern European teams would travel to their training camps in West Germany to fine-tune themselves for the World Cup. Joe Mercer would fly back with his England squad to Heathrow, where he would shake their hands and wave them goodbye after his 36 refreshingly uplifting days in charge. In his brief tenure, Mercer had shown the way forward for England but eyes were blind.

The FA's succession plans had taken an unlikely turn when Don Revie personally canvassed them for the vacant position, and impressed by an approach from the country's currently most successful club boss, they appointed him to the post. Revie had long entertained the dream of leading England – what top-class English manager wouldn't? But in truth he was the perfect man for Leeds United at the time; in hindsight, perhaps the last man who should have been offered the England job. The team's style of play, so refreshing under Mercer, immediately reverted to the late-period pragmatism of Alf Ramsey. As he had done for over a decade at Leeds, Revie pieced together exhaustive and detailed player dossiers for all of England's upcoming internationals, instructing his men how to nullify, negate and cancel out their opponents' best talents. But he didn't really know any of them as players, unlike his Leeds men – what made them tick or unlock their best skills or how they should be assembled to bring out the best of their own natural game.

In over a decade in charge at Elland Road, Revie's carefully built squad had got used to his dossiers and demands, and through time they had learned how to incorporate this detailed information into their own playing styles. But that had taken time, training together every day and playing as a team every week. And undoubtedly, the Leeds players had huge respect and loyalty for their manager but this too grew over time. Like Alf Ramsey, Revie was phlegmatic and fairly dictatorial in his man-management style. But now, as England boss, he had to learn how to integrate the personalities of very different players from many different clubs, playing very different styles and formations, who he would only meet up with seven or eight times a year for a few days at a time. Revie had only ever managed one club, albeit very successfully, and the national job took him completely out of his comfort zone. From the very beginning of his England reign, his international players were totally turned off by Don's dossiers.

England's strong Liverpool contingent of Ray Clemence, Emlyn Hughes, Alec Lindsay and Kevin Keegan were used to the Shankly and Paisley regimes, where simplicity and clarity of message had brought, and were still bringing, repeated success. Liverpool didn't worry too much about what their opponents could bring to the fight, only what they wanted to do to win. Similarly, Colin Todd and Roy McFarland grew up under Brian Clough at Derby being told to read the game, adapt tactically on the pitch and trust what you feel is right in the moment. Ditto Colin Bell under Joe Mercer and Malcolm Allison at Manchester City; and Trevor Brooking with Ron Greenwood and John Lyall at West Ham. Where Mercer had similarly offered up a simple tactical clarity that allowed him to draft in flair players like Worthington and Bowles, and trust in their skills, Revie's first matches in charge at the end of 1974 already revealed a destabilised confusion within the England ranks. Caution had returned with a vengeance.

Though England missed out on the World Cup, a good number of English footballers continued to play professional sport throughout the summer and many of them with bat and ball. There has been a long tradition of footballer-cricketers going right back to Victorian times, often because there has always been a rare breed of individual who shines at everything that is sporting and athletic. As the 20th century progressed and because of the vagaries of the maximum wage system in professional football, it was often also a case of needs must. Up until the 1960s, players were not allowed to earn above a set amount during the football season, but then during the non-playing summer break they had their wages reduced by around a third. Those who were good enough supplemented their lower off-season income by playing county and top local-league cricket, many at the highest level.

By 1974, and largely thanks to the continued efforts of the PFA, players were freed from the unfair maximum wage system and earned a decent living all the year round. But the tradition of footballer-cricketers continued to live on. During the 1974 county cricket season, Leicestershire's star performer was Carlisle United midfielder Chris Balderstone. Playing alongside him was Leicester City's Graham Cross. Manchester United defender Arnie Sidebottom turned his right arm over with great success for Yorkshire and England, while Sheffield United defender Ted Helmsley was a long-time Worcestershire regular. Aston Villa's first-choice goalie Jim Cumbes was a first-choice bowler for Lancashire, and in later years he became chief executive at the Old Trafford cricket club. In the summer of 1974, many other footballers were also turning out for top cricket league teams around the country.

It would not prove to be a particularly busy summer in the transfer market but there were several significant big-money moves. Liverpool shelled out £200,000 for a 22-year-old who already knew a fair bit about football's ups and downs. Aged 16, north-easterner Ray Kennedy had been signed up by no less a legend than Sir Stanley Matthews, then taking his first steps in management at Port Vale. But the young striker would have a brief and unhappy time at Vale Park. Matthews quickly decided that his young new acquisition didn't have what it took to play professionally, telling his board that Kennedy was 'too slow to be a footballer'. To his chagrin, Kennedy was released after a few months and returned to the north-east where he got full-time work in a local sweet factory. In his spare time, Kennedy continued to play competitive football but at a much lower amateur level for New Hartley Juniors in the East Northumberland Junior League. But then fate took a hand. An Arsenal scout had travelled north to run the rule over one of Kennedy's young team-mates, but in the end he was far more impressed by Ray and Arsenal signed him on. It took the young player a couple of seasons playing in the reserves before getting anywhere near the first team, but once he did, Kennedy established an impressive strike partnership with fellow forward John Radford. The older striker took the youngster under his wing and encouraged Kennedy to believe in himself. The duo would help power Arsenal to the First Division and FA Cup double in 1971, scoring 34 goals between them.

But despite the success, life at Arsenal was never easy for Kennedy. He struggled with his weight and was fined for lack of fitness. Manager Bertie Mee was never entirely convinced by Kennedy and replaced him with World Cup winner Alan Ball, keen to move him on. Bill Shankly, though, saw something in the young forward and made him his last signing before retiring in the summer. When Kennedy arrived at Anfield he weighed nearly 200lb and struggled to improve his fitness. During the 1974/75 season he played 37 games in all competitions with a modest strike return of 12 goals and the Anfield faithful remained distinctly unconvinced by Shankly's £200,000 signing.

But Liverpool's shrewd new manager Bob Paisley had been watching Kennedy's first touch and reading of the game, focusing on what he did best, and decided that he could transform the career of his striker. Fellow north-easterner Paisley sat Kennedy down in an office at the Liverpool training ground and offered him a new opportunity. He asked him to run the midfield. 'But first son, you need to lose some weight,' he said. Energised by the new faith being shown in him, Kennedy trained hard, lost the pounds and a man with an innate football intelligence soon adapted to his new role. In the coming years, Kennedy would indeed become Liverpool's midfield powerhouse, winning five league titles, three European Cups, the UEFA Cup, a League Cup and 17 England caps. His stellar career would, however, come to a depressing end. After experiencing a marriage break-up and financial troubles, Kennedy saw a specialist in November 1984 and was diagnosed, aged just 33, with Parkinson's disease.

Paisley and his scouting team once again showed their shrewdness by dipping down into the Fourth Division and make a £66,000 signing who would become a Liverpool legend. Young defender Phil Neal had made his debut for Northampton Town as a 17-year-old in 1968, and by the summer of 1974 he had made over 200 appearances for the Cobblers. Impressed by his composure on the ball and his abilities as an attacking defender, Paisley had bought Neal to eventually replace ageing right-back Chris Lawler. But once inside the Anfield camp, the coaching staff soon realised that the young player was already potentially ready for First Division football and Neal became a first-team regular.

On the way out of Anfield went giant Bristolian defender Larry Lloyd. Shankly, and now Paisley, realised they had a diamond in young new central defender Phil Thompson. Though Lloyd was tough-tackling and a big physical presence, the slighter, younger Thompson had already shown himself to be sharp and intelligent on the ball and could immediately turn defence into attack with his accurate passing skills; in many ways, a much more 'modern' player than the stop-them-at-all-costs Lloyd. Paisley and the Liverpool board were more than happy to pocket £240,000 from Coventry City for the big man's services.

Across the Pennines, Liverpool's major league rivals Leeds United, now under new boss Brian Clough, had signed a trio of new players in the summer – and none were made to feel particularly welcome. Clough had long been a big fan of midfielder John McGovern, having tried to tempt him away from Derby County the season before when he was manager at Brighton. McGovern was a fan of Clough but, still in his mid-20s, wasn't prepared to drop down to the Third Division. When Clough got the job at reigning league champions Leeds and came calling again, McGovern didn't think twice. But as McGovern admitted in later years, he really should have. Unaware of the psycho-drama that he was stepping into, the Scot soon realised that in the poisonous atmosphere that was now Elland Road, he was very much seen as a Clough man. He played four times under Clough during the manager's controversially brief 44-day sojourn and then no more.

Talking to the Youtube FC football channel, McGovern later said, 'When I arrived at Elland Road … I found out I was unwanted by anyone at the club and it was a very difficult time for me.

'I spent about six months at Leeds not being involved in the squad, and even in those days they used to have the players' names on the back of the squad tracksuits. Well I was there six months and I never got a tracksuit with my name on the back of it. I think it was a big hint from the club that I didn't really belong there.'

McGovern was joined at Leeds by former Derby team-mate John O'Hare for £125,000. The Scottish striker had fallen out with manager Dave Mackay and was happy to move on with McGovern to work under Clough. He too would be tarred with the 'Clough brush' and would only play six matches for Leeds. The third of Clough's signings, striker Duncan McKenzie, had a more successful spell at

Elland Road and cemented his place as a regular for the next few seasons.

Manchester City manager and former player stalwart Tony Book arguably pulled off the transfer steal of summer 1974. Big, brawny Scouser Joe Royle had been Everton's top scorer for the previous five seasons, striking 102 goals in 232 league games for the Goodison Park side. With a deal that promised Royle much-improved wages, a bargain £170,000 deal was agreed to bring him to Maine Road. And so the new 1974/75 season began. By the end of August, Liverpool were leading the First Division under Bob Paisley, already a seemingly seamless Anfield Boot Room transition. Across the Pennines at Leeds, Clough was having a nightmare. His new squad were resentful, truculent and openly rebellious, the toxic atmosphere at Elland Road badly affecting performances on the pitch.

United kicked off their season with a 3-0 away loss at Stoke City and then went on to win just one out of their first eight games. Now in open revolt, and led by Johnny Giles, Billy Bremner and Norman Hunter, the players delivered an unequivocal message to their board – Clough must go. Aware of the huge disquiet his appointment was causing among players, support staff and fans alike and realising the huge mistake they'd made, the club's directors decided to sack Clough after just 44 days in charge. After winning just one of his first six matches, Clough's Leeds were down near the bottom in 19th place and Don Revie's shadow followed him everywhere. He was given a huge £98,000 pay-off and three months later he took over at Nottingham Forest, where his Leeds nightmare became a City Ground dream. Years later, Clough would finally admit in his autobiography, 'I handled the whole thing badly. I was faced with a group of hardened and highly talented professionals who had been used to a father figure – nay, a godfather figure – a manager renowned for his attention to detail. In turn, they were faced with a new boss who had savaged them, on television and in print. It was perhaps not surprising that they failed to show the same dedication and commitment on the pitch.'

To this day, it's still a total head-scratcher as to why the Leeds board targeted Brian Clough for the job, not only the club's most vocal public critic but also the polar opposite of Revie in terms of personality and management style. Though clearly already a gifted manager and motivator in his own right, Clough was always going to be a round peg in a square hole at Elland Road and his short reign began a decline in Leeds' fortunes. Under new boss Jimmy Armfield, things didn't much improve for Leeds – by Christmas, the reigning league champions had lost ten times.

In the Second Division, the size, pull and history of relegated Manchester United led to few players wanting to leave the club to stay in the top flight and their First Division squad remained largely intact, still containing top internationals like Lou Macari, Willie Morgan, Sammy McIlroy, Stuart Pearson and Martin Buchan. The board considered the shock relegation to be a blip and continued to have faith in Tommy Docherty as boss. It didn't take long for the Red Devils to prove they were just too good for Second Division football. By the end of September, United were top having won seven, drawn two and lost just the once, scoring 18 goals and conceding just six.

15

The Kit

'For those watching in black and white, Spurs are in the all-yellow strip'

– John Motson

MOST OF the notable footballing events of 1974 seemed to involve Don Revie and Leeds United somewhere down the line, and this included some revolutionary new changes to strip that would pioneer not only the multi-million-pound replica kit market but also commercial shirt sponsorship. Revie was ever the conundrum. He looked old-fashioned with his Brylcreemed quiff, ever-shiny shoes and staid blue polyester suits. But when it came to the game itself, Revie was always prepared to consider the new and the different if it promised to offer his players even the smallest of advantages. His attention to detail was legendary. Convinced that team-bonding exercises would help create a Three Musketeers-like solidarity and togetherness out on the pitch, he regularly got his squad playing bingo, carpet bowls and darts together. He would take his players out for group trips and social get-togethers. He also believed that seemingly small changes could create new thinking, and that extended to what the players wore.

When Revie took over as Leeds player-manager in 1961, they were a mediocre Second Division side but he wanted his players to be inspired by the best. He persuaded the Elland Road board to change the club strip to all white, the colours worn by Europe's greatest team at the time, the multi-European Cup winners Real Madrid. Ironically, given United's later 'Dirty Leeds' tag, white was also the colour of purity and cleanliness.

Fast forward to 1973 and Revie sat down with directors and designers from Leicestershire sportswear company Admiral to discuss the idea of a trailblazing new kit design. He had been told by the board that the all-white home strip was off-limits, but Admiral had ideas for a new away kit and a custom-designed player tracksuit. Revie wanted his players to look individual and different from 'the rest' and he knew that Admiral had a track record for innovation.

The company started business in 1903 as Cook and Hurst, a hosiery business that expanded to make long johns, vests, swimming trunks and knickers. At the outbreak of the First World War, the firm won a lucrative government contract to provide the military with underwear – and also a deal with the Royal Navy to manufacture exercise and PE clothing for their sailors, their first foray into sports gear – and the inspiration for the company's name change to Admiral. The company proudly boasted, 'This is why we started to market our products with the stoic-looking Admiral's head: to signify superiority and to assure the wearer of high-quality British manufacturing.' The perhaps understandable tub-thumping patriotism changed through the decades and the admiral's head became a sleeker three-stripe Royal Navy admiral's uniform insignia brand logo by the 1960s.

Revie was aware that Admiral had designed an innovative new lightweight interlock football jersey for

England goalie Gordon Banks back in 1965 that featured elastication in the neck and cuffs, allowing for easier and greater freedom of movement. Banks wore it throughout the 1965/66 domestic season and was so impressed with his new lightweight shirt that he also wore it for every one of England's matches at the 1966 World Cup. Due to FA rules at the time, the shirt contained no sponsorship logo and Banks did not receive any payment for wearing it. The 1973 Leeds deal would be different. It would be worth £10,000 to the Elland Road club and in return, the away shirt featured a small Admiral crest on the right hand side of the chest. The shirts were indeed different in design, featuring a filled-in V at the neck with a small collar. The tracksuits were rather more full-on, with a big Admiral logo emblazoned across the top, but these had to be taken off by the players as soon as they reached the field of play because the FA were still vehemently opposed to kit sponsorship.

The new branded kit also proved to be a big hit with the Leeds fans and suddenly Admiral and the Elland Road board saw pound signs. Since the early 1960s, sportswear firms had produced novelty kit boxes for little children, containing a small shirt, shorts and socks, but the idea of replica kits for adults hadn't even been thought of. Ditto in 1974 and when Admiral suggested that they mass-produce the new kit and tracksuit to expand their market, it was to target kids and not adults. It went down a storm and soon adult fans were clamouring for replica kit in grown-up sizes. This once-small Midlands underwear company had become the trailblazers in what has now developed into a global market worth billions. And all thanks to their working relationship with Don Revie's Leeds.

But we all make mistakes. There was one idea that soon died a death and was rightly consigned to the grave of football crimes against sporting fashion – the Leeds sock tag. This creation of madness combined faux-satin cloth, frills hanging from the bottom and the player's team number in a two-and-a-half-inch square that was tied around the outside of the sock. It looked ridiculous, over-showy and cheap – the players hated them and eventually they were quietly retired, thankfully never to be seen again in English football. But Admiral went from strength to strength. For the 1974/75 season, Manchester United gave their kit contract to the firm, soon to be followed by West Ham, Sheffield United, Norwich and Leicester.

Later in 1974, Revie would of course become the new England manager and again, in an attempt to make his international players feel special, he called upon Admiral to create a new, modern, well-designed strip that was cutting edge. Rather like Revie's reign, it was not well-liked. Featuring a pointed collar and bold red and blue lines down the sleeves of the traditional white England shirt, it was over-fussy and ugly, and controversially, the first national strip to feature the manufacturer's logo. And like Revie, the design didn't last long.

In the early to mid-1970s, the FA remained resolute in their opposition to large-scale kit sponsorship. One club decided to take them on and defy the ban on paid-for shirt logos. No, not Manchester United, Arsenal, Liverpool or Chelsea, but Southern League Kettering Town. In 1976, the club had an extremely high-profile player-manager and chief executive in former Wolves legend Derek Dougan. One of football's true progressives, this man of many jobs was at the same time chairman of the Professional Footballers' Association, fighting for players' rights and loved a good old scrap against the authorities. Kettering were skint and Dougan used his extensive contacts to broker a money-spinning four-figure sponsorship deal to help ease their problems.

In January 1976, Kettering ran out to play Bath City wearing shirts that featured the brand Kettering Tyres. The FA came down upon Kettering like a ton of, well, very big tyres. They were warned that unless they removed the sponsorship slogan from their shirts, the club would be fined £1,000. Never a fan of the footballing establishment, Dougan cheekily changed the words on the shirts to 'Kettering T' claiming that the 'T' stood for Town. The FA were having none of it and gave the club one final chance to remove the slogan. Dougan told the press, 'It is inconceivable that petty-minded bureaucrats had only this to bother about.' Discussing the affair, Dave Moor, who runs the historicalkits.co.uk website, summed up the context to Dougan's trailblazing efforts succinctly, 'You've got to remember this was in the 70s – attendances were down, the game was losing its appeal and inflation was very high, so clubs were desperate for any kind of income.'

The truth was that all professional clubs in Britain were still hugely reliant on bums on seats to pay their bills and with attendances falling even the biggest clubs were anxious about raising their ticket prices. Many were now looking seriously at increasing their commercial activity away from the terraces to plug the financial gaps. Even the smaller clubs had begun to up their game in producing their own souvenir paraphernalia such as rosettes, scarves and club bobble hats, but this was piecemeal.

Dougan's pioneering move, albeit unsuccessful, illustrated the massive money-making potential of shirt sponsorship. If a non-league club like Kettering Town could broker a four-figure deal with a local tyre company, imagine the cash that could be made by bigger professional teams? Accordingly, several clubs began to lobby the FA to change their rules, pointing out that kit sponsorship was already legal in both Germany and France. In Germany,

Bayern Munich were earning a fortune after teaming up with Adidas. Under pressure, the FA caved in and from 1977 to 1980, 84 of the Football League's 92 clubs signed their first shirt sponsorship deals.

There were still some unexpected obstacles to overcome. Both the BBC and ITV refused to screen matches or highlights packages that featured teams wearing advertising slogans on their kit. But clubs soon found a way around this. Liverpool signed a £100,000 shirt deal with Japanese electronics giant Hitachi – written into the contract was a clause that the sponsorship logos could not be worn on the shirts for televised domestic games. That, of course, would all soon change and to bring us up to date, for the 2023/24 season, Chelsea signed a £40m shirt sponsorship deal with American sports technology company Infinite Athlete. Up on Merseyside, Liverpool are reported to have a £50m deal with Standard Chartered. At the other end of the East Lancs Road, Manchester City wear the Etihad brand on their shirts for a cool £70m a season. And they should all be thanking the vision and bloody-mindedness of Derek Dougan.

By the early 1970s, there was serious money to be made in boot endorsements. For decades, the major players in the market were both German, Adidas and Puma, and theirs is an everyday tale of Nazis, murderous sibling rivalry, betrayal and corporate intrigue. Back in the Weimar Republic of 1924, two Bavarian brothers, Rudolf and Adolf – Adi for short – both sons of a shoemaker, set up their own business, the Dassler Brothers Shoe Factory. The business-savvy siblings had spotted a gap in the market for mass-produced sports shoes and hit pay dirt. By the 1930s, their company was knocking out 200,000 pairs a year and the brothers had joined the Nazi Party. Now with friends in high places, the Dassler brothers landed a huge contract making army boots for the Wehrmacht and made a lot of money out of the Second World War. In peacetime, the firm once again concentrated its efforts on producing sports shoes, and particularly football boots. With money they'd made from the war, the brothers were able to spend big on research and development and created a range of popular boot designs.

But they had grown to loathe one another, disagreeing on what direction their company should take and finally falling out big time in 1948 when they decided to part ways. Rudolf set up a new venture, Puma, while Adi created the sports shoe firm Adidas. From that day onwards, they would be in fierce and sometimes thoroughly bitter rivalry. Ironically, this intense competitiveness would lead to some of the football boot's greatest innovations. In 1952, Puma launched the revolutionary Pro-Atom, the first boot to feature screw-in studs.

The bitter Dassler family rivalry finally came to a head, first in 1972 and then again at the 1974 World Cup. Brazil of course had won the 1970 Mexico World Cup and Pelé was now indisputably the best footballer in the world. In 1972, the player's boot contract was up for renewal, which was a big deal commercially. To the surprise of many, Puma and Adidas signed a bizarre document that became known as 'The Pelé Pact', an agreement that the Brazilian's new boot contract should be regarded as 'out of bounds' for both companies, who were worried that a protracted bidding war between the two rivals would become prohibitively expensive. The deal was sealed but soon after, Rudolf Dassler's Puma firm broke their word and negotiated a $120,000 contract with Pelé plus a generous share of Puma King boot sales. Adidas were outraged, but worse was to come.

Another of Puma's most high-profile clients was the Netherlands' star player, Johan Cruyff, who had become a leading marketing tool for the company across Europe. At the 1974 World Cup in West Germany, this threw a major spanner in the works, because the Dutch national team was sponsored by, you guessed it, Adidas. Cruyff's Puma Kings boot deal was extremely lucrative and his shrewd father-in-law agent Cor Costers was not going to allow his most valuable client to be seen on the world's biggest stage wearing Adidas kit. Desperate to keep their talismanic striker onboard, the Dutch FA agreed to a compromise. Cruyff would be allowed to wear his Puma Kings and his shirt was re-purposed. The iconic Adidas three stripes on the sleeves design became two stripes and the Adidas logo was removed from Cruyff's shirt. Arguably, however, Adidas would eventually win the marketing battle that summer: in the final, West Germany's Gerd Müller would thump home the tournament winner from the toe of a custom-made Adidas boot.

Alongside the German giants, a new British company was making headway in capturing a substantial share of the football boot market – step forward Stylo Matchmakers. Back in 1964, the Bradford-based company bought out the high street shoe company Barratt's and their innovative board looked immediately to expanding the business into the sports shoe market, specifically in the worlds of tennis, golf and football. Thinking big, their first marketing move in 1966 was a pretty impressive one; to wit, signing up Pelé to a Stylo Matchmaker exclusive boot deal. The company followed this up two years later with a further eye-catching coup, taking on George Best to promote the launch of their new 'football shoe', the Heirship 68. Best was so impressed with his new boots that he soon persuaded team-mates Brian Kidd and Sammy McIlroy to wear them. By 1974, Stylo Matchmakers were being worn by the entire Celtic, Leeds, Liverpool, Sunderland and Fulham squads, and emerging new star Kevin Keegan agreed to launch their brand new boot design, Heirship 1974.

In an increasingly crowded and competitive market, product endorsements from top players and clubs were all well and good, but new brands were forced to find different 'wow' factors to convince the buying public to purchase their 'untried' brands. In 1970, Hummel was a relatively unknown German company who were keen to get a foothold in the British marketplace and set up a UK franchise. They made two key signings – World Cup winner Alan Ball and a former Slazenger marketing expert called Brian Hewitt. To make Hummel's products stand out against their competitors, Hewitt came up with a genius of an idea. Ball was due to play in the 1970 Charity Shield at Wembley and with it being televised live, the marketing guru realised this offered the perfect shop window for something a little different. To wit, the Hummel boots that Ball put his name to would not be black or brown, but brilliant white. They were rushed into production, but disaster struck. Ball was uncomfortable with the final result and not happy wearing a pair of boots he didn't yet fully trust, so was less than keen about using them in such a high-profile game.

Roll on Brian Hewitt's second stroke of genius. According to the splendid footy-boots.com website, Hewitt arranged for Ball's regular Adidas boots to be painted white and then had Hummel's distinctive chevron brand design stitched on the sides. Ball wore these in the Charity Shield game and Hewitt effectively earned Hummel a free 90-minute advert on the determinedly non-commercial BBC.

So unusual were Ball's white boots that they became the talk of the game. TV commentator Kenneth Wolstenholme mentioned them again and again, with BBC cameramen dutifully showing the boots in close-up to illustrate his comments. For Hewitt, it became a marketing triumph. As footy-boots.com pointed out, 'The Monday after the game, the Hummel sales line was ringing off the hook. Twelve thousand pairs of white boots were sold, more than doubling Hummel's entire sales quotas in one morning.' The firm then worked overtime to adapt and develop a genuine white Hummel boot that Ball was totally happy with and he was soon wearing the real thing. By 1974 he would be joined in the Hummel white boot camp by several other top players, including Arsenal's flamboyant forward Charlie George.

16

The Media

'I am unable to understand how a man of honour could take a newspaper in his hands without a shudder of disgust'

– French writer and poet Charles Baudelaire

IN THE early 1970s, Fleet Street editors had begun to realise that football sold newspapers – not just for match reports and news on the back pages but with stories, increasingly salacious and shock horror, on the front. The tabloids hit pay dirt prior to the 1970 Mexico World Cup when England captain Bobby Moore was arrested in Colombia for allegedly stealing a £600 gold and emerald bracelet from the team hotel's jewellery shop.

In a bid to acclimatise to the high altitudes they would experience at the finals, England were in town to play a friendly against the Colombian national team. Settling into their Bogotá hotel, Moore and Peter Thompson accompanied Bobby Charlton to an upmarket jeweller's shop in the building, to help him choose a gift for his wife. As they left without a purchase, an assistant ran after them, accusing Moore of slipping a bracelet into his inside jacket pocket without paying. Moore protested his innocence and offered to be searched. But soon the police had arrived and the man who lifted the World Cup four years earlier was arrested.

The World Cup was just days away and Britain's national press went into overdrive. For days, Moore's plight filled the tabloid front pages and a legion of reporters were despatched to South America to dig up new angles on the story. The *Daily Mirror* ran an exclusive about a 'mystery woman' who was rumoured to have tried to sell the 'Bogotá Bracelet' to members of the local Colombian underworld, and other tabloids came up with several colourful conspiracy theories. Unknown South Americans within the football community were trying to sabotage England's campaign by 'taking out' their iconic World Cup-winning captain; it was an attempt by the Colombian mafia to frame and then blackmail the world-famous player. Several 'witnesses' offered up wildly varying descriptions of what happened but ultimately, after pressure from British PM Harold Wilson, Moore was given a conditional discharge and allowed to travel on to Mexico. Bizarrely, it would take two years for the Colombian courts to decide that Moore was the totally innocent victim of a frame-up. But Britain's tabloid press had a field day and it was proof positive that football on the front pages sold copies. From then on, non-sporting journalists began to take a serious interest in the private lives of Britain's footballers.

By 1974, the player above all others that they pursued was the one-man soap opera called George Best. Once used to playing alongside fellow stellar talents like Bobby Charlton, Denis Law and Brian Kidd, Best had become increasingly disenchanted with the quality of players now arriving at Old Trafford and was fast falling out of love with football. By 1974, his life had become a dysfunctional, drink-fuelled saga. Without the stern hand of Sir Matt Busby to keep him in line, the abundantly gifted Northern Irishman had become a problem for himself and for Manchester United. First Wilf McGuinness, then Frank O'Farrell and finally Tommy Docherty struggled with Best's increasingly contrary ways. After a series of disciplinary fines from the club, Docherty was in despair but continued to persevere. On 1 January 1974 the Scotsman picked Best to start against Queens Park Rangers at Loftus Road and it ended in tears. United were beaten 3-0 and it should have been by more. Best looked unfit and well off the pace and compounded his poor performance by then not turning up for training three days later. This was the final straw for Docherty, who dropped Best for the following weekend's FA Cup tie against Third Division Plymouth Argyle. Enraged by his manager's decision, Best quit and left Old Trafford for ever.

The following month, he was all over the tabloid front pages for days on end, after two Met policemen were sent up from London to question him at Slack Alice's, the club he co-owned in Manchester city centre, over theft allegations. This was not any old theft and in true George Best style it involved booze and beauty queens. It was alleged that the twinkle-toed, and now it was alleged, light-fingered winger had broken into the London flat of his former girlfriend, Miss World Marjorie Wallace, and made off with a fur coat, a passport and bottles of spirits. The paparazzi followed Best everywhere, to give constant coverage of the latest episodes in his hedonistic, champagne-fuelled lifestyle, and some weeks later he appeared in front of Marylebone Magistrates' Court to answer the charges; a no-show from Miss World meant they were dropped. The whole protracted affair filled hundreds of column inches in the red tops and helped circulation no end, as did Slack Alice's. The venue had become a regular haunt for a lot of top north-west footballers and thus became a magnet for tabloid reporters and photographers keen to sniff out any scandal.

The 1970s was the heyday of the tabloids and a massive circulation war, particularly between the country's best-selling red top, Robert Maxwell's *Daily Mirror*, and Rupert Murdoch's newly relaunched *The Sun*, was under way. Footballers were now fair game. The media was changing. George Best aside, who was a tabloid gift that just kept giving, news reporters – as opposed to football journalists – were ever on the lookout for potential new footballing icons to build up and then knock down. In 1974, the next man to find himself on the conveyor belt was rising new star Kevin Keegan. During the summer, England had embarked upon a short friendly tour of eastern Europe. After beating Bulgaria in Sofia, the squad flew to Belgrade to play Yugoslavia. Their plane arrived at the airport an hour early and there was no one present to officially greet them. Still cock-a-hoop from their win in Sofia and bored with having to hang around for the Yugoslav welcoming party to arrive, some of the England players clowned around on the baggage reclaim conveyor belt waiting for their luggage.

Keegan had slept all the way through the flight and, still knackered, sat down on the edge of the luggage rack. Minutes later, half a dozen armed guards appeared and aggressively shooed the players off the conveyor belt then, spotting Keegan dozing and prone, grabbed him by the neck and dragged him off to a nearby customs office. And then they locked the door. On his return to Merseyside, Keegan told the *Liverpool Daily Post* the rest of the story, 'I was hit in the face and that started my nose bleeding … I was made to kneel in the corner. I was hit eight or nine times and kicked twice. They did not know I was a footballer and when they did find out, they told me to wipe my face so the blood wouldn't show. I did absolutely nothing wrong and said nothing. I don't hold grudges. But I don't have to tell you the satisfaction I felt when I scored our equaliser against Yugoslavia.'

Weeks earlier, Keegan had been served notice by the tabloid press that his life was no longer his own. In September, he'd secretly married his long-term girlfriend Jean in front of 14 close family relatives at a Catholic church in Doncaster, keen to enjoy their ceremony in private, away from the public spotlight. It didn't stay secret for long. Two days later, the *Daily Mirror* splashed the story all over its front pages in a piece that contained an old tabloid trick. Buried a good few paragraphs into the story was a short, seemingly innocuous line that let the reader know that not one single member of the Liverpool squad had been invited to the wedding. In other words, Keegan had 'snubbed them' on his big day. The truth was that Keegan and his new wife wanted the wedding to be a small, private affair. But once again, the England striker realised that his personal life was now totally up for grabs. Football was becoming a spectator sport in more ways than one.

By 1974, there was more and more football on television, but few live matches. The Football League remained ever-fearful that showing full 90-minute match coverage of games would have a devastating impact on attendances and continued to stonewall the TV companies – as they had done back in 1927, to stop BBC Radio covering full live matches. As a result, the only live games shown on television were almost exclusively cup finals and internationals. The order of the day was the slickly edited 'highlights package' – ten to 15 minutes culled from the weekend's best, usually top-flight, games.

Television coverage was becoming ever more sophisticated. The BBC and most of the ITV regions had been broadcasting in colour since 1969 and filming at many grounds was multi-camera. The Beeb's *Match of the Day* was far and away the most popular football show on TV and in 1974 it was averaging a viewing audience of 12 million, despite going out late at night at 10pm. Rather cutely, figures always went higher when viewers realised that the night's programme was to feature a high-scoring game from the afternoon. The world's longest-running football television programme first aired on 22 August 1964 on BBC2 and it was far from an instant hit. The debut show featured highlights of Liverpool v Arsenal and drew a miserable audience of just 20,000 – less than half the amount of people who'd turned up at Anfield in the afternoon to watch the game proper. But it began to grow in popularity to such an extent that by the late 1960s, BBC controllers decided to move it on to BBC1.

In 1969, *Match of the Day* pioneered the use of slow-motion replays, and in 1973 it scored a famous victory by poaching Jimmy Hill from ITV as the show's main presenter – he would stay in the *MOTD* chair until 1988. Each edition engaged a small army of technicians and production specialists. The average top-flight match that the team covered involved a large mobile studio van parked right up next to the stadium and five different camera vantage points – four inside the ground and one atop a crane 90 feet above the pitch. Lead commentator Barry Davies gave an expert blow-by-blow account of the entire 90 minutes and the feed and various different camera angles were transmitted from the mobile unit back to BBC Television Centre, where the rest of the production crew made careful notes about the game's best moments and their precise timings. After the final whistle blew, the mobile crew packed up for the day and the hard yards were now down to the team back at Television Centre. Their task, to turn 90 minutes of live football into a seamlessly edited 25-minute highlights segment in under four hours. As the film editors furiously cut and spliced, script editors consulted with Hill and then put the final touches together for his script. As if by magic, the show was always ready to roll come 9.59pm every Saturday night.

In 1974, *Match of the Day* gained a sister programme, *Football Focus*. Broadcast live and put out on Saturday lunchtimes to preview that coming day's football fixtures as part of the BBC's regular five-hour *Grandstand* sports show, it was presented by Sam Leitch and Arsenal's legendary ex-goalie Bob Wilson, the latter of whom would remain a fixture on the show for the next 20 years. Not to be outdone, the ITV network launched its own half-hour-long national football show soon after, *On the Ball*. Presented by the perennially cheerful Brian Moore, it would form the first segment of their weekly Saturday *World of Sport* programme. The ITV network in 1974 was still strongly regionalised, so apart from *On the Ball*, virtually every area had its own dedicated local football show.

In the footballing hotbed of the north-west they had three, all produced by the mighty Granada. The weekend kicked off with a 30-minute Friday evening preview programme, *Kick Off*, that covered the following day's fixtures for no fewer than 19 local professional clubs – Manchester's United and City, Liverpool, Everton, Burnley, Blackpool, Preston North End, Bolton Wanderers, Blackburn Rovers, Oldham Athletic, Bury, Stockport County, Rochdale, Tranmere Rovers, Chester, Crewe Alexandra, Southport, Barrow and Wigan Athletic. On Sunday afternoons, viewers got to watch a full highlights package simply entitled *Football*, and then during the week there was a football game show, *Kick Off Quiz*. The presenter of all three programmes throughout the 1970s was the avuncular Gerald Sinstadt.

Down in London and the south-east, two TV companies shared the local football action. On Sundays, London Weekend Television broadcast a 30-minute highlights show, *The Big Match*, with Brian Moore both presenting and commentating. In 1974, Thames Television were responsible for the Greater London area's broadcasting from Mondays to Fridays and they ran a regular football highlights show, *The Mid-Week Match*. Like LWT, Thames covered 13 different clubs: Arsenal, Tottenham Hotspur, West Ham United, Chelsea, Fulham, Queens Park Rangers, Crystal Palace, Charlton Athletic, Millwall, Orient, Watford, Brentford and Wimbledon.

ATV represented the Midlands with their 30-minute Sunday afternoon highlights package, *Star Soccer*, with a young Gary Newbon operating as interviewer and link man, and match commentary coming from the highly respected broadcaster Hugh Johns, who'd delivered the commentary for ITV's 1966 World Cup Final coverage. Their remit was to cover 15 different clubs – West Bromwich Albion, Wolverhampton Wanderers, Derby County, Stoke City, Notts County, Nottingham Forest, Birmingham City, Aston Villa, Leicester City, Coventry City, Oxford United, Shrewsbury Town, Hereford United, Walsall and Port Vale.

Over to the east, Anglia TV offered a Sunday afternoon show that mainly followed Norwich City, Ipswich Town, Peterborough United, Luton Town and Hull City, though Grimsby Town and Colchester United did get the odd look-in. Throughout the 1970s, the voice of Anglia TV football was Gerry Harrison. Starting out in print journalism, most notably with the *Daily Express*, Harrison entered the BBC's Find a Commentator competition and though he finished in the top six, the Beeb passed on his talents. Their loss was Anglia's gain and Harrison became a much-loved commentator and then, in 1985, head of sport for Anglia TV.

Tyne Tees Television had a long-running football show called *Shoot*, that started off in the early 1960s as a

30-minute Saturday night programme, but by 1974 and by popular demand, this had expanded to 55 minutes and aired on Sunday afternoons. Tyne Tees only had five professional clubs to cover and of those, it was only really Newcastle United, Sunderland and Middlesbrough that got a look in. During the 1973/74 season, Hartlepool were featured on just one single occasion with highlights from their clash against Swansea City on 13 April. Poor old Darlington didn't feature once. In 1974, Tyne Tees pulled off a rare coup and engaged BBC legend Kenneth Wolstenholme as their lead commentator. This was the man who had commentated on 23 successive FA Cup finals, five World Cups, and of course, at Wembley in 1966, delivered possibly the most famous line of football commentary in sporting history, 'Some people are on the pitch – they think it's all over.' And then as Geoff Hurst struck his hat-trick and England's fourth, Wolstenholme delivered the *coup de grâce*, 'It is now.'

Like Granada, Yorkshire TV offered no less than three football programmes every week. In 1974, Yorkshire football was on the up and up. Alongside the stellar achievements of Don Revie's Leeds United, Sheffield United were more than a half-decent First Division side, and Jack Charlton's Middlesbrough had steamrollered the Second Division with a record-breaking points total. Interestingly, Boro received way more TV coverage than any other club outside the top flight because of their geographical position. Though in the north-east, the Middlesbrough of 1974 was still inside the Yorkshire boundary, and indeed regularly staged first-class matches for Yorkshire County Cricket Club. As a consequence, Big Jack's games were alternately seen on both Tyne Tees and Yorkshire TV.

Border TV was a strange fish indeed. When it was awarded a licence back in the early 1960s, a lot of media experts scratched their heads. Based in Carlisle and Selkirk, the local channel served two very distinctly different cultural areas – to the south, Cumbria, the Lake District and small industrial towns like Barrow, Workington and Maryport plus the area's only city, Carlisle, which had a population of less than 100,000. To the north and into Scotland, the rural wilds of the border counties, tiny towns like Hawick and Selkirk and hundreds of small villages and hamlets. Border's budget was small and compared to other ITV channels, resources were extremely limited. From the off, it produced a lot of good local news coverage but hardly any football or sport-related programmes. What its station controllers did extremely well was to cleverly find Border TV a unique niche within the ITV network, by using its studios to churn out daytime television quiz shows, most notably the hugely popular *Mr and Mrs*, which to keep costs down was hosted by their assistant controller Derek Batey. But in 1974, virtually all of its football highlights coverage was bought in from other regions, most notably Granada, Tyne Tees and Yorkshire. Which was a shame for Carlisle United, who in 1974/75 were enjoying their one and only season in the top flight.

In 1974, Britain's top-selling football magazine was the weekly *Shoot!*, which pretty much had the field to itself until *Match* was launched in 1979. *When Saturday Comes* would not emerge until a decade later and magazines like *FourFourTwo* wouldn't arrive until the Premier League boom of the 1990s. Aimed fairly and squarely at the youth market, *Shoot!*'s very first masthead in 1969 declared itself to be 'a terrific new football paper for boys' though it quickly became an adult footie fan favourite too. Former Newcastle and England star Chris Waddle even recalled the magazine being much read by fellow footballers on team coaches to games. It was launched in an age of colour – the same year, both the BBC and ITV had switched over from monochrome black and white – and was packed with photographs. Each issue featured a two-page colour centrefold of a team plus full-page colour photos of not just top players, but those playing further down the leagues. Regular features included 'Focus On…' which was a weekly questionnaire where an individual player was asked about their likes and dislikes, food they enjoyed, music they listened to and what their favourite films and TV programmes were. Mick Channon told readers that his 'best friend' was his bank manager, while Arsenal's John Radford declared his favourite actors to be Tom and Jerry. Players like Kevin Keegan and Billy Bremner 'wrote' regular columns about issues within the game and a perennial favourite was 'You Are The Ref' – a weekly cartoon strip that presented a hypothetical on-the-field situation and asked the reader to make the correct refereeing decision based upon the information given.

Refreshingly, *Shoot!* credited its young target readership with intelligence and between the shorter pop culture pieces were features that were often lengthy, text heavy and detailed in their analysis. On the eve of each season, the magazine also gave away free cardboard 'league ladders' plus movable cardboard tabs containing the name of each Football League and Scottish league team. Every week readers would check the latest scores and rearrange their league ladders accordingly. In the pre-internet analogue era of the early 1970s, the magazine was an important source of football information and by 1974 was selling well over 200,000 copies a week. Its only real competition was *Charles Buchan's Football Monthly*, which by now was 23 years old and still named after a player who had ceased playing back in 1928 and died in 1961. *Charles Buchan's Football Monthly* had been stuck in the mud for years and, compared to the exciting new kid on the block, it was a little worthy and outdated.

Another important source of information continued to be the Saturday evening newspaper sporting 'pinks' and 'greens', so-called because of the colour of the paper they were printed upon. Produced by local and regional evening newspapers, these swiftly put-together publications would hit the street often less than an hour after Saturday games had finished, complete with match reports, results, attendances and goal details. Hot off the press was an understatement. Although most of the features, interviews and stories on the inside pages were written and prepared earlier in the week were pre-internet, they were the most up-to-date information football fans could get about their local teams.

The work that went into producing the pinks and greens was testament to the ingenuity and organisational skills of the local press. Match reporters at the ground would arrive early to do their homework then phone in some introductory paragraphs and team line-ups just prior to kick-off, and then continue to phone in every 15 to 20 minutes to relate the latest action to copy typists back in the newsroom. Subeditors would rapidly edit through each new set of paragraphs and then they would be run down to the printing presses and marked up on hot metal print, ready to be published at full time. This was of course a long time before the emergence of the mobile phone and although the press boxes in some football grounds contained landlines, many did not. Particularly when covering away matches, the reporter's first job was to locate the nearest public telephone box or persuade a nearby local householder to let them use their phone and reverse the charges back to the newsroom.

In the 1980s I worked as a journalist for the *Sheffield Star* evening newspaper and early in my career was dispatched to cover a couple of Worksop Town games in the old Northern

Premier League, knowing nothing much about the team or its players. I can safely tell you that was the least of my problems. The stress and tension of first finding a nearby phone box that wasn't out of order and then racing out of the ground every 15 minutes or so to ring over my latest copy was nerve-wracking in the extreme. There was a public phone box just outside the ground but as I soon discovered, it was out of order. After a frantic search, I found a fully functioning box a five-minute jog from the stadium. So every 15 minutes, I would take ten minutes running to and from the phone box, spend five minutes phoning over my copy and then return to the ground, to anxiously interrogate the local *Worksop Guardian* reporter about what had happened during my absence. In total, I probably only saw about ten minutes of the match, but thank goodness I had my friendly press colleague to keep me up to speed. He was an affable elderly man and generous with his help and support – but as I was soon to discover, not wildly accurate. He had a few days to correct any details about the match before his weekly deadline – I did not. I phoned everything over and left the ground drenched with nervous sweat eternally grateful just to go home.

At eight o'clock on Monday morning I turned in for work as usual, and discovered what I can only describe as an angry note on my desk in the *Sheffield Star* newsroom. All written in capital letters and containing many exclamation marks, it was a less than jolly missive from my newspaper's sports editor. 'Great match report Marvin,' it began, instantly wrong-footing me. Wow, I thought, I've passed muster for my first live football coverage. But then I read on, and of course realised that the first four words were marinaded in sarcasm. I, or more to the point my elderly reporting colleague, had got not only the score wrong – it was a 2-2 draw which I had written up as a 2-1 win for

Worksop – I'd wrongly identified two of the scorers and missed two yellow cards.

The sports journo's final job was to ring through the full-time score, scorers, attendance, bookings and sendings-off and any late newsworthy details. And then the presses began to roll. Within minutes, the pinks and greens were being bundled and launched into the back of vans to be driven to newsagents around the region, where fans would already be forming long queues, expectantly awaiting their arrival. Some newspapers, like the Wolverhampton *Express and Star*, the *Shropshire Star* and the Birmingham dailies all shared overlapping circulation patches and covered the same regional matches, and then the race to deliver quickest was vital to sales. In some further-flung areas, the job of the delivery driver could be a long-distance one. The last stops for the Aberdeen evening newspaper pink were over 40 miles away in Fraserburgh. The halcyon days of the sports green and pinks was the early to mid-1950s, when hundreds of thousands of copies were sold up and down the country every Saturday. By 1974, circulation figures had dropped but the pinks and greens were still immensely popular.

In 1974, the quickest way to get up-to-date football news and hot-off-the-press results was to tune into a truly revolutionary new television service. Launched in September of that year, the BBC's Ceefax became the world's first teletext information service. As well as carrying pages of interactive general news, features and recipes, viewers could key in a page number to get running football scores before they appeared on the five o'clock TV results shows. It wasn't the internet, but for the time Ceefax was a game-changer.

17

The Grounds

'Be it ever so humble, there's no place like home'

– Old English proverb

FOR THE committed football fan, your team's ground is that second home. The place where you feel welcomed and comfortable. But like many of our own homes, which might need some TLC, serious work on a tired-looking old bathroom or kitchen, essential repairs on that leaking roof or proper attention to the DIY improvement jobs that we started but never finished, most grounds in 1974 were similarly neglected and worse. In fact a lot were aged, dilapidated basket cases. The last new stadia to be built, and then only a handful, were now over 20 years old and much of the rest had been constructed in Victorian days and in the early decades of the 20th century. Most had been kept in any semblance of order with make-do-and-mend repairs, the odd stand extension and minor ground rebuilds. At best, any progress in improving grounds was spasmodic and piecemeal, largely reactive, seldom part of any new vision to make life safer or more comfortable for the fans.

Before he died, my late uncle Albert told me of his experiences watching Bradford City at Valley Parade during the 1973/74 season and life in the ground was far from salubrious, 'The place was dropping to bits. There were holes on the top of the stands so if you were in the wrong place, you'd get wet through on rainy afternoons. A lot of the seats were broken and unsittable upon, just left to rot. Nothing ever seemed to get cleaned, it was all grime and dirt.' And as Albert told me – don't get me started on the toilets, 'You could smell the stench from 20 yards away. I mean we put up with it because City was our club. But you did now and again think, well they treat us like shit. Yet we're their fans, the people who pay money to keep them afloat. Can that be right? But you were just used to it and had been for years. You put up with it but it did often rankle with me, how bad the club treated us.'

Albert was not alone in this feeling. Many clubs simply took their supporters for granted. They habitually turned up, paid their money, so why worry? Most football fans know what happened at Valley Parade 11 years later, but for those who don't, here are the facts behind one of English sport's most harrowing modern-day tragedies.

The club were on the up, having just won the Third Division championship, their first major silverware for 56 years. On 11 May, Bradford played their last home game of the season against Lincoln City, having already secured the title. The afternoon was to be one of celebration for the success-starved supporters and the ground was packed with 11,076, nearly double the Valley Parade season average of 6,610. Before the game kicked off, Bradford-born captain Peter Jackson and his players paraded the Third Division trophy around all four corners of the ground. The match finally started at 3.04pm, in front of the watching Yorkshire TV television cameras, who were recording the game for their edited football highlights show.

The first 40 minutes proved to be a fairly dull affair on the pitch, but at 3.44pm local TV sports commentator John Helm spotted something off it – concerned, he reported that a small fire had started three rows from the back of the old wooden Midland Road stand in Block G. Within four minutes, the structure was completely ablaze, clouds of thick black smoke billowing up into the Bradford sky from the tar-covered wooden roof. Fifty-six fans were killed and nearly 300 injured, many seriously. The Popplewell Inquiry into the tragedy heard that prior to the match, the fire brigade had twice written to Bradford City warning them about a major build-up of rubbish and litter that filled a cavity beneath the dilapidated old wooden stand. It represented a major fire risk, but nothing was done about the warnings because 48 hours after the Lincoln match, demolition was due to begin on the old stand to make way for a new concrete and steel structure. The inquiry was told that the fire had been caused by a discarded lit cigarette falling through a gap in the wooden flooring and on to the tinderbox that lay heaped up in the cavity below.

In 1974, the pitches were often dire. Mud heaps throughout the winter months and into spring, almost devoid of grass. Go on to YouTube and watch highlights from any game during the 1973/74 season at whatever level, and what most have in common is crap pitches, Wembley included. Indeed, the FA were so concerned about the state of the playing surface at the national stadium that they'd approached Doncaster Rovers about buying their pitch off them for £10,000. Belle Vue had a reputation for maintaining a really good standard of turf reliability and even in the worst of weathers, most Rovers matches went ahead. The deal was never done, because as Doncaster pointed out to the hopeful naives at the FA, the pitch was so good thanks to what was underneath it. Their playing surface had been built on top of ash clinker, which allowed for excellent drainage when the weather was bad. So the very idea of the FA just buying Doncaster's turf was a nonsense. But it did reveal the ignorance at the very top about what was needed in creating the most important part of playing football – a good pitch.

Modern-day fans are so used to the manicured, well-drained, often undersoil-heated lawns that most of our clubs play on, watching footage of games from the period often appears laughable because of the state of the pitches. I recommend you go on to YouTube and watch Derby County v Velež Mostar from the UEFA Cup in 1974. This was an important top-level European game, but check out the muddy ploughed Baseball Ground pitch that the two sets of players got the green light to play on. Spare a thought though for Derby's long-suffering 1970s groundsman Bob Smith, who took on one of the toughest jobs in football at the time. Talking in later years to the *Derby Evening Telegraph*, Smith described the enormity of his task. The Baseball Ground pitch was four feet below street level, which caused severe and permanent drainage problems. In a match against Manchester City, Derby were awarded a penalty but the pitch was in such a state that the penalty spot had disappeared under a sea of mud. The game had to be halted, for Smith to jog on with a pot of white paint, measure out the 12 yards from the goal line and mark a new penalty spot on top of the muck. The penalty was successfully dispatched in what would turn out to be a 4-0 Derby win, but minutes later, the new penalty spot had been squelched into the mud and lost again. Smith recalled, 'There was one match around Christmas time when there wasn't a single blade of grass on the pitch.'

At most grounds, the go-to solution for drenched and muddy pitches was sand, and lots of it. By the turn of the year, most playing surfaces looked like Margate beach and a lofted ball would never bounce or run true when it finally reached the deck, just plop on to the sand and stay there. And yet it was rare in 1974 for matches to be called off because of the state of the ground. So just imagine the condition of some of the pitches down in the Third and Fourth Divisions throughout the winter of 1973/74. It's perhaps no coincidence that the 1960s and 1970s were full of FA and League Cup giant-killings. When the pitches were so poor they became match-levellers, with the silkier skills and more advanced technique of top-level players being lost in the mud and poor conditions. This created a different form of match, one based upon raw-boned physical endeavour, toughness and sheer bloody-minded do-or-die attitudes.

Despite these many shortcomings, it was a quiet year for ground improvements – and we'll soon discover why. Sunderland did open a new suite of private boxes and installed an underground sprinkler system; Arsenal spent £30,000 on undersoil heating to improve the state of their pitch. The three biggest developments of 1974 were at Chelsea, Liverpool and Burnley. Chelsea's largely homegrown young team had challenged for honours under manager Tommy Docherty for much of the 1960s, and under his successor Dave Sexton, won the FA Cup Final 2-1 against Leeds (after a replay) in 1970; a year later, they overcame the mighty Real Madrid to win the UEFA Cup Winners' Cup. Confidence at the club was high and off the back of these successes, chairman Brian Mears headed up an ambitious plan to revamp a now very tired-looking Stamford Bridge. The ground may have been large but it was far from pretty. A hotch-potch of jarringly different stands that included the aptly named Shed End, the east side of the Bridge contained a structure that had seen better days. Though designed by the illustrious football ground architect

Archibald Leitch, the old east stand was also limited in capacity, contained many poor sight lines and in the many years since its opening had become run-down and scruffy.

The Chelsea board's plan was to trash the old stand and in its place, build an edifice worthy of a top First Division club. They employed top architects Darbourne and Darke, who had made their name designing innovative new social housing, and charged them with creating a new stand that would impress. Mears proudly boasted, 'We believe this is the biggest reconstruction ever undertaken at a British football ground. We are not just building a new stand, but virtually a new stadium.' The ambition was clear, the timing unfortunate. Work on the new stand began in 1972, which meant that Stamford Bridge was only able to allow fans into the other three sides of the ground for well over two seasons. At a time when they most needed matchday cash to help fund the new venture, Chelsea's attendances dropped dramatically.

In 1970, the average gate at Stamford Bridge was 40,342. Thanks to an economic downturn, industrial action and ultimately, the challenges of the three-day week, the supposed one-year project was heavily delayed and dragged on well into the 1973/74 season. With one side of the ground still a building site, Chelsea's average home gate had dwindled to 25,983. Allied to this morale within the squad was not good. Unhappy with the pokey and basic temporary dressing rooms, players were also growing disgruntled with manager Sexton; star performers Peter Osgood and Alan Hudson had fall-outs with him that led to both leaving and signing on for Stoke City. Though their transfers put some much needed cash into the dwindling coffers, it damaged the quality of the squad and on the pitch, the team went into a sharp decline. Chelsea would end the 1974/75 season relegated into the Second Division. The magnificent new

East Stand was officially opened in August 1974, its sheer height completely dwarfing the rest of Stamford Bridge. But any further development on the other three sides had to wait. The wonderful new stand was now threatening the very financial stability of the club; to help pay for it, Chelsea needed to average at least 31,000 for each of their home games – in 1974/75, the average gate was 27,366. Up on the season before, but still well short of the club's break-even.

Further north, Burnley and Liverpool both showed their ambition by opening two new stands. Burnley chairman Bob Lord had long been a Marmite figure in English football. The son of a barber, he wheeled and dealed his way to become the owner of a meat factory and 14 local butchers shops around north Lancashire and was a man of multiple contradictions. A passionate Burnley fan, he became club chairman in 1955 and remained in the post for the following 26 years. Throughout the late 1950s and into the 60s, he oversaw the most successful passage in Burnley's history. Coming from a relatively small industrial town, his beloved club continued to cock a snook at the big-spending, big-city clubs, winning the First Division championship in 1960 and continuing to compete well at the highest level. There's no doubt that Lord was clever in knowing which direction the wind was blowing when it suited his interests best. A regular at the Burnley Conservative Club and a friend of Tory leader Edward Heath, the only political contributions he ever made were to the Labour Party. As a chairman, Lord was passionately opposed to the abolition of the maximum wage for footballers; and then when the PFA won their long campaign, he immediately made his star Burnley player Jimmy McIlroy the best-paid performer in the Football League on £100 a week. Described as the Khrushchev of Burnley after the then Soviet Union's autocratic leader, he banned numerous sports journalists and broadcasters from

Turf Moor if he disagreed with their reporting and fined his players if they talked to those of whom he disapproved.

He was short-sighted and yet sometimes visionary. Lord remained utterly opposed to televised football which he believed would destroy clubs financially, though successive TV deals brought vast new tranches of money into the professional game. He even banned TV coverage at Turf Moor. But he also predicted that greed for more cash would lead to attempts to form a European super league over 40 years before it was ever attempted. Though a hard-nosed businessman who checked every penny that went in and out of Burnley FC, he had the vision to sign off a substantial amount of money to create and build one of Europe's most forward-looking and modern training grounds, and facilities at Turf Moor were among the best in the top flight. Lord was anti-trade union but paid his workers what were very good local wages by any comparison. In return, he demanded total loyalty and hard bloody work.

The *Burnley Express* related a Christmas Bob Lord tale that seems to perfectly sum up his pragmatic attitude to life, almost echoing Charles Dickens' Scrooge. One Christmas Eve, his company's van drivers had all arrived back at base after spending an early start to the day delivering a massive consignment of Lord's turkeys, chickens, pork and beef. The day had made their boss a huge amount of money. It was mid-afternoon and after cleaning out their vans, the drivers decamped to the works canteen to start celebrating their Christmas. When Lord learned that they'd knocked off early, even though it was Christmas Eve afternoon, he was apoplectic. According to the *Burnley Express* writer David Thomas, 'Down he marched to the canteen, polished shoes thumping on the cobbles. Face set like a bulldog, fists clenched. And when he gets there and confronts them all, he sacks them on the spot. At least Ebenezer Scrooge had an ounce of feeling left in him and didn't actually sack Bob Cratchit.'

By all accounts, his meat factory foreman took Lord to one side and pointed out one tiny logistical snag, 'Nah thee has sacked yon lads, who will thee get to do the deliveries when we get back after Christmas?' Lord mulled it over, thought twice and then sent a message to all his drivers that they were reinstated and should report for work as normal after Christmas. And just for good measure, he sent them all a free Christmas turkey.

Lord was determined to stamp his mark on Burnley and what better way than to build a big new stand and name it after yourself? The 2,500-seater construction also included several luxury executive boxes and though simple in design – a plain flat roof over steeply raked seating – the Bob Lord Stand was a welcome addition to Turf Moor. Though Lord's name was writ big along the top of the new stand, Burnley wags soon renamed it 'The Martin Dobson Stand' – so-called because the unpopular £300,000 sale of their star performer to Everton went a long way to paying for the work. More of Burnley's best players followed him out of the door and two years later, the Clarets were also relegated to the Second Division.

Over at Anfield, Liverpool were one of the few top clubs whose attendances had risen season upon season, and to help house more fans the board decided to partially demolish the old Main Stand and then extend it out backwards underneath an enormous new roof. Opened by the Duke of Kent in March 1973, the new Main Stand housed 8,600 in the upper section and 2,150 in the paddock underneath. Unlike Chelsea and Burnley, Liverpool's new development was prudently budgeted, delivered on time and led to neither player sales nor relegation. Indeed, the Reds further strengthened an already First Division championship-winning squad and went on to win multiple European and domestic trophies.

Most other clubs were holding back on making ground improvements because of two important developments. With attendances falling generally, many were simply skint – desperate for money, Swansea were forced to sell their Vetch Field ground to the local council for £50,000 plus a £150,000 grant to help keep them in business. From then on, it was a case of short-term, day-to-day repairs only. The ailing, flailing and failing Bradford Park Avenue had crashed out of the Football League the season before, unable to gain re-election for the fourth time on the trot, and were so hard-up they had to sell their fine old historic Park Avenue home to property developers, and ground-share Valley Parade with their arch-rivals Bradford City. Many lower-league sides were deeply in the red, and some bigger clubs had overreached in the hope of success and spent unwisely. And the second element?

In 1974 a bill was going through parliament that would cause a financial revolution in British football and clubs were nervously holding back on prematurely spending money on their grounds, in anticipation of it becoming law. Three years earlier, 66 people were killed and over 200 injured at the end of an Old Firm derby at Ibrox Park. Around 80,000 fans had packed into the ground on a foggy 2 January and all the match action came right at the end. With a minute left on the clock, the game was goalless but then up stepped Jimmy 'Jinky' Johnstone to fire in what looked to be the Celtic winner. But seconds later, Rangers' Colin Stein scored an unlikely last-gasp equaliser. At the Rangers end, the fans went mental and as the whistle blew, thousands of them clattered boisterously down the uneven five flights of steps on the already notorious Stairwell 13. Ten years previously, two fans had died in a fatal crush at the same exit and throughout the following decade, dozens of Rangers supporters had been injured in incidents on the stairwell. On 2 January, it tragically became the location for Scotland's worst sporting disaster.

According to the resulting inquest, one or two fans had lost their footing in the surging crush of bodies, tripped and made other supporters around them fall. As they fell, hundreds more plummeted down the stairs and landed on top of them. Pathologist Professor Giles Forbes told the inquest that 60 of those killed had died from asphyxiation, the remaining six from suffocation. At one point on the stairs, the dead were piled prone and crushed on the ground six feet deep. Everyone who perished was under 50 years of age.

One man who survived was 27-year-old *Daily Express* sports journalist John Hodgson, who wrote a chilling eyewitness account of the tragedy: 'I clung frantically to a fence and as the seething mass crushed past me, I saw the first of the white handkerchiefs waved in terror. Further down some fans had fallen and the crowd was piling on top of them, but it was impossible to slow the crowd up; to let them know they were singing and dancing their way towards a horrible death … I did what I could. With brave, weeping policemen and heroic ambulancemen, I pounded the chests of those who showed small stirrings of life, in an effort to get their hearts moving. I pulled youngsters from the jumbled pile of bodies. We laid the dead aside and covered their faces. It was a frantic fight to save the living … I saw two policemen carry a small covered bundle to the top of the stairs and one of them wept as he repeated over and over again, "It's only a wee boy."'

It stirred horrific memories for Hodgson. As a young Rangers fan he had been badly injured on the very same stairwell during the fatal 1961 tragedy. Nineteen-year-old

Celtic player Kenny Dalglish would later experience an awful déjà vu of his own again and again, an anguished witness to the tragedies at Heysel and Hillsborough. Prime Minister Edward Heath called for an immediate inquiry into not only the Ibrox tragedy, but safety in general at Britain's professional football grounds. Though there was never any suggestion that the awful events at Ibrox had been caused by any form of hooliganism, the government was becoming increasingly nervous about the depressing headlines that football violence was bringing on to the front pages of the nation's national newspapers. Senior Scottish judge Lord Wheatley was tasked with producing an inquiry into the state of safety measures at English and Scottish league grounds. For 12 months, expert members of his investigating team, which included former England manager Walter Winterbottom, collected evidence and information from over 60 clubs; what they discovered was hardly surprising.

With the lack of any uniform strategy or framework, the clubs all ploughed their own individual furrows in ensuring safety inside their grounds. Most held an annual inspection involving local fire and police forces and usually an architect to check on the state of walls, exits, entrances and stairwells. Some checks were fairly thorough, mainly in the bigger grounds; others, a light touch, simply a catch-up on what running repairs were required to the stands and facilities. In other words, some stadiums were safer than others. Some clubs vigilant, others complacent; quite a few trying to find shortcuts to save money. One fact was clear above all else – most clubs were struggling big time to cope with the increasing scourge of hooliganism.

What the Wheatley Inquiry concluded was that there should be a nationally enforced uniform set of safety standards that all clubs must satisfy. After consulting at length with health and safety experts in building design and crowd control, it recommended a series of measures specifying the number, size and location of entrances to and exits from the stadium and any part of it plus the means of access to any such entrances and exits; the increased number, greater strength, size and situation of crush barriers; not only the maximum attendances to be allowed into each ground but exactly how many should be admitted into specific areas of the stadia. The inquiry also discovered that there was a general lack of coordination between police, St John Ambulance staff, stewards and club officials and poor facilities within many grounds for them to undertake their important work on matchdays. A new framework was suggested for how they could become more unified in their efforts.

Crucially, the inquiry also identified the increase in hooliganism and violence in and around football grounds as a further driver for the vital importance of change. It was, the inquiry concluded, essential for a central technical code of standards to be drawn up, so that a minimum standard of safety at all grounds would eventually be reached. Improved public safety was the first priority, but from the off, the inquiry realised that their recommendations would cost clubs a lot of money to implement. Many would need to do serious rebuilding work to bring their grounds up to standard. However, the inquiry's report made clear to the government that action had to be taken without delay and throughout 1974 a parliamentary bill was pieced together based on the Wheatley Inquiry's findings. According to Hansard, and during debates over the bill in the House of Lords, Viscount Simon stated the obvious, 'If there are any noble Lords who know less about football than I do, they will be as surprised as I was to find that there has not been any regulation up to now'.

The following year the bill became enshrined in law as the Safety of Sports Ground Act; the financial impact it had upon Britain's football clubs was huge. Henceforward, they were all required to obtain a safety certificate from their local authority or ultimately have their ground closed down. A lot of clubs were now facing heavy new bills. Although a new body called the Football Grounds Improvement Trust was set up to offer financial aid and grants to help fund the safety measures, the majority of the cost had to be borne by the clubs themselves. The general agreement was that the major risks to public safety were caused by overcrowding in bigger grounds and as a result, the new act put stadia into different categories. Those in category one, which included national stadiums, the English First and Second Division and Scottish Division One, were required to undertake work as soon as possible. Category two grounds further down the English and Scottish leagues were deemed to be less of an immediate risk and told they were to be dealt with further down the line, to also give them a chance to plan for the financial inevitability.

In the meanwhile, the top clubs had to bite the bullet and get on with it. At Sunderland, the Roker Park club had to shell out £250,000 on new safety barriers, access points, improved lighting and legally licensed refreshment bars. At nearby St James' Park, Newcastle United faced a bill of £150,000 to comply with the new recommendations.

Though the new legislation may have been a major drain on many clubs' resources, it was long overdue. For decades, fans had been treated like cattle, crammed into crumbling stadiums with insufficient thought for their safety or wellbeing. Conditions in many league grounds had been grim for years and as long as fans continued to turn up and pay for their tickets, clubs remained complacent, happier to spend their money on player wages and transfer fees.

For once, the government had the will and determination to look seriously at football and force truly radical change on the domestic game; it was the correct thing to do. The Safety of Sports Grounds Act helped to change the culture of the way fans are treated more than any government measure before or since.

18

End of Year Report

'O wind, if winter comes, can spring be far behind?'

– Poet Percy Bysshe Shelley

THE FINAL round of matches in 1974 was played out on Saturday, 28 December, and an ill wind blew – mainly across the North Sea from Siberia. It hit Scotland and England's north-east coast from Berwick down to Lincolnshire in the hours of darkness the night before and then lashed inland through most of northern England. Two people died, hit by falling trees as gusts became gales and then 90mph winds. In Yorkshire, scores of homes and buildings were destroyed, and on Humberside, firemen worked overtime, answering dozens of calls to make safe roofs and chimney stacks, after a vicious wind tore away bricks and tiles. Over on Scotland's west coast, the Sealink ferry service between Stranraer and Larne was cancelled as winds reached 80mph.

In football, three matches wrote themselves into the record books – Newcastle United v Liverpool in the First Division, Barnsley v Rotherham United in the Second Division, and the Fourth Division's Hartlepool v Northampton Town. They became the first in the 20th century to be postponed because 'wind stopped play'; the last in the league was at Bolton in 1894. Yorkshire and the north-east were particularly being battered good and proper. In explaining to the press why Newcastle had no alternative but to call off the game, secretary Russell Cushing said that a 90mph wind had blown straight down the pitch and buffeted and rattled the not insubstantial stands at St James' Park, adding 'It would have been madness to go ahead.' Down the coast in Hartlepool, the concerned local emergency services stepped in to make the club's decision for them. The *Sunday People* reported, 'Risk to the spectators from the storm-battered stand at Hartlepool made police tell the club to postpone the game. Part of the stand roof was blown into the main road, while other sections shook dangerously in the gale.'

Once again, the stands at Hartlepool received a right old wrecking. During the First World War, a German Zeppelin appeared through the fog and gloom to bomb the crap out of their Victoria Park ground. At the end of the Great War, the club's board sent a series of letters to the peace-time German government demanding they pay for the damage. They never received so much as a reply and then to add insult to injury, the Luftwaffe attacked the north-east and bombed out the ground again during the Second World War. At Barnsley's Oakwell ground, club officials clocked gusts of over 90mph, with referee Walter Johnson telling the press, 'A game would have been a farce.' This, after Johnson had placed a football on the centre spot and then watched it blow unaided across the pitch and roll at speed over a far distant touchline.

Among the games that did go ahead in the top flight, Harry Haslam's Luton Town, Bobby Robson's young Ipswich Town team and Dave Mackay's Derby County ended the day as the happiest of campers. Hitherto, Luton's return to the First Division had proved to be a tough old struggle and coming into Christmas, the Hatters had been in rock bottom for over two months, winning just the once, and were already eight points adrift. Back in the days before transfer windows, Haslam went to his board and told them his scouts had identified two gifted young players who might help the club start to turn things around; the toughest problem would be trying to tell them apart. The directors signed off on the transfers and 18-year-old identical twins Ron and Paul Futcher arrived from Fourth Division Chester for a joint fee of £125,000. The two young signings had somewhat underwhelmed Luton fans, who were scratching their heads. Six-feet-tall centre-forward Ron had only played four games for Chester and was yet to score a league goal. Defender Paul had made his debut as a 16-year-old but had still only managed 20 appearances for the basement club. The Luton faithful then began to question Haslam's sanity when his two untried lower-league signings walked straight into the first team; soon the fans would be hailing his genius.

With the introduction of the Futcher twins, Haslam's team suddenly hit form and in eight gloriously festive days they beat high-flying Ipswich and Derby. In their last match of the year, they overcame Wolves 3-2 at Kenilworth Road in a thrilling end-to-end encounter. Ron Futcher scored a hat-trick, with Paul setting up the second. According to the gloriously hyperbolic *People* newspaper, 'Not since Dracula has anyone risen so frighteningly from the grave as Luton Town.' Ron would go on to score seven in 17 appearances, while Paul took to top-flight football as though to the manor born. Cool and calm beyond his tender years, the young centre-back brought a steadiness to Luton's hitherto shaky defence. Both would continue to be first-team regulars for the rest of the season, bringing a youthful energy and vigour to Haslam's side. In the end, their inspired introduction would not be enough to save Luton from relegation straight back into the Second Division, but damn, they came close. Their last ten games saw them win six, draw one and lose just three. Agonisingly, Luton finished just a single point behind fourth-bottom Spurs.

Following the surprise defeat to Luton, Ipswich got back into winning ways thanks to a first-minute Roger Osborne goal at Birmingham City's St Andrew's ground. Once the lead was in the bank, Town pressed high and defended well to regain the top spot. Man of the match was 19-year-old defender John Peddelty, yet another young player Robson had fast-tracked into the Ipswich first team. His starting 11 against Birmingham also included 18-year-old defenders George Burley and Dale Roberts, in front of 23-year-old goalie Laurie Sivell, and in midfield, 21-year-old Brian Talbot. The oldest player on the pitch was Clive Woods, who'd only turned 27 a fortnight before the Birmingham game. From the day in 1969 that Robson took over at Portman Road, his mantra was 'bring on the kids'. Partly through pragmatism, as his new chairman John Cobbold let him know the club had little money to spend, but mainly because of a strong belief that homegrown talent would lay important foundations and sustain Ipswich Town for years to come; Robson was in it for the long haul. He would manage at Portman Road for 13 years and in that entire time he only signed 14 players. The young stars he would bring through into the first team included Eric Gates, Terry Butcher, Mick Mills, Kevin Beattie, Colin Viljoen, John Wark, Alan Brazil and Trevor Whymark as well as Talbot and Burley – all of whom would go on to play international football. By his own admission, Robson did not regard himself as a tactical genius, but what he had in spades was the power to inspire. A superb motivator, the 41-year-old treated his young charges with respect and understanding and in return, they ran through walls for him. His team would end the 1974/75 season in third place, just two points behind eventual champions Derby, and qualify for the UEFA Cup.

On 28 December 1974, Derby took on Manchester City at Maine Road. On Boxing Day, Mackay's team had ended a poor run of results, beating Birmingham City 2-1 at their Baseball Ground – their previous ten games had featured five losses and a draw and the Scot was feeling under pressure. Previous boss Brian Clough had unexpectedly set the bar extremely high at Derby. Before his arrival as manager, the club had languished in the Second Division for a decade, their only previous major honour having been winning the FA Cup way back in 1946. Clough and his talented sidekick Peter Taylor came into their new jobs like gangbusters. They saw the size and potential of the club but also a mediocre side and backroom setup. With ruthless precision, Clough and Taylor showed 11 players the door, leaving only striker Kevin Hector, midfielder Alan Durban, goalie Colin Boulton and Ron Webster in the building. Out went the club secretary, chief scout and the groundsman. It's rumoured that Clough even sacked two tea ladies, who he'd heard laughing after a defeat. A series of shrewd signings soon followed – Roy McFarland, John McGovern, Alan Hinton, Dave Mackay, Willie Carlin, Les Green and, later, Colin Todd. The management duo raised a hitherto underperforming side to new heights. After winning the Second Division championship, it took Clough and Taylor just three more seasons to win the First Division. After much-publicised rows with the Derby board Clough and Taylor left.

Mackay was the man charged with the job of keeping Derby at English football's top table. In his first season he made a good fist of it, Derby competing right to the last match of the season to end in a very creditable third place. Clough's championship win had been deliberately built on strong defensive solidity and knowing Mackay's reputation as a player, most Derby fans had expected him to carry on in the same vein. A tough sweeper and on-the-field enforcer, the Scottish international was ruggedly defensive in the extreme. George Best memorably described Mackay the player as 'the hardest man I have ever played against – and certainly the bravest'. But his managerial approach at Derby surprised many. Yes, he had pure class at the back with Roy McFarland, David Nish, Colin Todd and Welsh international Rod Thomas. But for the 1974/75 season and with Kevin Hector, Roger Davies, Francis Lee and Bruce Rioch in the side, Mackay knew he had an embarrassment of attacking talent, too; Derby went for the jugular and played on the front foot throughout the campaign. Hector would end up as the club's top league scorer with 18 goals, midfielder Rioch would hit 17, Lee 14, and Davies 12. Derby scored the second-most goals, 67, in the First Division (only Burnley scored more but defensive frailties meant the Clarets only finished tenth) and would finish as champions once again, two points clear of Bob Paisley's Liverpool.

By Christmas, the First Division's surprise package continued to be Jack Charlton's newly promoted Middlesbrough. Once again, he had shown himself to be a great man-manager and a shrewd judge of his players' abilities. During the close-season he made no moves in the transfer market and showed admirable loyalty to the squad who had walked away with the Second Division championship, reasoning that they deserved the chance to prove themselves at the highest level. And it should be borne in mind that only four of his squad had any experience of playing top-flight football – Bobby Murdoch in Scotland for Celtic, Alan Foggon and John Spraggs at Newcastle and John Hickton at Sheffield Wednesday, albeit eight years previously.

Middlesbrough's first game back in the First Division – an impressive 3-0 away win at Birmingham on 17 August 1974 – contained ten of the players Charlton had fielded in his last Second Division game against brother Bobby's Preston. Big Jack's confidence in them was well justified.

On 28 December, Middlesbrough drew 1-1 with Everton, having beaten Sheffield United 1-0 48 hours earlier on Boxing Day. Three 3-0 wins on the bounce against high-flying Ipswich, Birmingham and Leicester plus a 1-1 away draw at Burnley saw Middlesbrough cruise through the month of December unbeaten and equal top on 30 points with Ipswich. Along the way, they'd won 11, drawn eight and lost just six times. Charlton's starting 11 remained largely unchanged throughout, as his championship-winning side stepped up in style. By Christmas, nine outfield players had got on the scoresheet and striker Foggon was into double figures on 12 goals. At the back, they'd kept nine clean sheets and conceded just once on a further eight occasions. Big Jack's side would end the 1974/75 season in a very creditable fourth place and make it through to the quarter-finals of both the FA Cup and League Cup.

The day's fixtures threw up great drama at Stamford Bridge. Three months previously, the club had sacked likeable manager Dave Sexton and he now rocked up at Chelsea in charge of nearby rivals Queens Park Rangers.

Now run by Sexton's Chelsea assistant Ron Suart, the Blues came into the game hovering around the relegation zone. They were out-thought and outplayed, losing 3-0 to a lively, but crucially, well-organised QPR. Despite containing proven top performers like Scottish internationals David Hay and Charlie Cooke, Wales keeper John Phillips and Republic of Ireland defender John Dempsey plus exciting new young players like Ray Wilkins, Gary Locke and Kenny Swain and brutal enforcers Ron 'Chopper' Harris and giant centre-back Mickey Droy, Chelsea continued to play like headless chickens. After the match, the ever-honest Sexton told a press conference, 'Before the game I felt like a player who has been released by a club and then returns to play against them. More nervous than usual, more anxious to succeed.' The win put QPR just five points behind league leaders Ipswich, while the chic, fashionable Chelsea of Fulham Road fame found themselves in the bottom five.

By the end of the 1974/75 season that would be bottom three and after ten years in the top flight, Chelsea were relegated to the Second Division, 21st out of 22. It would be with an embarrassing whimper. Their run-in was miserable in the extreme. Chelsea's last 12 matches saw them win just once, 1-0 against West Ham, draw four and lose seven, including a 7-1 thrashing at Wolves. Their top league goalscorer Ian Hutchinson only found the net seven times and the team managed just nine wins all season, the only team in the top division not to get into double figures with victories. Just as galling for the Stamford Bridge faithful, Chelsea scored the fewest goals, 42, and conceded the joint-most with 72. This was the club that under Sexton had won the 1970 FA Cup Final, the 1971 European Cup Winners' Cup, and had been losing finalists in the 1972 League Cup. But as we explored earlier in this book, Chelsea's increasing success had led to damaging moments of hubris from chairman Brian Mears and his board. Desperate to secure their place among the very top rank of English clubs, the plan to turn Stamford Bridge into one of the country's finest grounds had gone badly wrong. The impressive new East Stand had been built but at a depressing cost. As John Moynihan observed in his book, *The Chelsea Story*, 'That giant construction of steel and concrete was already bleeding one of the country's great clubs to death.'

The upshot: Chelsea were mired in debt and had no choice but to develop promising young players of their own rather than compete with other top-flight clubs in the transfer market. Chelsea were fortunate to have several fast-improving performers in their youth team, but obviously new talent needs time to bed in, particularly at the highest level. By 1974 the Blues had run out of time. Star players like Peter Osgood and Alan Hudson had moved on, to be replaced by raw, untried youngsters like Ray Wilkins, Gary Locke and Kenny Swain. After seven years of significant progress under David Sexton, Chelsea fell into a decade of comparative decline.

Carlisle United had started their first season in the top flight like a dream as a brace of 2-0 wins against Chelsea and Middlesbrough and a 1-0 victory over Spurs put them top of the table. After the Tottenham win, Carlisle's characteristically modest manager Alan Ashman told the *Newcastle Journal*, 'We are unaccustomed to a lot of publicity and the amount we have had recently has put a lot of pressure on the lads. But they all did a tremendous job. It'll get harder. Clubs are bound to give us a lot more attention after the start we have made but I've no qualms about our ability to compete.' The shrewd Ashman was right on all counts. His spirited, hard-working side could never have been accused of not giving their all but they offered few surprises. Once other teams had worked out their simple, uncomplicated style, the defeats soon began to rack up. Much to their credit, Carlisle often lost by just the odd goal, and apart from a 5-2 defeat at Stoke, Carlisle's small, well-organised squad were, as Ashman predicted, competitive throughout the season. However, lose they did, again and again.

In the 20 games following their three-match winning start, Carlisle lost 13, drew three and won just four. Despite an end-of-season surge with three wins and two draws in their last six matches, it was all too little too late. Carlisle finished bottom, suffering 25 defeats. But to hell with all that. The Cumbrians and their loyal fans had had their season in the sun and though the taste of success was fleeting and bittersweet, they wouldn't have swapped it for all the mint cake in Kendal. This was a team of players who'd largely plied their trade in the lower leagues. Only five of their squad had ever played in the top flight before and apart from striker Frank Clarke who turned out 66 times for Ipswich, the other four had been bit-part players with fewer than 80 appearances between them in the First Division. Carlisle finished five points shy of survival, but oh my, what a ride.

On 28 December 1974, the Second Division's big shock of the day came high up in the Lancashire hills at a windswept Boundary Park in front of a bumper 26,384 crowd where newly promoted Oldham Athletic beat league leaders Manchester United 1-0. The Latics' return to the second tier had been a tough old battle and Jimmy Frizzell's side had not won since 15 October. Their big-city neighbours were overwhelming favourites but Oldham hadn't read the script. Defending impressively and attacking on the counter through the pacy Les Chapman and George McVitie, Oldham's turning point came in the 68th minute when hapless United defender Arnie Sidebottom, under pressure from George Jones, handled in the box. Left-back Maurice Whittle coolly stepped up and powered the ball past Alex Stepney to make it 1-0. Oldham hung on for the next 20 minutes to notch up a famous win against their mighty rivals and pulled themselves out of the relegation places into the bargain. Despite the defeat, United remained top, four points clear of Sunderland, six clear of Norwich in third and eight ahead of West Bromwich Albion in fourth spot. More depressingly, United's Red Army thugs continued to live up to their tiresome reputation and caused havoc in and around the ground and on their riotous route back to Oldham's two railway stations, Werneth and Mumps. Five months later, Oldham would escape relegation straight back to the Third Division in 18th place, just three points ahead of the drop zone – arguably, their unexpected two points against Manchester United massively helping them to stagger over the line.

The defeat at humble, far-smaller neighbours Oldham precipitated a mid-season wobble for Manchester United. Losing at Boundary Park seemed to have a psychologically destabilising effect on the hitherto rampant Reds. Over the next six games they went into their shell and temporarily lost any cutting edge. Three defeats, a draw and just two wins saw the ever-expectant Old Trafford fans begin to doubt whether the board's decision to keep faith with relegated manager Tommy Docherty had been the right one. But the Doc dug in, galvanised his dressing room and from 1 March onwards, United's run-in was peerless – eight wins, three draws and champions of the Second Division, thank you very much. United fans were not the only ones to be jubilant. Towns and cities with Second Division clubs up and down the nation breathed a sigh of collective relief, more than happy to wave goodbye to United's thuggish away fans.

Arguably, eventual Second Division runners-up Aston Villa would enjoy a more successful season than United, though it didn't seem likely on 28 December 1974. After a strong start to the season, Ron Saunders' Villans had endured a dreadful November and December and coming into their away game at Cardiff City, their last nine games had seen them win just three times, lose five and draw one. Confidence in the squad was at a low ebb and it soon showed at Ninian Park. Three down inside the first 34 minutes, Villa lost 3-1, their sixth defeat in ten. The result saw the Midlanders drop into seventh place, 11 points off leaders United and five points away from Norwich in the third promotion spot. A frustrated and furious Saunders sat his men down for a long talk after the match and demanded they turn over a new leaf in the new year. The 'pep talk' helped shock the players into action and from January until the final day of the season Villa went on an incredible 18-match run, winning 15, drawing twice and losing just the once, 1-0 away at Orient. Along the way, they also managed to win a major trophy. On 1 March Villa stepped out on to the Wembley turf to contest the League Cup Final against eventual promotion rivals Norwich, thus taking part in the only major final in the history of England's national stadium not to feature a team from the top flight.

Pre-match, the press had made much of the threat posed by Canaries striker Ted McDougall, dubbing him 'The Man With the Golden Gun'. On the day, the centre-forward forgot to load up with bullets and a calm, well-organised Villa defence effectively snuffed him out of the game. The only goal came in the 81st minute and it was a sickener for Norwich keeper Kevin Keelan. Villa were awarded a penalty and up stepped Ray Graydon and struck it to the right, but Keelan guessed correctly and pushed it against the post. The ball could have gone anywhere; unfortunately for Keelan, it rebounded off the woodwork straight back out to Graydon's right foot. With Keelan now prone on the turf, Graydon coolly stroked it home. And as the final whistle blew, it remained 1-0 to Villa. At the other end of the pitch, Villa keeper Jim Cumbes had pulled off an amazing achievement. He had had little to do throughout the match, touching the ball only twice in the second half, neither an actual save. But as he climbed the 39 steps up to the Royal Box, Cumbes became the first man ever to win Wembley final and county cricket championship medals during the same season. In a withering assessment of Norwich's largely ineffectual performance, the *Sunday People* observed, 'Jim Cumbes has worked harder waiting to bat for Worcestershire than keeping goal [today] for Villa.'

Docherty's United may have ended up winning the 1974/75 Second Division, but Villa were not only runners-up and League Cup Final winners – their Wembley win qualified them for Europe and the following season's UEFA Cup. Norwich may have been second-best in the League Cup but they were more than happy to be third-best in the Second Division, an achievement that saw them promoted to the top flight for only the second time.

The 28 December fixtures also saw Blackburn Rovers cement their place at the top of the Third Division with a 2-1 win at hapless Huddersfield Town, who remained second-bottom. Manager Gordon Lee had had a summer clear-out and signed six key new players including Don Hutchins, Ken Beamish and Graham Oates, and by Christmas, the hard-working, well-organised Ewood Park side were playing with confidence and consistency. But it was a division with no particular standout sides and after the 28 December round of games, only five points separated top from tenth place. By the end of the season, a good old war of attrition between the top teams saw Blackburn lift their first silverware since winning the Second Division in 1939, ending up just a single point ahead of runners-up Plymouth Argyle. Charlton Athletic were promoted in third.

In the Fourth Division, Mansfield continued their unexpected good form and in the last of their Christmas fixtures they beat Newport County 3-0 in front of the division's biggest crowd of the day, 7,930. The season before, new manager Dave Smith had come in towards the end of a depressing campaign and narrowly saved Mansfield from having to apply for re-election. Over the summer close-season, he made some astute signings and set about transforming Mansfield into an attractive, attacking side. Key to their success was the acquisition of 22-year-old striker Ray Clarke from Swindon, one of the scorers in the 28 December Newport win. Clarke was something special. The Hackney-born player came through the Tottenham Hotspur youth and reserve team setups alongside Graeme Souness and Steve Perryman, scoring an astonishing 155 goals in 228 matches. Legendary Spurs boss Bill Nicholson loved the lad, but with seasoned internationals Alan Gilzean and Martin Chivers up front, Clarke found it impossible to break into the first team. The avuncular Nicholson suggested he move on to develop his career and recommended him to Swindon.

Clarke only played a dozen games for the Wiltshire side before Smith became aware of his huge potential and made him a priority signing for Mansfield. He ended his first season at Field Mill as the club's top marksman, firing in 27 of the 90 goals that would power Mansfield to the Fourth Division championship. It would prove to be a landmark year for the unfashionable East Midlands club – their first league trophy; most league wins in a season with 28 and their best home record, ending the campaign unbeaten at Field Mill with 17 wins and six draws.

Ray Clarke remains an enigma to this day, one of modern English football's largely unsung heroes. A year before 'Mighty Mouse' Kevin Keegan exchanged a garlanded career at Liverpool for life with Hamburger SV in the German Bundesliga, the Third Division striker moved from Mansfield to the Netherlands in 1976 to play for top-flight side Sparta Rotterdam. In the days when it was rare for English footballers to play in Europe, Clarke made a massive impact in the Netherlands' second city. In 65 Eredivisie games the prolific striker scored 35 times and caught the eye of mighty Ajax, who had recently become the first club to win three consecutive European Cups since Real Madrid in the 1950s. He was signed by the Amsterdam side and continued to score goals for fun. His first came after just one minute in his debut against NAC Breda and in 31 matches for Ajax that season Clarke scored 26 times, and was a major reason the club won that year's Dutch league and cup double.

As a footballer it was a life-changing time for Clarke. Speaking in later years to the tottenhamhotspur.com website, he described the culture shock, 'Everything about Ajax was totally new to me. Everything that was done at Ajax – the way they trained and played, the fitness levels, technical ability, mental application and of course the culture of "Total Football" was on a different level to any other club I'd been a part of previously. I was playing with some unbelievably good players like Ruud Krol, Frank Arnesen, Søren Lerby.' And he was loving it. Clarke had become an instant hit with the De Meer Stadion faithful and they, in turn, were overjoyed when the Englishman was offered a new contract in the close-season. But as is so often the case in football everywhere, club politics led to Clarke's contract offer being withdrawn and he was sold on to Club Brugge in Belgium for £220,000. Despite a stellar first season at Ajax, a new chairman decided to rebuild the squad with young players and the money from Clarke's sale would help sign and develop them. The fans were outraged and at the start of the next season, the terraces were draped with banners that read 'Ray Must Stay' and 'Clarke, King of Ajax'. Even club legend Johan Cruyff, who'd now moved on to Barcelona, publicly said the board were 'idiots' for letting Clarke go.

He would not have a happy time in Belgium. His wife Cindy had become ill with a heart complaint and after a dozen or so games at Club Brugge, Clarke decided to cut short his European adventure and return home to Britain. He enjoyed a successful season at Brighton and First Division Newcastle United soon stepped in to sign him. But Clarke had been struggling increasingly with recurring hip problems and he made few appearances for his new club. After seeking expert medical advice, Clarke was forced to make the heartbreaking decision to retire from football aged just 28. He would go on to run pubs and restaurants and scout for several clubs including Celtic, Coventry City and Southampton, but it was a highly promising career cut sadly short. His 96 games in the Netherlands' top flight had brought him 61 goals. By comparison, fellow English striker Kevin Keegan played 90 games for Hamburger SV, scored 32 goals and won the European Footballer of the Year trophy twice.

The very fact that so few English players moved abroad in the mid-1970s said much about the ever-ongoing insular nature of our nation's football culture at the time. 1974 had undoubtedly been a year of great change in British football domestically. The managerial merry-go-round had seen most of the country's top managers sacked, move on or retire; Sunday football was controversially introduced; non-league football had a massive shake-up. But in terms of world football, the British game was once more in decline. Between 1966 and 1970, a short golden age had seen England win the World Cup and excite at the 1970 finals in Mexico; Celtic and then Manchester United had won the European Cup; and players like Bobby Moore, Bobby Charlton, George Best and Denis Law were universally regarded as among the best in the world. But by 1974, the England national team had quickly become a shadow of its former self and failed to qualify for the World Cup in Germany. Moore and Charlton had retired and the England side contained just one world-class player in Kevin Keegan. The rest? An ever-rotating squad of decent enough domestic club performers, many of whom only gained a cap or two here, a substitute appearance there but never meaningful or lengthy England careers.

The FA still banned non-British nationals from playing in the Football League and though managers like Jock Stein and Bobby Robson were keen students of foreign coaching and management methods, most English, Scottish and Welsh clubs were looking at football in an insular, inward-looking way. Leeds United had got to the 1973 European Cup Final, and lost, but the tournament had been dominated by the Dutch and Italians for the previous decade.

The economic and political greyness that seemed to hold Britain in its depressing grip was reflected in football's grimy goings-on. The game's biggest, most notorious stories in 1974 generally involved shocking acts of football hooliganism off the pitch and increasingly grim acts of violence on it. But there were reasons to be cheerful. Bob Paisley was quietly getting into his stride at Anfield. After his Leeds debacle, Cloughie would start to make something extraordinary happen at Forest and by the late 70s, English teams began to dominate Europe. 1974 was a year on a down, but the ups were soon to return.

Selected Bibliography

Books:

Bagchi, R. & and Rogerson, P., *The Unforgiven: Don Revie's Leeds United* (Aurum, 2004)

Best, G., *Blessed: The Autobiography* (Ebury, 2002)

Chapman, D., *100 Years of Leeds United 1919–2019* (Icon Books, 2019)

Charlton, B. with Lawton, J., *My Manchester United Years* (Headline, 2007)

Clough, B., *Clough: The Autobiography* (Transworld, 2011)

FA Yearbooks, 1973–75

Frosdick, S. & and Marsh, P., *Football Hooliganism* (Willan, 2005)

Goldblatt, D., *The Ball is Round: A Global History of Football* (Viking Press, 2007)

Hodkinson, M., *The Longest Season: A Winter With England's Worst Ever Football Team* (Pitch, 2022)

Holt, R., *Sport and the British: A Modern History* (Oxford University Press, 1985)

Inglis, S., *Football Grounds of England and Wales* (Willow Books, William Collins Sons & Co. Ltd., 1983)

Korr, C., *West Ham United: The Making of a Football Club* (University of Illinois Press, 1987)

League Journal 1974

Marr, A., *A History of Modern Britain* (Pan, 2017)

McKinstry, L., *Jack and Bobby: A Story of Brothers in Conflict* (Willow, 2011)

Moynihan, J., *The Chelsea Story* (Arthur Barker Limited, 1982)

Nicholson, B., *Glory, Glory: My Life With Spurs* (Pan Macmillan, 1984)

Peace, D., *The Damned United* (Faber and Faber, 2006)

Royle, E., *Modern Britain: A Social History 1750–2011* (Bloomsbury, third revised edition, 2012)

Shankly, B. with Roberts, J., *Shankly: My Story* (Trinity Mirror Sports Media, 2009)

Stott, R., *Dogs and Lampposts* (Metro Books, 2002)

Taylor, P., *With Clough* (Biteback, 2019 edition)

Turner, A.W., *Crisis? What Crisis?: Britain in the 1970s* (Aurum, 2009)

Wilson, J., *Brian Clough: Nobody Ever Says Thank You* (Orion, 2012)

Wilson, J., *Inverting the Pyramid: The History of Football Tactics* (Orion, 2013; new edition)

Archives, collections and government papers:

British Newspaper Archive

Hansard

National Football Museum archives

National Museum archives

Scottish National Museum archives

The Grecians (Exeter University)

The Safety of Sports Ground, Bill 1974, and Act 1975

Newspapers, magazines and periodicals:

Aberdeen Evening Express

Birmingham Daily Post

Birmingham Evening Mail

Bradford Telegraph and Argus

Burnley Express

Coventry Evening Telegraph

Daily Mail

Daily Mirror
Daily Telegraph
Derby Evening Telegraph
Evening Standard
Exeter Express and Echo
Folha de São Paulo
Glasgow Evening Times
Glasgow Herald
Irish Independent
Lancashire Post
Liverpool Daily Post
Liverpool Echo
Manchester Evening News
Melody Maker
Newcastle Journal
Northern Echo
Nuevo Diario
Our Game
Shoot!
Sports Argus
Sunday People
Sunday Times
The League
The People
The Sun
The Times
West Lancashire Evening Gazette

Television, audio and podcasts:

Clough and Revie Yorkshire TV Calendar Special
Jack Charlton: The Boss BBC TV documentary
My Moment in History: Kicking Off the Women's Game (BBC podcast series)

Websites and online channels:

arsenal.com
englandfootballonline.com
englishfootballstats.co.uk
footy-boots.com
footballhistory.org
footballsite.co.uk
football-stadiums.co.uk
Highbury's Heroes
historicalkits.co.uk
liverpoolfc.com
Off The Ball
RochdaleAFC.com
stats.football.co.uk
Theanfieldwrap.com
The Pink News
Tottenhamhotspur.com
YoutubeFC

Appendix I

Football League tables 1973/74

First Division	*P*	*W*	*D*	*L*	*F*	*A*	*Pts*
Leeds United	42	24	14	4	66	31	62
Liverpool	42	22	13	7	52	31	57
Derby County	42	17	14	11	52	42	48
Ipswich Town	42	18	11	13	67	58	47
Stoke City	42	15	16	11	54	42	46
Burnley	42	16	14	12	56	53	46
Everton	42	16	12	14	50	48	44
Queens Park Rangers	42	13	17	12	56	52	43
Leicester City	42	13	16	13	51	41	42
Arsenal	42	14	14	14	49	51	42
Tottenham Hotspur	42	14	14	14	45	50	42
Wolverhampton Wanderers	42	13	15	14	49	49	41
Sheffield United	42	14	12	16	44	49	40
Manchester City	42	14	12	16	39	46	40
Newcastle United	42	13	12	17	49	48	38
Coventry City	42	14	10	18	43	54	38
Chelsea	42	12	13	17	56	60	37
West Ham United	42	11	15	16	55	60	37
Birmingham City	42	12	13	17	52	64	37
Southampton	42	11	14	17	47	68	36
Manchester United	42	10	12	20	38	48	32
Norwich City	42	7	15	20	37	62	29

Second Division	*P*	*W*	*D*	*L*	*F*	*A*	*Pts*
Middlesbrough	42	27	11	4	77	30	65
Luton Town	42	19	12	11	64	51	50
Carlisle United	42	20	9	13	61	48	49
Orient	42	15	18	9	55	42	48

Blackpool	42	17	13	12	57	40	47
Sunderland	42	19	9	14	58	44	47
Nottingham Forest	42	15	15	12	57	43	45
West Bromwich Albion	42	14	16	12	48	45	44
Hull City	42	13	17	12	46	47	43
Notts County	42	15	13	14	55	60	43
Bolton Wanderers	42	15	12	15	44	40	42
Millwall	42	14	14	14	51	51	42
Fulham	42	16	10	16	39	43	42
Aston Villa	42	13	15	14	48	45	41
Portsmouth	42	14	12	16	45	62	40
Bristol City	42	14	10	18	47	54	38
Cardiff City	42	10	16	16	49	62	36
Oxford United	42	10	16	16	35	46	36
Sheffield Wednesday	42	12	11	19	51	63	35
Crystal Palace	42	11	12	19	43	56	34
Preston North End	42	9	14	19	40	62	31
Swindon Town	42	7	11	24	36	72	25

Third Division	*P*	*W*	*D*	*L*	*F*	*A*	*Pts*
Oldham Athletic	46	25	12	9	83	47	62
Bristol Rovers	46	22	17	7	65	33	61
York City	46	21	19	6	67	38	61
Wrexham	46	22	12	12	63	43	56
Grimsby Town	46	18	15	13	67	50	51
Watford	46	19	12	15	64	56	50
Aldershot Town	46	19	11	16	65	52	49
Halifax Town	46	14	21	11	48	51	49
Huddersfield Town	46	17	13	16	56	55	47
Bournemouth	46	16	15	15	54	58	47
Southend United	46	16	14	16	62	62	46
Blackburn Rovers	46	18	10	18	62	64	46
Charlton Athletic	46	19	8	19	66	73	46
Walsall	46	16	13	17	57	48	45
Tranmere Rovers	46	15	15	16	50	44	45
Plymouth Argyle	46	17	10	19	59	54	44
Hereford United	46	14	15	17	53	57	43
Brighton & Hove Albion	46	16	11	19	52	58	43
Port Vale	46	14	14	18	52	58	42
Cambridge United	46	13	9	24	48	81	35

Shrewsbury Town	46	10	11	25	41	62	31
Southport	46	6	16	24	35	82	28
Rochdale	46	2	17	27	38	94	21

Fourth Division	*P*	*W*	*D*	*L*	*F*	*A*	*Pts*
Peterborough United	46	27	11	8	75	38	65
Gillingham	46	25	12	9	70	49	62
Colchester United	46	24	12	10	73	36	60
Bury	46	24	11	11	81	49	59
Northampton Town	46	20	13	13	63	48	53
Reading	46	16	19	11	58	37	51
Chester	46	17	15	14	54	55	49
Bradford City	46	17	14	15	58	52	48
Newport County	46	16	14	16	56	65	45
Exeter City	45	18	8	19	58	55	44*
Hartlepool	46	16	12	18	48	47	44
Lincoln City	46	16	12	18	63	67	44
Barnsley	46	17	10	19	58	64	44
Swansea City	46	16	11	19	45	46	43
Rotherham United	46	15	13	18	56	58	43
Torquay United	46	13	17	16	52	57	43
Mansfield Town	46	13	17	16	62	69	43
Scunthorpe United	45	14	12	19	47	64	42**
Brentford	46	12	16	18	48	50	40
Darlington	46	13	13	20	40	62	39
Crewe Alexandra	46	14	10	22	43	71	38
Doncaster Rovers	46	12	11	23	47	80	35
Workington	46	11	13	22	43	74	35
Stockport County	46	7	20	19	44	69	34

* Exeter City deducted two points for failure to appear for game at Scunthorpe United
** Scunthorpe United awarded game against Exeter City and two points for a win

Appendix II

Scottish tables 1973/74

Scottish Football League Division One

	P	*W*	*D*	*L*	*F*	*A*	*Pts*
Celtic	34	23	7	4	82	27	53
Hibernian	34	20	9	5	75	42	49
Rangers	34	21	6	7	67	34	48
Aberdeen	34	13	16	5	42	26	42
Dundee	34	16	7	11	67	48	39
Heart of Midlothian	34	14	10	10	54	43	38
Ayr United	34	15	8	11	44	40	38
Dundee United	34	15	7	12	55	51	37
Motherwell	34	14	7	13	45	40	35
Dumbarton	34	11	7	16	43	58	29
Partick Thistle	34	9	10	15	33	46	28
St Johnstone	34	9	10	15	41	60	28
Arbroath	34	10	7	17	52	69	27
Morton	34	8	10	16	37	49	26
Clyde	34	8	9	17	29	65	25
Dunfermline	34	8	8	18	43	65	24
East Fife	34	9	6	19	26	51	24
Falkirk	34	4	14	16	33	58	22

Scottish Football League Division Two

	P	*W*	*D*	*L*	*F*	*A*	*Pts*
Airdrieonians	36	28	4	4	102	25	60
Kilmarnock	36	26	6	4	96	44	58
Hamilton Academical	36	24	7	5	68	38	55
Queen of the South	36	20	7	9	73	41	47
Berwick Rangers	36	16	13	7	53	35	45
Raith Rovers	36	18	9	9	69	48	45

Stirling Albion	36	17	6	13	76	50	40
Montrose	36	15	7	14	71	64	37
Stranraer	36	14	8	14	64	70	36
Clydebank	36	13	8	15	47	48	34
St Mirren	36	12	10	14	62	66	34
Alloa Athletic	36	15	4	17	47	58	34
Cowdenbeath	36	11	9	16	59	85	31
Queen's Park	36	12	4	20	42	64	28
Stenhousemuir	36	11	5	20	44	59	27
East Stirling	36	9	5	22	47	73	23
Albion Rovers	36	7	6	23	38	72	20
Forfar Athletic	36	5	6	25	42	94	16
Brechin City	36	5	4	27	33	99	14

Appendix III

British Home Championship 1973/74

	P	*W*	*D*	*L*	*F*	*A*	*Pts*
Scotland (C)	3	2	0	1	4	1	4
England (C)	3	2	0	1	3	2	4
Northern Ireland	3	1	0	2	1	2	2
Wales	3	1	0	2	1	4	2

11 May 1974: Scotland 0 Northern Ireland 1 (Cassidy); Hampden Park, Glasgow

11 May 1974: Wales 0 England 2 (Bowles, Keegan); Ninian Park, Cardiff

14 May 1974: Scotland 2 (Dalglish, Jardine) Wales 0; Hampden Park, Glasgow

15 May 1974: England 1 (Weller) Wales 0; Wembley Stadium, London

18 May 1974: Wales 1 (Smallman) Northern Ireland 0; Racecourse Ground, Wrexham

18 May 1974: Scotland 2 (Pejic og, Todd og) England 0; Hampden Park, Glasgow

Appendix IV

Selected non-league tables 1973/74

Northern Football League

	P	*W*	*D*	*L*	*F*	*A*	*Pts*
Spennymoor United	38	30	4	4	87	37	64
Blyth Spartans	38	30	4	4	95	32	64
Willington	38	21	6	11	87	60	48
Bishop Auckland	38	19	9	10	68	43	47
Billingham Synthonia	38	20	7	11	67	50	47
North Shields	38	17	8	13	68	52	42
Tow Law Town	38	18	4	16	62	63	40
Ashington	38	16	6	16	60	56	38
Penrith	38	15	8	15	56	62	38
Durham City	38	16	5	17	74	60	37
Whitley Bay	38	14	8	16	48	48	36
Evenwood Town	38	13	10	15	63	65	36
Consett	38	14	7	17	61	63	35
Ferryhill Athletic	38	14	7	17	47	69	35
Shildon	38	12	9	17	59	62	33
Whitby Town	38	11	9	18	52	76	31
Crook Town	38	9	9	20	44	75	27
South Bank	38	8	7	23	43	77	23
West Auckland Town	38	5	11	22	37	83	21
Stanley United	38	4	10	24	41	86	18

Northern Premier League

	P	*W*	*D*	*L*	*F*	*A*	*Pts*
Boston United	46	27	11	8	69	32	65
Wigan Athletic	46	28	8	10	96	39	64
Atrincham	46	26	11	9	77	34	63
Stafford Rangers	46	27	9	10	101	45	63

Scarborough	46	22	14	10	62	43	58
South Shields	46	25	6	15	87	48	56
Runcorn	46	21	14	11	72	47	56
Macclesfield Town	46	18	15	13	48	47	51
Bangor City	46	19	11	16	65	56	49
Gainsborough Trinity	46	18	11	17	77	64	47
South Liverpool	46	16	15	15	55	47	47
Skelmersdale United	46	16	13	17	50	59	45
Goole Town	46	14	15	17	60	69	43
Fleetwood	46	14	15	17	48	68	43
Northwich Victoria	46	14	13	19	68	75	41
Mossley	46	14	11	20	53	65	41
Morecambe	46	13	13	20	62	84	39
Buxton	46	14	10	22	45	71	38
Matlock Town	46	11	14	21	50	79	36
Great Harwood	46	10	14	22	52	74	34
Bradford Park Avenue	46	9	15	22	42	84	33
Barrow	46	13	7	20	46	94	33
Lancaster City	46	10	12	24	52	67	32
Netherfield	46	11	5	30	42	88	27

Isthmian League Division One

	P	*W*	*D*	*L*	*F*	*A*	*Pts*
Wycombe Wanderers	42	27	9	6	96	34	90
Hendon	42	25	13	4	63	20	88
Bishop's Stortford	42	26	9	7	78	26	87
Dulwich Hamlet	42	22	11	9	71	38	77
Leatherhead	42	23	6	13	81	44	75
Walton & Hersham	42	20	12	10	68	50	72
Woking	42	22	6	14	63	55	72
Leytonstone	42	20	9	13	63	44	69
Ilford	42	20	8	14	60	44	68
Hayes	42	17	14	11	65	43	65
Oxford City	42	15	16	11	45	47	61
Sutton United	42	13	16	13	51	52	55
Hitchin Town	42	15	10	17	68	73	55
Barking	42	14	12	16	57	58	54
Kingstonian	42	12	15	15	47	46	51
Tooting & Mitcham	42	14	9	19	57	62	51
Enfield	42	13	11	18	50	57	50

Walthamstow Avenue	42	11	13	18	50	57	46
Bromley	42	7	9	26	37	81	30
Clapton	42	8	3	31	36	128	27
St Albans City	42	4	7	31	30	92	19
Corinthian-Casuals	42	3	4	35	31	107	13

Isthmian League Division Two

	P	*W*	*D*	*L*	*F*	*A*	*Pts*
Dagenham	30	22	4	4	68	23	70
Slough Town	30	18	6	6	46	23	60
Hertford Town	30	17	5	8	46	29	56
Chesham United	30	16	6	8	61	43	54
Aveley	30	16	5	9	50	28	53
Tilbury	30	14	5	11	47	36	47
Maidenhead United	30	12	11	7	36	30	47
Horsham	30	12	9	9	47	35	45
Harwich & Parkeston	30	11	9	10	46	41	42
Staines Town	30	10	8	12	34	41	38
Carshalton Athletic	30	8	8	14	34	51	32
Hampton	30	6	10	14	33	51	28
Harlow Town	30	6	9	15	33	48	27
Finchley	30	6	7	17	29	52	25
Southall	30	3	10	17	17	52	19
Wokingham Town	30	3	8	19	30	74	17

Athenian League Division One

	P	*W*	*D*	*L*	*F*	*A*	*Pts*
Boreham Wood	34	25	6	3	68	20	56
Cheshunt	34	18	11	5	58	24	47
Ruislip Manor	34	18	10	6	61	29	46
Ware	34	16	8	10	55	47	40
Hornchurch	34	15	9	10	48	44	39
Croydon	34	14	12	8	49	34	38
Erith & Belvedere	34	14	9	11	41	32	37
Edmonton & Haringey	34	12	12	10	40	35	36
Hounslow	34	13	9	12	55	46	35
Worthing	34	14	7	13	47	51	35
Lewes	34	11	12	11	50	43	34
Redhill	34	13	8	13	46	45	34
Grays Athletic	34	8	12	14	34	40	28

Wembley	34	11	6	17	42	55	28
Eastbourne United	34	8	9	17	34	60	25
Marlow	34	8	6	20	23	48	22
Letchworth Town	34	7	7	20	28	58	21
Herne Bay	34	1	7	26	16	86	9

Athenian League Division Two

	P	*W*	*D*	*L*	*F*	*A*	*Pts*
Alton Town	30	19	7	4	54	23	45
Rainham Town	30	17	7	6	48	33	41
Leyton	30	14	11	5	55	30	39
Uxbridge	30	14	11	5	36	23	39
Faversham Town	30	14	7	9	47	31	35
Wingate	30	15	5	10	42	37	35
Molesey	30	15	5	10	36	33	35
Harrow Borough	30	11	9	10	44	37	31
Addlestone	30	12	5	13	41	38	29
Aylesbury United	30	8	10	12	42	45	26
Hemel Hempstead	30	8	9	13	37	41	25
Edgware	30	9	6	15	33	54	24
Eastbourne Town	30	8	7	15	31	46	23
Feltham	30	7	5	18	29	50	19
Dorking	30	5	7	18	38	67	17
Windsor & Eton	30	6	5	19	25	50	17

Index